Introducing
New Testament
Interpretation

Guides to New Testament Exegesis
Scot McKnight, General Editor

Introducing
New Testament
Interpretation

Edited by Scot McKnight

BAKER BOOK HOUSE
Grand Rapids, Michigan 49516

Copyright 1989 by
Baker Book House Company

Printed in the United States of America

Library of Congress Cataloging-in-Publication Data

Introducing New Testament interpretation / edited by Scot McKnight.
   p. cm. — (Guides to New Testament exegesis ; 1)
   Includes bibliographical references.
   Contents: New Testament background / Warren Heard — New Testament
textual criticism / Michael W. Holmes — New Testament Greek
grammatical analysis / Scot McKnight — New Testament word analysis
/ Darrell L. Bock —Sociology and New Testament exegesis / Thomas
E. Schmidt — New Testament theological analysis / L.D. Hurst — The
function of the Old Testament in the New / Craig A. Evans.
   ISBN 0-8010-6260-8
   1. Bible. N.T.—Criticism, interpretation, etc. I. McKnight,
Scot. II. Series.
BS2361.2.I58 1989
225.6′01—dc20   89-28390
                                          CIP

Contents

Editor's Preface to Series

Four literary types (genres) comprise the New Testament: the Gospels, the Acts of the Apostles, the Letters, and, finally, the Apocalypse. Each genre is distinct, and, as has been made abundantly clear by contemporary scholars, each requires different sensitivities, principles, and methods of interpretation. Consequently, applying the same method to different genres will often lead to serious misunderstandings. Consequently, students need manuals that will introduce them both to the specific nature of a particular genre and to basic principles for exegeting that genre.

The Guides to New Testament Exegesis series has been specifically designed to meet this need. These guides have been written, not for specialists, but for college religion majors, seminarians, and pastors who have had at least one year of Greek. Methods and principles may change, but the language of the New Testament remains the same. God chose to speak to people in Greek; serious students of the New Testament must learn to love that language in order better to understand the Word of God.

These guides also have a practical aim. Each guide presents various views of scholars on particular issues. Yet the ultimate goal of each is to provide methods and principles for interpreting the New Testament. Abstract discussions have their proper place but not in this series; these guides are intended for concrete application to the New Testament text. Various scholars, specializing in given areas of New Testament study, offer students their own methods and principles for interpreting specific genres of the New Testament. Such diversity provides a broader perspective for the student. Each volume concludes with a bibliography of twenty essential works for further study.

Previously the point was made that different genres require different methods and principles. A basic exegetical method which can be adapted to various genres, however, is also essential. Because of the inevitable overlap of procedures, this introductory volume to the series covers the basic methods and principles for each genre. The individual exegetical guides will then introduce the student to more specific background procedures for that particular genre.

The vision for this series comes from Gordon Fee's introduction to New Testament exegesis.[1] Without minimizing the important contribution Fee has made to New Testament study, this series goes beyond what he has presented. It intends to develop, as it were, handbooks for each of the genres of the New Testament.[2]

Finally, this series is dedicated to our teachers and students, in thanksgiving and hope. Our prayer is that God may use these books to lead his people into truth, love, and peace.

Scot McKnight

---

1. *New Testament Exegesis: A Handbook for Students and Pastors* (Philadelphia: Westminster, 1983).

2. A helpful introduction to the various genres of the New Testament is D. E. Aune, *The New Testament in Its Literary Environment*, Library of Early Christianity (Philadelphia: Westminster, 1987).

Editor's Preface to *Introducing New Testament Interpretation*

Guides to New Testament Exegesis is based on the important premise that different genres deserve their own handbooks of interpretive principles. Hence, *Guides* plans volumes on each genre in the NT: synoptic Gospels, the Gospel of John, Acts, Pauline letters, Hebrews, and a finale on apocalyptic for the Revelation given to John.

If it is true that different genres deserve their own methodological discussions, it is also clear that the methods for each genre overlap to some extent. No one doubts that grammatical analysis, word studies, textual criticism, etc., are required for each type of literature. *Introducing New Testament Interpretation* presents the steps of NT exegesis that are common to any kind of writing found in the NT. The essays presented here were assigned to scholars in the field. Each essayist was given the freedom to present the material as seemed best. Since the subject matter was evaluated in the light of what most students need to know, various procedures were followed. Whereas some survey the field, others have dug more deeply into one corner of that field.

Beginning students usually encounter a teacher who contends that the NT cannot be understood (very well, at least) without a comprehensive understanding of the Jewish and Graeco-Roman backgrounds. Students generally agree with this assertion and are stimulated to poke around in the sources. But where does one begin? The Old Testament? OT pseudepigrapha or Apocrypha? Dead Sea Scrolls? Josephus? Philo? The Greek magical papyri? Suetonius? The rabbis? Dr. W. Heard offers to the student a brief survey of the literature, events, and ideas that comprise NT background; further, he appends ample bibliography for those who have a mind to plow deeper in a given area. A careful reading of his essay will introduce the student to most of the facts and all of the sources the beginning student needs.

Every student of the Greek NT has had to learn the various sigla found in the apparatus of the Greek NT. But textual criticism finds few devoted participants. As one of the last doctoral students supervised under the brilliant eye of B. M. Metzger, M. W. Holmes ranks among the finest of young scholars who have walked the special path of textual criticism. His essay is designed to present the basic facts and procedures for doing textual criticism and he includes the most up-to-date charts for classifying external evidence.

Along with the vagaries of background and textual criticism, the student of exegesis also has to master the essential categories of Greek syntax. The third essay, written by the editor, is built on a statement heard when in seminary. I was told, by my Greek teacher, that exegesis is essentially understanding the genitive case, the article, and the aorist tense. Perhaps this is an overstatement; but from my own teaching experience I can say that if the student comes to terms with these features of the Greek sentence, that student will reap abundant harvests. To encourage systematic grounding in the features of grammar, an introduction to diagramming Greek sentences is also provided.

Of all the features of exegesis, none has been used (or abused) more than word study. In the light of the latest progress in word analysis, Dr. D. L. Bock presents and illustrates the essential steps of doing a word study. Students need to give special heed to the author's instructions on the fallacies commonly committed and to the careful attention given to "meaning."

Recent NT study has turned toward integrating traditional methods with the humanities. In his doctoral thesis, Dr. T. E. Schmidt demonstrated the ability to utilize the methods now associated with NT sociology and evaluate current theories in light of those methods and the ancient texts. His essay in this volume presents a lucid introduction to the approaches associated with NT sociology. His careful definitions, comprehensive survey of the more influential studies to date, and judicious advice regarding integration will introduce students and teachers to the discipline and enable them to appreciate and assess this field now in full bloom.

Caught at the "right time," Dr. L. D. Hurst willingly offered an essay for students surveying NT theology. His essay is bound to provoke reaction among evangelical students, although he presents the issues pertaining to the field in a comprehensive and even-handed manner. Dr. Hurst recently completed editing G. B. Caird's posthumous New Testament theology as well as a festschrift in his memory.

The final essay hails from Dr. C. A. Evans. Christians have traditionally read the OT exclusively from the angle of "predictive prophecy." Without denying the importance or legitimacy of such an approach, one must also note that the last forty years of NT scholarship have brought to the surface the complex nature of hermeneutics among the earliest Christians (and first century non-Christian Jews). In this technical essay Dr. Evans explores the many factors at work as the NT authors emerged from an OT heritage. Besides some important observations regarding the terms and hermeneutical procedures associated with the discussion of the function of the OT in the NT, he works out his procedure of analysis with examples from the NT authors. If his bibliography is full, it is only because the discussions today are "full throttle" and the topic significant for theology.

Since the publication of his dissertation, *Baptism in the Holy Spirit* (Philadelphia: Westminster, 1970), Professor James D. G. Dunn has continued to offer scintillating summaries of scholarship and studies in the nature and development of earliest Christian theology. His books have challenged and provoked. Perhaps the greatest disservice that can be done to a scholar is to ignore his writings. I can think of no book written by Professor Dunn that has not implored immediate attention and discussion. His Foreword to *Guides to New Testament Exegesis* offers a refreshing proposal and I, one of his doctoral students, am grateful for his remarks.

A brief bibliography, composed by the editor, concludes the essays.

I am especially thankful to Tammy Thomas for her cheerful willingness to type a late essay quickly and efficiently. A special word of appreciation belongs to Gary Knapp, of Baker Book House, for his careful attention to these essays. Our gratitude also reaches out to Jim Weaver and Allan Fisher, also of Baker, for their steady and insightful implementation of this series, once just an idea of two young teachers.

Scot McKnight

Contributors

Darrell L. Bock. Assistant professor of New Testament literature and exegesis, Dallas Theological Seminary. Ph.D., University of Aberdeen.

James D. G. Dunn. Professor of divinity, University of Durham. Ph.D., Cambridge University.

Craig A. Evans. Associate professor of biblical studies, Trinity Western University. Ph.D., Claremont Graduate School.

Warren Heard. Adjunct assistant professor of counseling and New Testament, Trinity Evangelical Divinity School. Ph.D., University of Aberdeen.

Michael W. Holmes. Associate professor of biblical studies, Bethel College. Ph.D., Princeton Theological Seminary.

L. D. Hurst. Associate professor of religion, University of California, Davis. Ph.D., Oxford University.

Scot McKnight. Assistant professor of New Testament, Trinity Evangelical Divinity School. Ph.D., University of Nottingham.

Thomas E. Schmidt. Assistant professor of New Testament, Westmont College. Ph.D., Cambridge University.

Introduction
James D. G. Dunn

The Challenge of New Testament Study for Evangelicals Today

The challenge of New Testament study for evangelicals today can be summed up in the words "evangelical" and "scholarship." An evangelical believes that Scripture is the Word of God—that God speaks through the Scriptures and that the New Testament in particular is a normative expression of God's Word spoken and definitive for Christianity. Scholarship begins from the recognition that these scriptural texts were written many centuries ago, in different languages from our own, in different cultures and societies, in different worlds of meaning from our own, and is concerned to understand them across the historical divide.

What gives evangelical scholarship its distinctiveness and its characteristic cutting edge is the attempt to maintain a positive interaction between these two worlds. Evangelicalism alone without scholarship can easily become dangerously lopsided in its emphasis on Scripture as God's Word. The claim to hear God speaking directly through Scripture is quite proper. But it can easily become self-deceptive. Individual presuppositions can easily bracket out what one doesn't want to hear. Or a meaning can be heard in a text which is quite divorced from its original or scriptural sense. A text can become a pretext. Or strange teachings and actions can be justified by a selective hearing of Scripture. Some of the fringe sects around Christianity also claim to believe in the Bible as the Word of God. "The devil can cite Scripture for his purpose." "The Bible is the Word of God" can be a slogan of heresy as well as of orthodox Christian faith. The need to "test the spirits" is as relevant to a claim of Word-of-God authority in an interpretation of a scriptural text as it was in evaluating the original inspiration behind the text.

One important safeguard against such abuse is NT scholarship. For scholarship is concerned to uncover the meaning of the text in its original setting and significance. And this is bound to provide some check at least on the wilder flights of fancy which have laid claim to scriptural authority.

But equally, scholarship alone is not enough. The concern to understand the biblical text in its original setting is also quite proper. But if it is not wedded to a recognition that these words were heard speaking with Word-of-God authority, the point of the exercise is largely lost. It becomes, no doubt, an interesting historical exercise, a fascinating antiquarian study to be sure, but of little relevance beyond a small circle of academic specialists, and certainly not worth the vast amount of resources of time and money devoted to it. Since such scholarship has so little relevance to the present, it need not feel any constraint in the exercise of historical imagination or in the pursuit of novelistic and other curious speculations.

Evangelical scholarship therefore is marked out by this twofold concern. Evangelical scholars start with the recognition that the NT text was written at the prompting of God's Spirit and was heard to speak with more than local or incidental authority by those who first received it. It is precisely because it was heard to speak with Word-of-God authority that the text was preserved in the first place. This too is a historical datum which scholarship cannot ignore, since, apart from anything else, it explains the beginning of the process whereby only these texts were recognized in due course as canonical.

But evangelical scholars also recognize the historical character of the text—written by (a) certain individual(s), addressed to particular situations(s), using forms, language, and idioms that would be meaningful to the first readers, drawing on a common store of knowledge, the taken-for-granteds of "what everyone knows" (and so does not need to say explicitly), and so forth. To set that text in its historical context, to hear it as it was intended to be heard, and was in fact first heard by those who received and cherished it, is therefore one of the chief tasks of evangelical scholarship.

That requires hard work—knowledge of original language, not just of NT Greek, but of the wider usage of the time as well, awareness of the difficulty of recovering the original text, appreciation of the significance of different genre, awareness of the broad social, political, and religious context of the time (without which we cannot begin to hear the less explicit allusions let alone the taken-for-granteds), developing hermeneutical method and skills, and so on. Hard work, but necessary. Only so will we be in a position to straddle the divide of the centuries, to enter sympathetically into lines of thought and situations so far removed in time and culture from our own. Only so will we have some check on whether what we hear from the text is in fact the Word of God as it was heard by those for whom these texts were originally intended.

Just as important is the fact that such study enables the evangelical scholar to recognize the particularity of the Word of God. The fact of four Gospels is itself a reminder that the same gospel could be presented in different ways, with different structurings and emphases, because it was being addressed to different situations and needs. The letters of the NT likewise have different emphases because they were addressed to different churches in different stages of development. Only if these different objectives and situations are borne in mind can we hope to recognize the Word-of-God significance of the text which it was originally intended to bear. To generalize too quickly, or to read every text as though its teaching had universal application could actually mean denying or disregarding the historical specificity of the Word of God. Rather, the evangelical student, by means of the tools of scholarship, is enabled more adequately to recognize and illuminate that particular Word-of-God force of the text in its original context. And by thus demonstrating how the Word of God spoke with different emphases to different needs in the beginning of the Christian era, the student can help facilitate the recognition of how the Word of God may speak with similarly different emphases and specific force to the different and diverse needs of today.

All this is not to imply that only scholars can hear the Word of God properly, or that the apparatus of scholarship is necessary for any hearing of the Word of God. Nonspecialists may hear the Word of God with clarity when students' ears have become dulled by the noise and confusion of academic debate. And to be "made wise unto salvation" requires no knowledge of Greek. God can still speak through even mistaken exegesis and despite highly questionable interpretations.

But this in turn should not be allowed to distract from the normative function of the NT, namely, its role as the principal yardstick by which one may measure faith and life. For those who want their conscience to be subject to the Word of God, the normative meaning of a NT text cannot be dispensed with. And that normative meaning is to be found primarily in the meaning intended by the author who wrote it for the people to whom he sent it.

So the role of evangelical scholarship is crucial. That is why pastors and teachers must go through the sometimes wearisome business of studying ancient languages and texts, of familiarizing themselves with theories of origin of the biblical documents, with questions of source and genre, form and redaction, word studies and specialist monographs, the theology and ethics of this NT writer or that. Because they share the responsibility with Christian NT scholarship generally of expounding the NT text with its original Word-of-God force in such a way that those they minister to may hear the Word of God for themselves and may have some of their misconceptions, including those about the Word of God, clarified and explained.

So in sum, what is the challenge of NT study for evangelical students of today? First, it is the challenge of recognizing the strangeness of the Word of God in the NT. It speaks to us across the centuries in a foreign language, with very different idiom, from long dead cultures. Unless it comes to us as something alien, from another world, there is something wrong! For then we have domesticated the Word of God, made it familiar and comfortable, and robbed it of its power. To recognize the historical distance of the NT writings is a first step towards acknowledging the holy otherness of the Word of God.

Second, it is the challenge of recognizing the different ways in which God was heard to speak in the past to those who shared the same faith in Jesus Christ as Lord. It spoke to Jew and Gentile, Greek and Roman, to slave and free, man, woman, and child, a word which met them where they were and which enabled them to own Jesus as Lord through or despite their diverse situations in life. To enter into these different settings so far as we may, to hear again something of the force of that diverse word as it first captivated and commanded mind, heart, and will, is another crucial step towards hearing the Word of God with contemporary force.

And third, it is to bring that strange disturbing word to reexpression in its rich diversity through our own word and life so that it can be heard to speak with something of its original and still living power today. At least, that is the goal. The challenge is the hard work, the study, the learning individually and jointly, and the prayer which may make that goal possible of attainment.

1

New Testament Background
Warren Heard

The NT was written in a particular political, social, cultural, and theological milieu. The exegete must be immersed in this milieu so that the NT can be understood on its own terms; too often the texts in question are studied from the horizon of the twentieth century instead of the horizon of the first. The purpose of this chapter is to introduce the student to this area of study and hopefully stimulate an interest in NT background so that whenever any text is approached the exegete will attempt to listen to the text from the standpoint of one living in the first century.

The NT is more than the recorded religious experience of certain individuals, though it is that; it is more than the literary production of several creative writers, though it is that, too; indeed, it is no less than the authoritative written Word of God. Though these truths are rightly emphasized, it is not uncommon to observe that another facet of the NT is often overlooked, namely, the NT is also a record of the forming of Christian consciousness, which was shaped by the life and teachings of Jesus but also by the world that received it. That world gave the church its language as well as its literary forms for expressing its faith. The church's Scriptures and ancestors were Jewish; its political and legal frameworks were Roman; among its religious antecedents were a curious blend of several Near Eastern traditions. The NT reflects this background, and the careful exegete will consider all of these aspects.

In this chapter we will survey the period from Alexander the Great to the Bar Kochba revolt.[1] First, we will identify and list the major primary sources. Second, we will briefly survey the people and events of Judean history. Third, we will outline the major forms of Jewish religious expression by focusing upon Judaism's parties and sects. Finally, we will survey Hellenistic forms of religious expression in order to give the student an overview of the milieu. Throughout each of these discussions we provide ample references in the notes for further study.

Sources for Background Studies

Literary

The OT is an important Jewish source, particularly the portions of certain books which relate to the Maccabean period (e.g., Daniel). The OT apocrypha and pseudepigrapha are also valuable background documents. Although the historical value of many of these documents remains in question, they reflect social, religious, cultural, and theological developments and are therefore highly significant.[2] 1 and 2 Maccabees are exceptions

---

1. Some of the more important secondary works covering this period include: G. F. Moore, *Judaism in the First Centuries of the Christian Era*, 3 vols. (Cambridge, Mass.: Harvard University Press, 1927–30; W. Foerster, *Palestinian Judaism in the New Testament Times* (Edinburgh: T. & T. Clark, 1964); J. Jeremias, *Jerusalem in the Time of Jesus* (Philadelphia: Fortress, 1969); A. Schalit, *The World History of the Jewish People*, vol. 6 (New Brunswick, N. J.: Rutgers University Press, 1972); E. Schürer, *The History of the Jewish People in the Age of Jesus Christ*, rev. and ed. G. Vermes et al., 3 vols. (Edinburgh: T. & T. Clark, 1973–86); M. DeJonge and S. Safrai, eds., *Compendia Rerum Judaicarum ad Novum Testamentum. Section One: The Jewish People in the First Century*, ed. S. Safrai and M. Stern, 2 vols. (Assen: Van Gorcum, 1974, 1976); M. Hengel, *Judaism and Hellenism*, trans. J. Bowden, 2 vols. (Philadelphia: Fortress, 1975); R. A. Kraft and G. W. E. Nickelsburg, *Early Judaism and Its Modern Interpreters* (Atlanta: Scholars, 1986); cf. also E. P. Sanders, *Paul and Palestinian Judaism: A Comparison of Patterns of Religion* (Philadelphia: Fortress, 1977).

2. The two standard works on this literature are R. H. Charles, ed., *The Apocrypha and Pseudepigrapha of the Old Testament*, 2 vols. (Oxford: Clarendon Press, 1913), and J. H. Charlesworth, ed., *The Old Testament Pseudepigrapha*, 2 vols. (Garden City, N.Y.: Doubleday, 1983, 1985). See also Charlesworth, *The Pseudepigrapha and Modern Research with a Supplement* (Chico, Calif.: Scholars, 1981); M. McNamara, *Intertestamental Literature* (Wilmington, Del.: Michael Glazier, 1983); G. W. E. Nickelsburg, *Jewish Literature Between the Bible and the Mishnah* (Philadelphia: Fortress, 1981); M. E. Stone, ed., *Jewish Writings of the Second Temple Period* (Philadelphia: Fortress, 1984).

to this generalization and as such are helpful historical documents.[3] Other important Jewish sources include Philo of Alexandria (ca. 20 B.C.–A.D. 50)[4] and Flavius Josephus (A.D. 37–100).[5]

In general, the Greek and Latin authors paid relatively little attention to matters in Palestine. Nevertheless, some writers did mention this and other regions that are of enough general importance that they merit reading. These authors include: Polybius (ca. 203–120 B.C.; Polybius wrote a forty-volume world history); Diodorus Siculus (1st century B.C.; Diodorus recorded an historical survey); Strabo (ca. 64 B.C.–A.D. 21; Strabo included commentary on Palestine); Livy (ca. 59 B.C.–A.D. 17; Livy particularly concerned himself with foreign policy, and mentioned Palestine); Tacitus (ca. A.D. 55–110; besides general history Tacitus included a survey of Jewish history to the First Jewish War); Suetonius (A.D. 69–140; Suetonius included biographies of the Roman emperors from Augustus to Domitian); Appian (2d century A.D.; Appian wrote about the period from ca. 133–27 B.C.); and Dio Cassius (ca. A.D. 155–235; Dio concerned himself with the events from 69 B.C.–A.D. 46).[6]

Since 1947 many scrolls, fragments, papyri, and ostraca discovered near the Dead Sea have been studied. These artifacts date from about 200 B.C. to A.D. 135. The information gleaned from these materials is invaluable because it gives an insight into Jewish religion and politics, especially when the Hasmoneans ruled.[7] Because of the difficulty in generalizing the situation at Qumran to the whole of Palestinian Judaism, this background

---

3. For the value of these documents see the good introduction in J. A. Goldstein, *1 Maccabees* (Garden City, N. Y.: Doubleday, 1976); idem, *2 Maccabees* (Garden City, N. Y.: Doubleday, 1982). See also Nickelsburg, *Jewish Literature*, 114–21; idem, "1 and 2 Maccabees—Same Story Different Meaning," *Concordia Theological Monthly* 42 (1971): 515–26.

4. On Philo, see F. H. Colson et al., *Philo*, 12 vols. (Cambridge, Mass.: Harvard University Press, 1929–62); S. Sandmel, *Philo of Alexandria* (New York: Oxford University Press, 1979).

5. Important works on Josephus include: H. St. J. Thackery et al., *Josephus*, 9 vols. (Cambridge, Mass.: Harvard University Press, 1926–65; L. H. Feldman, *Josephus and Modern Scholarship (1937–1980)* (Berlin: de Gruyter, 1984); T. Rajak, *Josephus and Historian and His Society* (Philadelphia: Fortress, 1984).

6. For text and translations of these Greek and Latin writers, see the Loeb Classical Library (LCL); see also M. Stern, ed., *Greek and Latin Authors on Jews and Judaism*, 3 vols. (Jerusalem: Israel Academy of Sciences and Humanities, 1976–84); all quotes in this chapter from these Greek and Latin writers are from the LCL unless otherwise indicated.

7. For text and translation see D. Barthélemy and J. T. Milik, et al., eds. *Discoveries in the Judean Desert*, 5 vols. (Oxford: Clarendon Press, 1955–68). See also G. Vermes, *The Dead Sea Scrolls: Qumran in Perspective* (London: Collins, 1977).

should be dealt with judiciously and conclusions from this material must be carefully nuanced.

Rabbinic literature includes the Mishnah, the Tosephta, the Talmuds, the Midrashim, and the Targums. This material originated after A.D. 70 and must be used carefully because of the danger of drawing conclusions about Jewish traditions in the NT era from sources written after the destruction of Jerusalem. The Mishnah had its final redaction around A.D. 200 and contains a collection of laws and legislation purportedly based on the OT. The rabbis taught that the Mishnah was derived from Moses via oral tradition.[8] The Tosephta (final redaction about A.D. 500)[9] contains sayings which, for some reason, were omitted from the Mishnah.

Thinkers who concerned themselves with explicating the Mishnah produced works called the Gemara. The combined work of the Mishnah and the Gemara is known as the Talmud. There are, however, two Talmuds: the Jerusalem or Palestinian Talmud (final redaction about A.D. 500) and the Babylonian Talmud (final redaction about A.D. 700). The latter is generally regarded as more significant.[10] The Midrashim are commentaries on the OT produced in the first few centuries A.D.[11] The Targums are translations of the OT into Aramaic, though at certain points it is better to call them paraphrases. Since such Targums were found among the discoveries along the Dead Sea, it seems likely that their existence goes back into the intertestamental period. The two princi-

8. H. Danby, trans., *The Mishnah* (Oxford: Clarendon Press, 1954); P. Blackman, *Mishnayoth*, 3d ed., 7 vols. (New York: Judaica, 1965); J. Neusner, *The Mishnah* (New Haven: Yale University Press, 1988).

9. See M. S. Zuckermandel, *Tosefta* (Jerusalem: Bamberger and Wahrmann, 1937); S. Lieberman, *The Tosefta*, 13 vols. (New York: 1955); J. Neusner, *The Tosefta Translated from the Hebrew*, 6 vols. (New York: Ktav, 1977–81).

10. The standard English translation of the Babylonian Talmud is by I. Epstein, ed., *The Babylonian Talmud*, 35 vols. (London: Soncino, 1935–52). An English translation of the Jerusalem Talmud, *The Talmud with English Translation and Commentary*, edited by A. Ehrman is forthcoming, and one by J. Neusner, *The Talmud of the Land of Israel* (Chicago: University of Chicago Press, 1982–), has begun to appear. See also J. Neusner, *The Talmud of Babylonia, An American Translation*, 26 vols. (Chico, Calif.: Scholars, 1984).

11. H. Freedman and M. Simon, eds., *Midrash Rabbah*, 10 vols. (London: Soncino, 1951); J. Z. Lauterbach, *Mekilta de-Rabbi Ishmael*, 3 vols. (Philadelphia: Fortress, 1949); J. Neusner and R. Brooks, *Sifra: The Rabbinic Commentary on Leviticus* (Atlanta: John Knox, 1985); J. Neusner and W. S. Green, *Sifre to Numbers* (Atlanta: John Knox, 1986); R. Hammer, *Sifre: A Tannaitic Commentary—the Book of Deuteronomy* (New Haven: Yale University Press, 1986); J. Neusner, *Genesis Rabbah* (Atlanta: John Knox Press, 1986); W. G. Braude, *The Midrash on the Psalms*, 2 vols. (New Haven: Yale University Press, 1959); idem, *Pesikta Rabbati*, 2 vols. (New Haven: Yale University Press, 1969).

ple Targums are Targum Onkelos to the Pentateuch and Targum Jonathan to the former and latter prophets.[12]

Archaeological

Through archaeology we are able to partially reconstruct patterns of settlement, architecture, living conditions, cultural developments, and so on. Moreover, the study of ancient artifacts (e.g., inscriptions, coinage, ostraca, etc.) is a tremendous help in the reconstruction of an era. For example, numismatics (the study of coins) has revealed titles and claims of rulers, current ideas, religious and political symbolism, and chronology.[13]

Judean History[14]

The Greek Period

When the Israelites returned from their captivity in Babylon, the Persians were in power (539–331 B.C.), but their empire collapsed when confronted with Alexander III (the Great) at Issus in 333 B.C. Upon Alexander's death (323 B.C.) his empire was divided among his generals, the so-called Diadochoi, or "successors." By the third century B.C. three dynasties originat-

---

12. See J. W. Etheridge, *The Targums of Onkelos and Jonathan Ben Uzziel on the Pentateuch with the Fragments of the Jerusalem Targum from the Chaldee*, 2 vols. (New York: Ktav, 1968); M. L. Klein, *The Fragment-Targums of the Pentateuch According to then Extant Sources*, 2 vols. (Rome: Biblical Institute Press, 1980); A. Sperber, ed., *The Bible in Aramaic*, 4 vols. (Leiden: Brill, 1977). An English translation edited by Martin McNamara is forthcoming from Michael Glazier.

13. See E. M. Meyers and J. F. Strange, *Archaeology, the Rabbis, and Early Christianity* (Nashville: Abingdon, 1981); E. M. Yamauchi, *The Archaeology of New Testament Cities in Western Asia Minor* (Grand Rapids: Baker, 1980); M. Avi-Yonah and E. Stern, eds., *Encyclopedia of Archaeological Excavations in the Holy Land*, 4 vols. (Engelwood Cliffs, N. J.: Prentice-Hall, 1975); J. Wilkinson, *Jerusalem as Jesus Knew It: Archaeology as Evidence* (New York: Thames and Hudson, 1978); E. M. Blaiklock and R. K. Harrison, eds., *The New International Dictionary of Biblical Archaeology* (Grand Rapids: Zondervan, 1983).

14. This section is only a brief survey of these events. For a fuller treatment, see F. F. Bruce, *New Testament History* (Garden City, N. Y.: Doubleday, 1972); E. Schürer, *History of the Jewish People*; E. M. Smallwood, *The Jews under Roman Rule* (Leiden: Brill, 1976); H. H. Ben-Sasson, ed., *A History of the Jewish People* (Cambridge, Mass.: Harvard University Press, 1976); S. Freyne, *Galilee from Alexander the Great to Hadrian* (Wilmington, Del.: Michael Glazier, 1980); W. D. Davies and L. Finkelstein, eds., *The Cambridge History of Judaism*, 4 vols. (New York: Cambridge University Press, 1984–); H. Jagersma, *A History of Israel from Alexander the Great to Bar Kochba* (Philadelphia: Fortress, 1986).

ing from Alexander's generals were well established: (1) the Ptolemaic in Egypt and Coele-Syria; (2) the Seleucid in Babylon, upper Syria and Asia Minor; and (3) the Antigonid in Macedonia. A fourth dynasty, unrelated to the Diadochoi, the Attalids of Pergamum, also had been established in Asia at the expense of the Seleucids. This division remained fairly stable until the Roman invasion.

Ptolemaic rule over Palestine (301–246 B.C.) was important economically because it meant controlling trade and caravan routes. Militarily, Palestine was crucial for Egypt because it formed a strategic front line of defense against the Seleucids. In the first (274–271 B.C.) and second Syrian wars (260–253 B.C.) Egypt was successfully defending Palestine against the attacks of the Seleucids. Despite these wars, most of Palestine was left unscathed. Judging from the first fifty years of Ptolemaic rule, it is not impossible to believe Polybius's report that the people were pleased with Ptolemaic rule.[15]

The second fifty years of Ptolemaic rule (246–198 B.C.), however, was not as agreeable. When the third Syrian war (246–241 B.C.) broke out, Onias II, the acting high priest, refused to pay taxes. Ptolemy III then sent a delegation to pressure Onias to pay tribute. Joseph, Tobias's son, took a stand against Onias; he was pro-Ptolemaic, if not Hellenistic. This probably marked the beginning of the controversy between the Oniad and Tobiad families. Joseph apparently was appointed to collect taxes, and did so with abject cruelty. Along with the rise of Joseph, however, also came economic boom. From this time forward the classical authors paid attention to Jerusalem; it was no longer a nugatory state arranged around a temple and neglected by most of the world.[16] The fifth Syrian war (202–198 B.C.) brought Antiochus III, the Seleucid king, control of Palestine. Thus the Tobiads switched their allegiance from the Ptolemies to the Seleucids. Seleucus IV (187–175 B.C.), eldest son of Antiochus III, was the next king, but Antiochus IV, also the son of Antiochus III, who had been held hostage in Rome, was released and seized the throne.

15. Polybius, V, 86, 10.
16. Hengel, *Judaism and Hellenism*, I, 53.

The Maccabean Period

Antiochus IV (175–164 B.C.) inherited a kingdom that lacked political and economic stability. He therefore attempted to stabilize it through a vigorous program of hellenization. Antiochus also wished to restore the Seleucid kingdom to its former glory, so he launched a campaign against Egypt that proved so successful that Rome ordered Antiochus to withdraw. Meanwhile, Onias III, a conservative high priest, was displaced by his pro-Hellenist brother Jason after Jason bought the position from Antiochus. A short while later Jason was ousted by Menelaus, the brother of the captain of the temple. Menelaus offered Antiochus even larger sums of money. In order to pay Antiochus, Menelaus embezzled from the temple. Menelaus' pilfering caused a Jewish uprising that Antiochus quelled on his way back from Egypt. Smarting from humiliation by the Romans, Antiochus quelled this Jewish uprising with a strong hand and accelerated the process of hellenization. Since the Jews resisted, Antiochus decided to enact the final measure which, in effect, outlawed Jewish religion. He suspended regular sacrifices, banned all feasts as well as the Sabbath, outlawed circumcision, and prohibited the reading of the Torah. Jews were forced to eat swine, heathen altars were erected, and in December, 167 B.C., the altar of burnt offering was replaced by an altar to Zeus upon which a pig was sacrificed.[17]

These measures merely galvanized Jewish resistance. The resistance was basically nonmilitary until a priest named Mattathias, the father of a family called the Hasmoneans, killed one of the king's officials. After killing the official, Mattathias fled into the wilderness and organized guerrilla warfare against Antiochus. Mattathias died in 166 B.C., and his third son Judas became the leader of a victorious movement (see 1 Macc. 2:42–70). In December, 164 B.C., the temple was rededicated. With religious freedom secured Judas then sought political freedom, but he was killed in battle (160 B.C.) and his brother Jonathan took his place. Jonathan

17. 1 Macc. 1:41–64; 2 Macc. 6:1–11; Josephus, *Antiquities*, XII, 5, 4; Dan. 11:31–32; for more detail on the events of the Maccabean uprising also see Schürer, *History*, II, 151–63; Jagersma, *History*, 57–63; H. Koester, *Introduction to the New Testament*, 2 vols. (Philadelphia: Fortress, 1982), I, 210–15; E. Bickermann, *From Ezra to the Last of the Maccabees* (New York: Schocken, 1962), 93–127; D. E. Gowan, *Bridge Between the Testaments* (Pittsburgh: Pickwick, 1980), 89–112.

continued to fight against Syria until his death in 143 B.C. Simon, another brother, succeeded Jonathan and shortly thereafter gained complete political independence from Syria and signed a peace treaty with Rome. For the first time since the beginning of the Babylonian exile, the political yoke of the Gentiles had been broken.

In 1 Maccabees 14 Simon and his brothers are publicly praised for their political and military accomplishments. The crowd then elects Simon to be the high priest until a prophet should arise. Before 152 B.C. only bona fide descendants of Zadok had been allowed to be high priests; therefore, it is not surprising that the appointment of a non-Zadokite to the hereditary high priesthood caused significant controversy. Simon reigned until Ptolemy, his son-in-law, killed him in an attempted coup d'état in 135 B.C.[18] Simon's son John Hyrcanus succeeded him, and by the end of his reign he had secured a kingdom which, broadly speaking, was equivalent to Solomon's.

Aristobulus I, John's son, succeeded Hyrcanus, but died a year later in 103 B.C. Alexander Janneus (103–76 B.C.), the third son of Hyrcanus, followed with a reign of military conquest. Before he died (76 B.C.), Alexander had increased Israel's borders to include Judea, Samaria, Galilee, the Philistine coastal region, and a large portion of the Trans-Jordan. After Alexander's death, Salome Alexandra, his widow (76–67 B.C.), became Israel's political head. Since she could not be high priest, she appointed Hyrcanus II, her oldest son, to the post. All things considered, Salome's reign was fairly peaceful. In the international arena, Pompey, the Roman general, was flexing Rome's muscles, and in 64 B.C. Syria became a Roman province. Rome now was interested in Judean affairs more than ever.

The Roman Period

Aristobulus II (67–63 B.C.), younger son of Salome, defeated Hyrcanus II, his older brother and high priest, and succeeded Salome. In 63 B.C. the Roman general Pompey captured Jerusalem, which ended the Hasmonean dynasty and Jewish indepen-

---

18. 1 Macc. 16:11–22.

dence. Israel lost all its territory except Judea, Galilee, Idumea, and Perea. Antipater, whose father had been named proconsul of Idumea by Alexander Janneus, was the one with the political muscle. Antipater assigned his sons, Herod and Phasael, the task of governing Jerusalem and Galilee. In 40 B.C. Antigonius, son of Aristobulus II, gained power in Judea, imprisoned his uncle, Hyrcanus II, and claimed the titles king and high priest, the last Hasmonean to do so. Herod fled to Rome, was declared king of the Jews by the Senate and by 37 B.C. had conquered Jerusalem and executed Antigonius.

Herod had considerable ability as king, and his kingdom prospered through agricultural and commercial enterprises. Important for the Jews was Herod's rebuilding of the temple, but he also had many other architectural projects. Jewish by religion but Edomite by birth, Herod was never popular with the Jews. After Herod's death in 4 B.C., Rome divided his kingdom among his sons: Archelaus received Judea, Samaria, and Idumea; Philip received Iturea and Trachonitis; Herod Antipas received Galilee and Perea. Philip and Herod Antipas ruled about forty years, but Archelaus was dismissed in A.D. 6. Rome turned his empire into a province governed by procurators.[19] For the most part these rulers respected the Jews; Pontius Pilate, however, antagonized them and Vitellius, governor of Syria, removed Pilate from office in A.D. 36.

Agrippa, one of Herod's sons, was sent to Rome for an education. While there he became friends with the future emperor, Gaius Caligula.[20] In A.D. 37 Caligula became emperor and soon Agrippa was king over all of Palestine. Agrippa patronized the Jews by adopting their customs, minting coins without an image, and persecuting the early Christians (see Acts 12); but outside of Judea he behaved in a pagan manner. With Agrippa's death (A.D. 41) the governance of Judea returned to procurators because his son, Agrippa II, at age 17, was too young for the throne. About A.D. 50, however, Agrippa II succeeded Herod his uncle as king of Chalcis, a small territory in Lebanon. Agrippa

---

19. The early governors included Pontius Pilate, who ruled from A.D. 26 to 36.
20. The Roman Emperors for our period of survey were: Augustus (3 B.C.–A.D. 14); Tiberius (14–37); Gaius Caligula (37–41); Claudius (41–54); Nero (54–69); Vespasian (69–79); Titus (70–81); Domitian (81–96); Nerva (96–98); Trajan (98–117); and Hadrian (117–138).

died about A.D. 92, and with his death the Herodian family passed from history.[21]

In many ways the first Jewish revolt was the culmination of Jewish resentment and memories of political independence. In response Nero chose Vespasian to quell the revolt. By A.D. 67 Galilee fell and by A.D. 68 almost all of Judea was subjugated. After Nero died Vespasian went to Rome and left his son Titus to finish the campaign in Judea. Titus began the siege of Jerusalem in A.D. 70, and by August, Jerusalem had been razed. Some strongholds held out longer (Masada lasted until perhaps A.D. 74), but the Roman victory was complete. The devastation of the temple meant that the center of Jewish life was now destroyed. Sacrifices ceased, the priesthood was abolished, and the sacred temple to Yahweh was now a pile of rubble. The significance of A.D. 70 for Jewish religion and culture cannot be underestimated.

During the siege of Jerusalem, Rabbi Johanan ben Zakkai escaped and Vespasian later granted him permission to found an academy in Jamnia.[22] This academy became the administrative seat of Jewish life. Under the guidance of Johanan and Gamaliel II, grandson of Paul's teacher, post-70 Judaism was restructured. The Jamnia period witnessed a shift from a centralized temple-oriented religion to a decentralized synagogue-oriented one. About A.D. 115, during the reign of the Roman emperor Trajan, the Jewish communities in Cyrene, Egypt, and Cyprus revolted. The fighting was fierce, but by 117 the uprising had been suppressed. This revolt is the only known rebellion of the Diaspora, and it seems to have been prompted by civil rights issues rather than messianism.[23]

Apparently, two edicts by Hadrian—one forbidding circumcision and another allowing Jerusalem to be rebuilt with a temple to Zeus included in the plans—precipitated another Jewish re-

---

21. The later governors of Judea were Cuspius Fadus (A.D. 44–46; slaughtered Theudas and his followers; see Acts 5:36); Tiberius Julius Alexander (46–48; nephew of Philo and procurator during the Jerusalem famine; see Acts 11:27–29); Ventidus Cumanus (48–52); Antonius Felix (52–60[?]; held Paul prisoner in Caesarea; see Acts 24); Porcius Festus (60[?]–62; upon his appeal, sent Paul to Rome; see Acts 25); Albinus (62–64); and Gessius Florus (64–66; first Jewish war breaks out).

22. Aboth R. Nathan, iv, 11b–12a.

23. See A. Fuks, "The Jewish Revolt of 115–117," *Journal of Roman Studies* 51 (1961); 98–104; S. Applebaum, *Jews and Greeks in Ancient Cyrene* (Leiden: Brill, 1979).

volt in A.D. 132.[24] Simon ben Koseba, a Jewish leader who had studied at Jamnia, claimed to be Messiah and apparently received an endorsement from Rabbi Akiba. Fighting from caves and using guerilla tactics, the rebels experienced some early success, but when the Roman troops arrived, total defeat was inevitable. When the rebellion was finally put down, Hadrian erected a temple in Jerusalem to Jupiter Capitolinus, banned Jews from entrance, and erected a statue of himself. For the next 1800 years the Jewish people were divorced from their political homeland. Only their Torah, their traditions, and their hope bound them together.

Forms of Jewish Religious Expression

Parties and Persuasions

The Sadducees

The Sadducees first appear in our sources alongside the Pharisees and the Essenes.[25] Presently there is no extant writing that we can prove was written by a Sadducean, so we must cautiously derive our sketch of this group from those who wrote about them, often polemically. Exactly how, why, and when the Sadducees came into existence is impossible to know with certainty.[26] Whatever their origin, from at least the time of John Hyrcanus (and probably Jonathan) down to A.D. 70, they played an important role in Judea; they were the class with wealth and political power. Thus they had a vested interest in maintaining political stability in order to preserve their own personal interests. A policy of cooperation with foreign rulers was an integral part of their platform.

This conservatism was also manifested in their religious beliefs; the Sadducees accepted only the Pentateuch as authoritative. They rejected the oral tradition of the Pharisees, and even the rest of the OT was not generally used as a quarry from which

---

24. These edicts might have been the *result* rather than the *cause* of the revolt. See H. Mantel, "The Causes of the Bar Kochba Revolt," *Jewish Quarterly Review* 58 (1968): 224–42.

25. Josephus, *Antiquities*, XIII, 173.

26. For discussion see J. LeMoyne, *Les Sadducéens* (Paris: Lecoffre, 1972); H. Mulder, *De Sadduceeën* (Amsterdam: Buijten and Schipperheijn, 1973).

the Sadducees would mine doctrine. They did, however, have their own traditions vis-à-vis the sacrificial system and legal matters, but these were not binding. The Sadducees also denied the resurrection of the dead, as well as the existence of angels and spirits.[27] Even though the NT rarely mentions the Sadducees, this fact obscures the impact that this aristocracy had on the social setting of the first century.

The Pharisees

The origin of the Pharisees is unclear, though some associate the Pharisees with the Hasidim, the pious Jews who supported Judas Maccabeus in his struggle against Antiochus.[28] According to Josephus, the Pharisees contested John Hyrcanus's role as both high priest and king.[29] Their conflict with the Hasmoneans intensified until, under Alexander Janneus, the Pharisees were persecuted. Surprisingly, however, the Pharisees gained considerable power under Alexander's widow, Alexandra. With the establishment of the Herodian dynasty, however, the Pharisees' political power waned, so they concentrated on influencing the local level through their interpretation of the Torah. After the destruction of Jerusalem, the Pharisees initiated the establishment of Jewish religion in the post-temple era, and Rome recognized the political and religious position of these pharisaic scholars. The Judaism that survived the destruction of Jerusalem and the Bar Kochba revolt was primarily Pharisaic Judaism.[30]

---

27. See Acts 23:8. This verse has raised difficulties because there is no other source that confirms this Sadducean denial of angels and spirits; indeed there seems to be plenty of evidence in the Pentateuch to affirm the existence of these beings. In response, it has been suggested that they denied the elaborate angelology and demonology of the Pharisees. A second suggested solution is that the latter two negatives of Acts 23:8 are distributive, i.e., the Sadducees denied a resurrection (not only physical but) whether in the form of an angel or spirit. See D. Flusser, "Josephus on the Sadducees and Menander," *Immanuel* 7 (1977): 61–7.

28. For those scholars who support this view, see E. Lohse, *The New Testament Environment* (Nashville: Abingdon, 1976), 77; P. R. Davies, "Hasidim in the Maccabean Period," *Journal of Jewish Studies* 28 (1977): 127–40; Schürer, *History,* II, 400; Hengel, *Judaism and Hellenism,* I, 176.

29. Josephus, *Antiquities,* XIII, 288–298.

30. One must heed the caution of J. Neusner (*The Rabbinic Traditions About the Pharisees Before 70* [Leiden: Brill, 1971], III, 247), and not easily assume that the later rabbinic traditions are accurate descriptions of Pharisaism before A.D. 70. But see also E. Rivkin, *A Hidden Revolution: The Pharisees Search for the Kingdom Within* (Nashville: Abingdon, 1978), 72–75. Neusner believed that pre-70 first-century Pharisaism was quietistic and apolitical and concerned mostly with ritual, whereas Rivkin claimed this era of Pharisaism was revolutionary and concerned with a range of issues much broader than ritual purity.

Unlike the Sadducees, the Pharisees believed in the resurrection. Unlike the Qumranians who dwelt in isolation, the Pharisees lived in the towns, were interested in the world of the average Jew, and practiced a warm hospitality.[31] Josephus also noted the influence of the Pharisees on the townsfolk; the Pharisees were admired for their piety, their simple lifestyle, and their strict observance of their religion.[32] They did not restrict the authority of the Scriptures to the Pentateuch. The list of authoritative teachings also included the Writings, the Prophets and perhaps other oral traditions. It must also be noted that pharisaism was not monolithic. Various factions existed within the group, which at times even produced violent internecine confrontations. Nevertheless, pharisaism was the only Jewish sect that survived the crisis of A.D. 70.[33]

The Essenes

The Essenes' origin is enigmatic. Scholars often posit some sort of relationship with the Hasidim, but this is not certain.[34] Possibly the Essenes and the Qumran community are related, though this hypothesis also falls short of proof.[35] Josephus said that the Essenes repudiated slavery,[36] never took oaths,[37] and rigorously observed the Sabbath.[38] They rejected animal sacrifice in favor of bringing gifts to the temple,[39] paid close attention to personal purification rites, and preferred white clothing.[40] A simple life-style was endorsed in the context of communalism.[41]

31. Josephus, *Jewish War*, II, 166.

32. Josephus, *Antiquities*, 18:15.

33. For additional information on the Pharisees, see Schürer, *History*, II, 388–403; W. D. Davies, *Introduction to Pharisaism* (Philadelphia: Westminster, 1967); Neusner, *From Politics to Piety* (Englewood Cliffs, N. J.: Prentice-Hall, 1973); A. Finkel, *The Pharisees and the Teacher of Nazareth* (Leiden: Brill, 1974); Rivkin, *Hidden Revolution*.

34. So Hengel, *Judaism and Hellenism*, I, 175; B. Reicke, *New Testament Era* (Philadelphia: Fortress, 1968), 170.

35. Scholars who equate Qumran and the Essenes include E. Ferguson, *Backgrounds of Early Christianity* (Grand Rapids: Eerdmans, 1987); M. Black, *The Scrolls and Christian Origins* (Atlanta: Scholars, 1983), 45–47; Schürer, *History*, II, 583–85; A. Dupont-Sommer, *The Essene Writings from Qumran*, trans. G. Vermes (Oxford: Blackwell, 1961), 39–67.

36. Josephus, *Antiquities*, XVIII, 21.

37. Josephus, *Jewish War*, II, 135.

38. Ibid.

39. Josephus, *Antiquities*, XVIII, 19.

40. Josephus, *Jewish War*, II, 123, 149–150.

41. Josephus, *Jewish War*, II, 120; *Antiquities*, XVIII, 20.

The Essenes were apolitical and determined quietists.[42] Celibacy was practiced,[43] but not enforced.[44] Their various views of marriage suggest that perhaps the term "Essenes" was a broad one that included a number of subgroups, one of which may have been at Qumran. The Essenes generally were small farmers or craftsmen in small villages who avoided cities whenever possible because of injustice there.[45] Though their numbers were comparatively small,[46] the Essenes remained a part of Judaism until A.D. 70 when they disappeared from the historical record.

The Qumran Community

The Qumran community probably was in existence from about 150 or 140 B.C. until the Romans slaughtered it in A.D. 68.[47] At Qumran many Greek, Hebrew, and Aramaic writings have been found. These documents clearly show that they were rivals to the Jerusalem priests. Often a "godless priest" is mentioned who probably was the high priest in Jerusalem. Qumran apparently felt that worship at the temple was totally corrupt and regarded itself as the true Israel.

Leadership at Qumran consisted of twelve men who represented the twelve tribes of Israel, three priests (see 1QS 8:1f.), and the "teacher of righteousness." Attempts to identify this teacher are numerous (e.g., Jonathan, Alexander, John the Baptist, etc.), but all suggestions thus far are little more than conjecture.[48] As mentioned above, the Essenes and Qumran were described very similarly; however, Qumran put greater stress on purity and therefore on ritual washings (see CD 10:10–13; 12:12–14). The community also stressed discipline; for example, if one member answered another disrespectfully or impatiently, the offender was banned from the community for a year (1QS 6:26–27); for a verbal interruption, the sentence lasted ten days (1QS

42. Philo, *Quod omnis probus Liber sit*, 78.
43. Josephus, *Jewish War*, II, 120–121; *Antiquities*, XVIII, 21.
44. Josephus, *Jewish War*, II, 160–161.
45. Philo, *Quod omnis probus Liber sit*, 76.
46. Josephus (*Antiquities*, XVIII, 21) and Philo (*Quod omnis probus Liber sit*, 75) estimated their population at 4,000.
47. Cross, *The Ancient Library of Qumran* (Garden City, N. Y.; Doubleday, 1958), 57–60. But cf. E. M. Laperrousez, *Qumran, L'établissement essénien des bords de la Mer Morte* (Paris: A. J. Picard, 1976), 93–99, who argued that due to an earthquake Qumran was uninhabited from 67 B.C. until the beginning of Herod's reign.
48. For a survey of the views, see Vermes, *The Dead Sea Scrolls*, 160.

7:10); for loud or stupid laughter, a thirty-day penalty was enforced (1QS 6:14). An annual examination assigned rank to each member according to spiritual progress; each then sat in the assembly according to this rank.

The Zealots

Josephus seems to have reserved the term "Zealot" for the instigators of the revolt against Rome in A.D. 67; nevertheless, the party that instigated the revolt probably existed in at least embryonic form early in the first century (see Luke 6:15).[49] The Zealots argued that it was unlawful to pay taxes to Rome, for God alone was Lord (see Matt. 22:17). Since God himself would be outraged with the Romans' taxation of the Jews, God would fight with them if they would only take up arms and revolt. One branch of these revolutionaries was known as the Sicarii (lit. "dagger men"; see Acts 21:38). On festive occasions they would mingle among the crowds and stab prominent Jewish leaders who had collaborated with Roman officials, and then vanish among the crowds.[50]

The Herodians

The Herodians are not mentioned outside the Gospels, which themselves tell us little about this group. The name suggests that they were partisan to Herod and supporters of the Herodian dynasty. Others suggest that the Herodians were Essenes, but this is little more than conjecture.[51]

The People of the Land

In spite of the influence of the above mentioned religio-political parties, the majority of the Jews did not belong to any of them. This majority is often referred to as the "people of the land" (Heb. 'am hā'āreṣ). They did not deny Judaism or repudiate

---

49. See S. Freyne, *The World of the New Testament* (Wilmington, Del.: Michael Glazier, 1980), 120–21; D. Rhoads, *Israel in Revolution: 6–74 C.E.* (Philadelphia: Fortress, 1976).

50. Cf. Josephus, *Jewish War*, II, 254–257; IV, 400–405; *Antiquities*, XX, 186–187. For comprehensive works on the Zealots, see W. R. Farmer, *Maccabees, Zealots, and Josephus* (New York: Columbia University Press, 1957); M. Hengel, *Die Zeloten* (Leiden: Brill, 1961); R. A. Horsley, "The Zealots: Their Origin, Relationships and Importance in the Jewish Revolt," *Novum Testamentum* 28 (1986): 159–92. See also Schürer, *History*, II, 598–606.

51. See C. Daniel, "Les 'Hérodiens' du Nouveau Testament: Sont-Ils des Esséniens?" *Revue de Qumran* 6 (1967): 31–53.

the law, but they did lack the scrupulousness with which the other groups observed it. Most of the members of this group were farmers or day laborers. They were the ordinary people, the masses. Undoubtedly they were considered socially inferior and were ridiculed by the parties mentioned above.[52] By way of contrast, the Gospels portray Jesus not only as one who associated with these outcasts, but also as a leader who recruited most of his followers from among them. Indeed, Mark tells us that Jesus had compassion on them because they were "sheep without a shepherd" (Mark 6:34). Moreover, Jesus' concern for the lepers, handicapped, and sinners (members par excellence of "the people of the land") demonstrated his opposition to current social and religious prejudices.

The Samaritans

Within the context of the "people of the land," the Samaritans also should be mentioned because they too were victimized by Jewish prejudice. In the eighth century B.C., about two hundred years after Israel was split into north and south, the Assyrians subjugated the northern kingdom (later Samaria). Through a forced exchange program, Israelites were deported to Assyria and Assyrians were imported. Mixed marriages and syncretistic religion and culture were the result. The remaining Israelites in the southern kingdom regarded these inhabitants to the north as impure and unacceptable as coreligionists. After the inhabitants of the southern kingdom returned from the exile, they refused to let the Samaritans help with the rebuilding of the temple.[53] This refusal caused hatred, plots, killing, and even an attempt to assassinate Nehemiah the Judean leader.[54]

In the fourth century B.C. the Samaritans courted Alexander the Great, and were allowed to build a replica of the Jerusalem temple on Mount Gerizim. This act was viewed by the Judeans as a flagrant violation of the Torah.[55] The conflict and violence between these two groups even spread beyond Palestine into

---

52. Later rabbinic tradition advised against allowing one's daughter to marry one of the "people of the land" because the men among them were little more than sexual animals or worse yet, like Gentiles; see A. Oppenheimer, *The 'Am Ha-Aretz* (Leiden: Brill, 1977), 101–2.

53. Ezra 4:4; 1 Esdras 5:66–73; Josephus, *Antiquities*, XI, 87–88.

54. See Neh. 4:7; cf. Josephus, *Antiquities*, XI, 97, 174.

55. Josephus, *Antiquities*, XI, 322–324; see John 4:19–26.

the Diaspora.[56] When the Judeans experienced extreme suffering under Antiochus Epiphanes IV, the Samaritans told Antiochus that they were unrelated to the Judeans; they claimed that they were colonists from Persia! Furthermore, the Samaritans requested that their temple on Mount Gerizim be dedicated to Zeus Hellenios,[57] an act totally repugnant to the Judeans. Moreover, during the Jewish struggle with Antiochus, Apollonius, the governor of Samaria, led his soldiers against the Maccabean army.[58] Later that century Hyrcanus retaliated; he marched against Samaria, besieged it for a year, and then destroyed it.[59]

By the first century A.D., Pompey had liberated the Samaritans from Judean rule, rebuilt Samaria and stimulated enough goodwill that Samaria was clearly pro-Roman.[60] If this was not insulting enough to the Judeans, the Samaritans were also pro-Herod, who was bitterly opposed by the Judeans because he was not a purebred Jew. When Herod besieged Jerusalem in 37 B.C., the Samaritans actively aided the king.[61] Similar conflicts continued in the first century A.D. and tensions continued to escalate. With this background one can easily see that Jesus' parable about the good Samaritan is far more than a mere humanitarian statement. The parable is an incisive criticism of the deep racial and religious prejudice that had been festering for over seven hundred years. Obviously, this parable continues to speak with incredible force to contemporary society.[62]

Proselytes and God-fearers

Monotheism, high moral standards, synagogue worship, ancient Scriptures, and a sense of community all attracted Gentiles to the Jewish community. When a Gentile who had been favorably impressed by Judaism wished to become a part of the Jewish community, there were three requirements for initiation:

---

56. Josephus, *Antiquities*, XII, 7; XIII, 74–79.
57. Josephus, *Antiquities*, XII, 257–264.
58. 1 Macc. 3:10; Josephus, *Antiquities*, XII, 287.
59. Josephus, *Antiquities*, XIII, 273.
60. Josephus, *Antiquities*, XIV, 75; *Jewish War*, I, 156.
61. Josephus, *Jewish War*, I, 299.
62. On the Samaritans, see J. Macdonald, *The Theology of the Samaritans* (Philadelphia: Westminster, 1964); J. D. Purvis, *The Samaritan Pentateuch and the Origin of the Samaritan Sect* (Cambridge, Mass.: Harvard University Press, 1968); Schürer, *History*, II, 16–20; Ferguson, *Backgrounds*, 423–25; Koester, *Introduction*, I, 247–49.

circumcision, baptism, and an offering in the temple. When a family converted to Judaism all of the males were circumcised, regardless of their age. By way of contrast, both males and females were baptized. The earliest attestation of proselyte baptism is about A.D. 80. Nevertheless, most scholars feel that the practice is pre-Christian since the likelihood of Jews copying a Christian practice is slim. Proselyte baptism was by immersion and was self-administered. All family members were baptized, regardless of age.

Many Gentiles viewed circumcision as a mutilation of the body, which was not only painful but disgusting; therefore, it is not surprising to discover that many more women than men became Jewish converts. Often the men who were related to female Jewish converts were also attracted to Judaism, but stopped short of full membership because of circumcision. Those who wished to become a part of the Jewish community, but who did not want the stigma of circumcision, fit the special category of "god-fearer" (see Acts 10:2, 22, 35; 13:16, 26). These god-fearers attended synagogue, participated in imageless worship, and espoused monotheism. Furthermore, they adopted Jewish ethical standards and practiced Jewish piety (e.g., regular prayer and almsgiving).

The Apocalypticists

The apocalypticists are not a party per se, but many during the period from 200 B.C. to A.D. 100 became persuaded of apocalyptic eschatology. Russell has summarized its salient features:

1. The "future hope" of OT prophecy becomes strictly "eschatology".
2. The new eschatology is dualistic, expressing itself in a doctrine of two ages and involving a transcendental view of the coming kingdom.
3. The new order takes the form of a new beginning, free from corruption.
4. The transformation is cataclysmic, not evolutionary.
5. The transformation is brought about by supernatural power, not human or historical forces.

6. The transformation takes the form of a cosmic drama in which demonic and divine forces are engaged.
7. The transformation relates to the individual's eternal destiny and includes resurrection and judgment.
8. The consummation is wholly the work of God and is the fulfillment of His plan for the entire universe.[63]

Although some would argue that apocalyptic eschatology is discernible at least in embryonic form in some earlier writings,[64] this new genre of eschatology clearly did not reach its fully developed form until the period when most of the apocalypses were produced, namely, 200 B.C. to A.D. 100.[65] By 200 B.C. Israel had been back in their Promised Land nearly 350 years and had not yet attained the greatness promised by the classical prophets. Perhaps Israel was not the perfectly holy nation that the Law required; nevertheless, they had eradicated idolatry and could say with certainty that they were morally superior to their neighbors. Yet the promised kingdom never arrived. Israel was simply a pawn to be passed between subjugating nations.

Thus, for the apocalypticists Israel's situation looked funereal. It was a depressing period of unfulfilled hopes, shattered eschatological dreams, conflict with the ruling class, and lack of authorized prophetic spokesmen. Above all, periods of persecution plagued those who remained faithful to the Torah and traditional Hebrew religion, while prosperity flourished for the hellenized and severely compromised Jewish aristocracy. This crisis forced the apocalypticists to search for creative solutions, which gave rise to an apocalyptic eschatology that represented a new interpretation of human history and human destiny with new emphases and insights.

---

63. D. S. Russell, *The Method and Message of Jewish Apocalyptic* (Philadelphia: Westminster, 1964), 269. It must be noted that this is a description of apocalyptic eschatology, not of the literary genre of the apocalypses nor of the intellectual movement, both of which have been confusingly called "apocalyptic." See J. J. Collins, "Introduction: Towards the Morphology of a Genre," *Semeia* 14 (1979): 1–20, for a description of the literary genre of the apocalypses.

64. P. D. Hanson, *The Dawn of Apocalyptic* (Philadelphia: Fortress, 1975), 402–13, argued for the origination of an apocalyptic eschatology between 520 and 420 B.C. But Hanson himself contrasted this eschatological genre with preexilic and full-blown apocalyptic eschatology. We too would note the contrast but would stress continuity; indeed, we have argued that one is the antecedent of the other.

65. Hengel, *Judaism and Hellenism*, I, 217.

Faith and Practice

Monotheism

Israel interpreted the exile as God's discipline to teach Israel not to worship other gods. From the exile onward monotheism characterized Israel. The great Shema, "Hear, O Israel: The LORD our God, the LORD is one" (Deut. 6:4), became the basic creed for Jewish religionists and was never seriously questioned. Along with monotheism the Jews stressed God's holiness and transcendence. This stress, however, never precluded the possibility of a personal relationship with him. The insistence upon monotheism led to the slaughter of a great many Jews, but costly as it may have been, the repudiation of idolatry was considered a non-negotiable. All who suffered for standing firm were highly esteemed (see Test. Mos. 9–10; Mart. Isa.; 2 Macc. 6–7; 4 Macc. 4–19).[66]

Election

As with Israel's monotheism, the belief that the Hebrews were God's chosen people also intensified as a result of the exile. From the time of Ezra an exclusiveness and a strict separatism characterized the nation. This separatism manifested itself in specific religious practices in regard to circumcision, the Sabbath, the Law, priesthood, interracial marriages, etc. Israel's election was also related to the land of Palestine; the land was their permanent possession. Political ascendancy was theirs as soon as the requirement of obedience was met.[67]

The Law

The Pentateuch was Law in the primary sense and was absolutely binding; the rest of the OT was supplementary. The Law was offered to every nation but only Israel accepted it. The Law was a joy to follow—not a burden. Israel believed that it was

---

66. For a discussion of Jewish monotheism, see Hengel, *Judaism and Hellenism*, I, 261–67; J. R. Bartlett, *Jews in the Hellenistic World* (Cambridge: Cambridge University Press, 1985), 146–47; Schürer, *History*, II, 454–56; S. J. D. Cohen, *From the Maccabees to the Mishnah* (Philadelphia: Westminster, 1987), 79–87.

67. On Israel's election, see E. P. Sanders, *Paul and Palestinian Judaism* (London: SCM, 1977), 84–106, 257–69; Ferguson, *Backgrounds*, 427; W. D Davies, *The Gospel and the Land* (Berkeley, Calif.: University of California Press, 1974).

eternal and preexistent, and even that it had a share in creation. However, to what extent the nation of Israel kept the Law is difficult to know exactly. Certainly some sincerely tried to keep the Law, others apostatized, while still others argued that a strict interpretation of the Law was not really Moses' original intent. Many (perhaps the majority) lacked the time, energy, and education to practice the Law scrupulously. They probably concerned themselves more with health and harvests than with personal piety.

The Temple

The structure built by Solomon in the tenth century B.C. had been destroyed by the Babylonians in 586 B.C. but was rebuilt shortly after Israel returned from exile (520–516 B.C.). Herod, however, was the one who restored the temple to its former glory. The principal furnishings in the temple were the altar of incense, the table of shewbread, and the seven-branched candlestick. Between the sanctuary that held these articles of furniture and the Holy of Holies hung a curtain. Outside the temple lay a series of courts (from the innermost to the outermost): the Court of Priests (reserved for priests in the state of ritual purity), the Court of Israel (reserved for Jewish men), the Court of Women (reserved for any Jew), and the Court of the Gentiles (where any could enter; also, the site of Jesus' "cleansing" activity).

The temple was the central sanctuary where all of the sacrifices and Israel's three main festivals were to take place. Its explicit function was to focus Israel's attention upon their God. This centralized cult not only unified Israel and focused Israel's worship, but it also provided an opportunity for the Jews to express their loyalty in a tangible way, namely, in their offerings and sacrifices. Though not its original intent, the temple also functioned as a political center. As such the Jews often sought refuge from foreign armies within the fortified walls of the temple. In A.D. 70 the Roman armies sacked Jerusalem and destroyed the temple. Today, only the great stones of the outer wall and the supporting arches under the southeast corner of the platform remain.[68]

---

68. On the temple, see Safrai and Stern, *Jewish People*, II, 865–907; Schürer, *History*, I, 273–305; B. Mazar, *The Mountain of the Lord* (Garden City, N. Y.: Doubleday, 1975); Gowan, *Bridge*, 249–57.

Synagogue

The origin of the Jewish synagogue is unknown, but archaeological digs in Egypt indicate that synagogues were in use at least
by the third century B.C. By the first century, many synagogues
dotted Palestine and the Diaspora. The synagogue was the center
of the social and religious life of the Jewish community, functioning as the schoolhouse, place of prayer, meeting house, and judgment hall. The building was essentially a meeting hall; it probably
had a platform and chairs for the worship leaders, and the teacher
would sit during the time of instruction. There were two offices:
the ruler and the minister. The ruler conducted the meeting and
decided upon its participants while the minister was the ruler's
assistant and performed many of the mundane tasks, (e.g., bringing out and returning the scrolls after each service). The service
was simply structured: the Shema, prayer, reading of the Torah
with translation, reading of the Prophets with translation, sermon, and blessing. Many scholars feel that the synagogue provided a paradigm for worship in the early church.[69]

Sanhedrin

The earliest reference to the Sanhedrin occurs in Josephus
who mentioned a Jewish *gerousia*, "senate," composed of priests
and elders under the direction of the high priest.[70] During the
Hasmonean dynasty its powers were curtailed, but it continued
to function. Salome (76–67 B.C.) was the first to appoint Pharisees to the Sanhedrin; previously it had been primarily Sadducees. During the first century the Sanhedrin was composed of
the chief priests, elders, and scribes. In A.D. 6 when Judea became a Roman province, the Sanhedrin was granted almost exclusive control over Israel's internal affairs; apparently this authority also extended into the Diaspora. When Jerusalem fell in
A.D. 70 the Sanhedrin was permanently dissolved.[71]

---

69. J. Gutmann, ed., *The Synagogue: Studies in Origins, Archaeology and Architecture* (New
York: Ktav, 1975); J. Heinemann and J. J. Petuchowski, eds., *Literature of the Synagogue* (New
York: Behrman House, 1975); J. Gutmann, ed., *Ancient Synagogues* (Chico, Calif.: Scholars,
1981); Schürer, *History*, II, 52–80; Safrai and Stern, *Jewish People*, II, 908–44.

70. Josephus, *Antiquities*, XII, 138–140; see also Acts 5:21.

71. For more on the Sanhedrin, see H. Mantel, *Studies in the History of the Sanhedrin*
(Cambridge, Mass.: Harvard University Press, 1961); Safrai and Stern, *Jewish People*, I, 377–
419, 504–33; Schürer, *History*, I, 163–95; Gowan, *Bridge*, 295–97.

The Sabbath

The seventh day of the week, the Sabbath, was set aside as a holy day. The Sabbath was not only a day of rest, but also a day to attend synagogue and to gather family and friends for a common meal. Certain activities transcended the Sabbath and were allowed: circumcision, temple sacrifice, saving human life, etc. The regulations that clarified the keeping of the Sabbath quickly proliferated. Nevertheless, the Sabbath was intended to be a celebration. The best meal of the week was prepared for this day, fasting was forbidden, and even mourning and visiting the sick had restrictions. Rightly observed, the Sabbath was the highlight of the week.

Messianic Expectations

Jewish expectation of the future tended to be optimistic. Even when doom was impending in the form of the Babylonian captivity, there still was the hope that one day Israel would return and be a global power. However, it is not likely that many of the Jews in the OT period linked the Messiah with the optimism anticipated in Israel's future. During the intertestamental period heroic figures who would deliver Israel became more popular. The Samaritans' hope was the *Taheb* or "the restorer" (see John 4:25). The Psalms of Solomon 17–18 refer to a coming king who is the son of David and "the anointed of the Lord." In 1QS 9:11 two Messiahs are apparently mentioned: an Aaronic priest and a Davidic king. The Qumran Rule of Community also mentions an eschatological prophet along with these two Messiahs. In the similitudes of Enoch (1 Enoch 37–71) a supernatural "Son of Man" is described in terms similar to Daniel 7 (see 2 Esdras 13). The Testaments of the Twelve Patriarchs describe a person who saves the race of Israel (Test. Sim. 7:2), is filled with the Spirit and judges and saves all that call upon the Lord (Test. Judah 24:1–6), arises from Judah and Levi (Test. Dan 5:10), and destroys all of Israel's enemies (Test. Joseph 19:8), but never calls this person Messiah. Perhaps it is better only to speak of an eschatological priest and an eschatological prophet when referring to these Testaments.

Thus there was not a single, uniform, widespread messianic

expectation in pre-Christian Judaism. Moreover, the messianic expectation which was current in pre-Christian Judaism was generally a purely human figure whose functions were primarily political. Messiah was not spoken of in terms of God incarnate, nor was there any explicit mention of Messiah saving people from their sins. Furthermore, there is no evidence that Isaiah 53, the Christian proof text for a suffering Messiah, was ever interpreted messianically before it was applied to Jesus.

Eternal Destiny

In first-century Judaism there was no unanimity among Jewish writers concerning the afterlife. Sirach (ca. 175 b.c.) echoed the belief found in the majority of the OT that upon death one enters the underworld; this shadowy existence is left fairly undefined (see Ecclus. 14:16–19; 17:25–32; 38:16–23; 51:5–6). Both the Wisdom of Solomon (ca. 20 b.c.?) and Fourth Maccabees (ca. a.d. 35) affirm the immortality of the soul (Wis. Sol. 2:24–3:11; 8:13, 17; 15:2–3; 4 Macc. 14:6; 18:23). Resurrection, which is almost never mentioned in the OT (see Isa. 26:19; Dan. 12:2), is affirmed in Second Maccabees (see 2 Macc. 7:9, 11, 14, 23; 12:43–45). Those who affirmed resurrection had divergent views as to its nature. Some argued that the life to come was merely a glorious extension of the present age (see T. B. Sanh. 9lb; Sib. Or. 4:179–190; Gen. Rab. 14:5; 95:1). Others denied that physical pleasures (e.g., feasts, sex, etc.) would be included in the resurrection (T.B. Ber. 17a). Sheol or Hades increasingly became the abode of the wicked where its inhabitants would be tortured, usually with fire (T.B. Hag. 15a; Pesah. 54a). Sometimes this punishment is replaced with annihilation (Gen. Rab. 26 on 6:3) and for the more benign sinners release after a period of purging was even postulated (Tos. Sanh. 13:3–6). As is obvious, the Jewish theology of the afterlife was not a widespread systematic dogma.[72]

---

72. For additional discussion on the afterlife, see Russell, *Jewish Apocalyptic*, 353–90; G. W. E. Nickelsburg, *Resurrection, Immortality and Eternal Life in Intertestamental Judaism* (Cambridge, Mass.: Harvard University Press, 1972); H. C. C. Cavallin, *Life After Death* (Lund: Gleerup, 1974); Schürer, *History*, II, 539–47.

Forms of Hellenistic Religious Expression

Although Graeco-Roman religious expression took a variety of forms, some generalizations are possible. First, Graeco-Roman religion was inclusive; any nation's deity could have been added to the pantheon. Second, a spreading syncretism that began to blend deities together catalyzed a tendency toward monotheism. Third, the power of fate was emphasized; it found philosophical justification in Stoicism and was even worshiped as a deity. This belief in fate was often linked to the stars, so that astrology also received increased attention. Fourth, magic was a means of managing the world; the use of superstition, sorcery, amulets, healing formulas, and divination proliferated. Fifth, religion was not a private enterprise; rather it had a corporate nature and an active social side. Accordingly, piety was not privatized. Finally, religion and morality were not closely linked; rules of ritual purity were normally ceremonial and not ethical or moral.[73]

Greek Sacrifice

At the heart of the message of the NT is a message about one whose death was an atoning sacrifice. This message was one that the Graeco-Roman world would clearly understand; they regularly employed sacrifice in their worship, and the theology of human sacrifice was common knowledge, but a distinction must be made between Olympian and Chthonian worship.[74] The purpose of sacrifice to the Chthonians was to placate the evil

---

73. Ferguson, *Backgrounds*, 133–35. Some good works that survey religious expression in the Graeco-Roman world include: G. Murray, *Five Stages of Greek Religion* (Oxford: Clarendon Press, 1925); M. P. Nilsson, *Greek Piety*, trans. H. J. Rose (Oxford: Clarendon Press, 1948); E. R. Dodds, *The Greeks and the Irrational* (Berkeley, Calif.: University of California Press, 1966); W. K. C. Guthrie, *The Greeks and their Gods* (Boston: Beacon, 1951); F. C. Grant, *Roman Hellenism and the New Testament* (New York: Scribner, 1962); J. Ferguson, *The Religions of the Roman Empire* (Ithaca, N. Y.: Cornell University Press, 1970); R. MacMullen, *Paganism in the Roman Empire* (New Haven: Yale University Press, 1981); R. Parker, *Miasma* (Oxford: Clarendon Press, 1983); W. Burkert, *Greek Religion*, trans. J. Raffan (Cambridge, Mass.: Harvard University Press, 1985).

74. J. E. Harrison, *Prolegomena to the Study of Greek Religion*, 3d ed. (Cambridge: Cambridge University Press, 1922), 10. This distinction has been commonly accepted since her work. See R. K. Yerkes, *Sacrifice in Greek and Roman Religion and in Early Judaism* (London: Adam and Charles Black, 1953), 53–60, and esp. 221 n. 9: "While some of her conclusions have been questioned by scholars, minor differences of opinion have not affected the general recognition of the value of her penetrating evaluation of the sources." See also H. J. Rose, *Religion in Greece and Rome* (New York: Harper, 1959).

spirits who caused disease, old age, and death, as well as to
remove pollution and to appease the powers below. These ma-
levolent powers were not welcome guests at the religious ritu-
als. These rites were nocturnal and executed with dread, an
obvious contrast to the joyous daytime sacrificial festivals held
for the Olympians. The worship of the Chthonians is regarded
as the most primitive aspect of Greek religion.[75]

Sacrificial festivals were the traditional means utilized to
overcome all sorts of social crises. Extraordinary situations of
emergency, famine, and disease led to human sacrifice again
and again. Samples of popular atoning sacrifices are supplied
as examples:

> There is the myth as well as the memorial of two Boeotian
> sisters, Androcleia and Acis, who voluntarily sacrificed
> themselves in the place of Antipoinos, their father, in order
> to save Thebes.[76]

> Another pair of Boeotian sisters, daughters of Orion in Aeonia,
> were sacrificed to propitiate two underworld gods. They
> died on behalf of their fellow citizens.[77]

> In Athens a homicide in the temple brought a plague down
> upon the city. Two men voluntarily sacrificed themselves
> and expiated this "crime of Cylon."[78]

> The ancient blood guilt of Oedipus was atoned for by the
> human sacrifice of Menoeceus.[79]

> Attica, while about to be overrun by the Dioscurio, offered a
> foreigner, Marathon by name, who volunteered to be an
> expiatory sacrifice. As a result, Attica was victorious and a
> city was founded in the victim's honor.[80]

> An oracle from Apollo demanded a human sacrifice to save
> Athens from the enemy. Thus, Aglauros, Cecrops' priest-

---

75. F. M. Young, *The Use of Sacrificial Ideas in Greek Christian Writers* (Philadelphia: Patristic
Foundation, 1979), 13–14.
76. Pausanias, *Boeotia* 17.1–2.
77. Ovid, *Metamorphoses* 4.389.
78. Diogenes Laertius, *Lives of the Eminent Philosophers* 1:110; *Athenagoras,* 13.602C–602D.
79. Statius, *Thebias* 10.756–782; Hyginus, *Fabulae* 68.
80. Plutarch, *Theseus* 32.4.

ess daughter, cast herself to her death in order to deliver the city.[81]

Unquestionably, these examples are all expiatory sacrifices.

In five of Euripides' extant tragedies atoning human sacrifice plays a prominent role.[82] Indeed, voluntary self-sacrifice nearly becomes routine in the tragedies of Euripides.[83] The Greek tragedy writers Aeschylus and Sophocles also vibrate with this theme.[84] A final example comes from Lucan, nephew of Seneca and contemporary of the apostle Paul. In his *Pharsalia* he depicted Cato's death as an atoning sacrifice. At the climax of this work, Cato said: "May the strict gods of the Romans receive complete expiation . . . may the two armies pierce me through. . . . this, my blood, will ransom all the people; this, my death, will achieve atonement for all that the Romans have deserved through their moral decline." These words help us understand why the earliest Christian message made sense in a Graeco-Roman milieu.

Mystery Religions

With the steady decline in institutional and traditional religion, participation in the mystery cults increased. "Mystery" is defined as a secret rite by which selected individuals were brought into a special relationship with a god and were guaranteed certain benefits. For example, Dionysus was a god who died and was resurrected, and who assured the fertility of the earth and the fermentation of wine. The ambrosial nectar consumed by Dionysian worshipers caused an intoxicated state which, when combined with orgiastic rites, left the worshiper feeling touched by the power and mystery of Dionysus. In an agricultural context the mystery religions celebrated the death and resurrection of the god at seedtime and harvest. In an urban context the mysteries delivered the worshiper from banal existence; however, identification with the god's death and resurrec-

---

81. Philochorus, *Fragmenta Historicorum Graecorum*, ed. C. Müller, 5 vols. (Paris: n.p., 1841–70), 328 F105–106.

82. The five extant tragedies containing the theme of self-sacrifice are: *Alcestis, Heraclides, Hecuba, Supplices,* and *Phoenissae.*

83. W. Burkert, *Structure and History in Greek Mythology and Ritual* (Berkeley, Calif.: University of California Press, 1980), 71.

84. Aeschylus wrote about Iphigenia, and Sophocles wrote dramas about both Iphigenia and Polyxena.

tion enabled the celebrant to share the mystery of life and to merge with the cosmic order.[85]

Cynicism

Cynicism was another important development. One of Cynicism's preeminent spokesmen, Diogenes Laertius, attributed to Antisthenes, the precursor of the Cynics, the revolutionary insight that suffering had merit: "By means of the great Heracles and Cyrus, (Antisthenes) demonstrated that hardship is good."[86] Diogenes accepted, developed, expanded, and popularized the teaching of Antisthenes. Probably the most illuminating story about Diogenes was told by Dio Chrysostom (ca. A.D. 80). Arriving at the Isthmian games Diogenes was asked if he had come as a spectator; he replied that he was instead a participant. After some laughter and scorn from his questioners, they asked about the identity of his opponents. Diogenes responded succinctly: "The toughest opponent imaginable—hardships." Diogenes' goal in life was ". . . to despise wealth, reputation, pleasure, life; and to be superior in their opposites: poverty, ill fame, hardship and death."[87]

Four distinct elements were foundational to the Cynics' understanding of the nature of the universe: (1) a pessimistic Weltanschauung (worldview); (2) the wise one is part of a decided minority; (3) there is a tendency toward masochism; (4) suffering is believed to be part of nature and therefore beneficial to experience.

Undoubtedly the wandering Cynic philosophers colored the way citizens of the NT era viewed Christian missionaries. Cynic influence on Paul's radical style of missionary work is also arguable. The list of Paul's hardships (2 Cor. 11:23–29) possibly parallels similar catalogues in Cynic diatribes.[88] Other possible paral-

---

85. For important works on the mystery religions, see B. M. Metzger, "A Classified Bibliography of the Graeco-Roman Mystery Religions 1924–1973 with a supplement 1978–1979," *Aufstieg und Niedergang der römischen Welt*, II/17.3 (Berlin: 1984), 1259–1423.

86. Diogenes Laertius, *Lives of Eminent Philosophers* 6.2.

87. Flor 8.6.19 (translation from H. D. Rankin, *Sophists, Socratics and Cynics* [London: Athlone Press, 1983], 233). For a good summary of Diogenes, his relationship to Antisthenes and early Cynicism, see Rankin, *Sophists*, 229–37. See also R. Höistad, *Cynic Hero and Cynic King* (Uppsala: n.p., 1948), 5–21.

88. See H. D. Betz, *Der Apostel Paulus und die sokratische Tradition* (Tübingen: Mohr, 1972), 98.

lels include Jesus' nomadic existence (Luke 9:58), his instructions to travel lightly (Mark 6:8), and his teaching on anxiety and wealth (Matt. 6:19–34).

Stoicism

That Cynicism and Stoicism were closely connected is well attested.[89] The Stoics, however, attempted a more philosophical understanding of their world than the Cynics, and they endeavored to think systematically. It seems that Stoicism had three main intellectual preoccupations: physics, logic, and ethics. Stoic physics postulated a universe that was the embodiment of a nonmaterial force, partly active and partly passive; the active portion was soul. The divine logos principle controlled the cosmos and permeated all of creation. Often this divine logos was thought to be the soul of the universe, and the individual human soul was considered to be an emanation of this logos and therefore divine. Stoics believed that God determined the world and all of its events. Providence was his rationality, making the process purposeful: it provided for the maintenance and good order of the world and its beneficence to humanity.[90] Pain, suffering, and evil operated in a just and purposeful manner. Thus the Cynics viewed suffering positively.

Although foreign to the basic thrust of the OT (which affirms the retributive principle: good is rewarded, evil is punished), the notion that suffering is somehow beneficial is quite at home in the NT (see Rom. 5:3–5; Heb. 12:4–13; James 1:2–4). Stoic influence on Paul is almost certain from his use of the diatribe, a method of argumentation assuming a hypothetical objector (e.g., Rom. 6:1, 7:7; 9:14). Moreover, terms common in both the NT and Stoicism are easily demonstrated (e.g., self-sufficiency, Spirit, conscience, logos, virtue, etc.). Finally, the household codes (Eph. 5:21–6:9; Col. 3:18–4:1; 1 Pet. 2:13–3:7; etc.) in both form and content also suggest Stoic influence.[91]

---

89. A. A. Long, *Problems in Stoicism* (London: Athlone Press, 1971), 219; Rankin, *Sophists,* 250–52; J. M. Rist, *Stoic Philosophy* (Cambridge, Mass.: Cambridge University Press, 1969), 54–80. See also Diogenes Laertius, *Lives of Eminent Philosophers* 6.104–105; especially 7.2–3: "Indeed there is a definite and close relationship between the two schools."

90. F. H. Sandbach, *The Stoics* (New York: Norton, 1975), 79–80.

91. See J. E. Crouch, *The Origin and Intention of the Colossian Haustafel* (Göttingen: Vandenhoeck and Ruprecht, 1972); D. L. Balch, *Let Wives Be Submissive: The Domestic Code in 1 Peter* (Chico, Calif.: Scholars, 1981).

Gnosticism

Another important nontraditional religious system was Gnosticism. Each Gnostic teacher fashioned the Gnostic material with a sense of individuality so that "Gnosticism" is now a general term that covers a bewildering array of individual constructions. If we keep this caveat in mind, it is possible to outline some general characteristics of Gnosticism. Most Gnostics believed matter was evil, but spirit was good. Indeed, at the heart of Gnosticism lay a radical dualism between the world above and the world below, between truth and falsehood, knowledge and ignorance, light and darkness, spirit and matter. In Gnostic anthropology humans were believed to be ignorant and blind and destined to wander aimlessly in the darkness; yet some did possess a spark of the divine. A redeemer was sent from God who intervened and enlightened those who were lost; he revealed the way to escape from the material world. Once enlightened and in possession of special knowledge (Gk. *gnōsis*; hence, Gnostic), the Gnostics recognized their heavenly citizenship, their origin, and their destiny. Some of the common themes in Gnosticism include: (1) the existence of intermediate spirit beings, which are emanations from the first principle; (2) classes of humans, which determine their fate; (3) an emphasis on pneumatic experience; (4) freedom from the moral law, which leads either to asceticism or libertinism; (5) a desire to know the secrets of the universe; (6) a sense of alienation from the world and a preoccupation with the problem of evil.[92]

Some of the false teaching attacked in the NT was possibly some sort of incipient Gnosticism. Some of the themes in the Corinthian literature (e.g., wisdom, knowledge, freedom, pneumatic experience, etc.) sound strangely similar to Gnostic ideas. The dualisms in the Gospel of John (e.g., life and death, truth and falsehood, light and darkness) resemble those found in Gnosticism. The author of Colossians seemed to combat a heresy that was bent on cosmic speculation. The pastoral Epistles attack a false teaching devoted to asceticism, aeon speculation, an exclusive claim to a higher knowledge, and an inclination

---

92. H. Jonas, *The Gnostic Religion*, 2d ed. (Boston: Beacon, 1963), 42–47; A. D. Nock, "Gnosticism," *Harvard Theological Review* 57 (1964): 255–79; K. Rudolph, *Gnosis: The Nature and History of Gnosticism*, trans. R. McL. Wilson (San Francisco: Harper and Row, 1983), 53–272.

toward libertine behavior. These contours have a certain resemblance to religious themes in Gnosticism.[93]

This chapter is an introduction to the background of the NT. As limited as this discussion has been, it is apparent how invaluable backgrounds are for understanding the NT. Each area we studied is important because of the contribution it makes to the milieu from which the NT emerged. Other backgrounds are also significant to the NT exegete (e.g., Jewish Mysticism, Epicureanism, Neopythagoreanism, entertainment, education, social institutions, etc.), but because of the limits of this inquiry they were excluded. We have explored NT background area by area and theme by theme. This procedure is somewhat artificial since all of first-century reality hung together in a cohesive cultural matrix. The task of the NT exegete is to attempt to rebuild that matrix bit by bit, piece by piece, block by block, and then interpret the NT within the boundaries of that matrix. If we are able to rebuild that matrix accurately, then we will be better able to understand a particular text and unpack its meaning on its own terms. After uncovering the text's intended meaning, then, and only then, are we able accurately to draw significance from it for our own cultural matrix today.

---

93. On Gnosticism, see D. M. Scholer, "Bibliographica Gnostica, Supplementum," *Novum Testamentum* 13 (1971): 322–36, and succeeding autumn issues. See also R. McL. Wilson, *Gnosis and the New Testament* (Philadelphia: Fortress, 1968); E. Yamauchi, *Pre-Christian Gnosticism*, 2d ed. (Grand Rapids: Baker, 1983); A. Segal, *Two Powers in Heaven: Early Rabbinic Reports about Christianity and Gnosticism* (Leiden: Brill, 1977); P. Perkins, *The Gnostic Dialogue* (New York: Paulist, 1980); B. Layton, ed., *The Rediscovery of Gnosticism*, 2 vols. (Leiden: Brill, 1980–81); C. G. Strousma, *Another Seed: Studies in Gnostic Mythology* (Leiden: Brill, 1984); C. W. Hendrick, and R. Hodgson, eds., *Nag Hammadi Gnosticism and Early Christianity* (Peabody, Mass.: Hendrickson, 1986).

2

New Testament Textual Criticism
Michael W. Holmes

Textual criticism, the science and art of reconstructing the original text of a document, is a necessary step in the exegesis of the NT because the original documents are no longer extant and the existing copies differ (sometimes widely) among themselves. Thus the exegete must determine the precise wording of a text before attempting to interpret it. The threefold task of NT textual criticism involves: (1) gathering and organizing the evidence, including especially the collation (comparison) and manuscripts (– MSS) with one another, in order to ascertain where errors and alterations have produced variations in the text; (2) evaluating and assessing the significance and implications of the evidence to determine which of the variant readings most likely represents the original text; and (3) reconstructing the history of the transmission of the text to the extent allowed by the evidence.

This chapter will focus on the second task, the practice of evaluating variant readings and determining which of them most likely preserves the text of the original document. The discussion assumes that the reader has at least a passing acquaintance with such basics as the making of ancient books, the kinds of evidence (Greek MSS, patristic citations, early translations) available, the causes of errors in transmission, and a general idea of how to read the critical apparatus in Nestle-Aland, *Novum Testamentum Graece*, 26th edition (=NA[26]), and/or the United Bible Societies' *The Greek New Testament*, 3rd edition (=UBS[3]).[1] Before proceeding to the central focus of the chapter, it will be helpful to say a few words about contemporary approaches to textual criticism.

Contemporary Approaches to Textual Criticism

The classical method of textual criticism relied heavily upon a stemmatic or genealogical approach that sought to reconstruct a *stemma* or family tree of surviving MSS and thereby to determine the "best manuscript" upon which to base an edition. But in the case of the NT this classical approach has proven to be unworkable. Except in the case of certain small subgroups of MSS (e.g., f^1, f^{13}) it has not been possible to reconstruct a stemma for the textual tradition as a whole. This is due to (1) the relatively large number of MSS involved and (2) the widespread presence of mixture (or "cross-pollination") within the textual tradition, which means that at any given point even the most reliable MS or group of MSS may be wrong; conversely (at least in theory), even a MS of very poor quality may occasionally preserve a true reading. Consequently an approach has emerged that is best described as a *reasoned eclecticism*.[2] This approach seeks to apply all the tools and

---

1. Those who need additional information on these topics may consult the following: on the making of ancient books, see B. M. Metzger, *The Text of the New Testament* (New York/Oxford: Oxford University Press, 1968), 3–35, and J. Finegan, *Encountering New Testament Manuscripts* (Grand Rapids: Eerdmans, 1974), 19–46; on Greek MSS, early translations, and patristic citations, see Metzger, *Text*, 36–92, and K. and B. Aland, *The Text of the New Testament* (Leiden/Grand Rapids: Brill/Eerdmans, 1987), 72–217; on the causes of error, see Metzger, *Text*, 186–206. On the history of the text see B. M. Metzger, *A Textual Commentary on the Greek New Testament* (London/New York: United Bible Societies, 1971), xv–xxiv, G. D. Fee, "The Textual Criticism of the New Testament," in *The Expositor's Bible Commentary*, ed. F. E. Gaebelein, 12 vols. (Grand Rapids: Zondervan, 1979), 1:425–29, and Aland, *Text*, 48–71; on the history of printed editions of the NT, see Metzger, *Text*, 95–146, and Aland, *Text*, 3–47; on the history of scholarly study of the NT text, see Metzger, *Text*, 149–55; and on modern methods, see Metzger, *Text*, 156–85, and Fee, "Criticism," 430–31. For an introduction to the use of NA[26] and UBS[3] see Aland, *Text*, 218–62.

2. Sometimes referred to as "rational criticism" (Lagrange) or the "local-genealogical" method (Aland).

criteria developed by the classical method on a passage-by-passage basis. No one rule or principle can be applied nor any one MS or group followed in a mechanical or across-the-board fashion; each variation unit must be approached on its own merits and as possibly unique.

Differences in method today are largely a matter of differing judgments as to the relative weight to be given to *external* (or, in some cases, *which* external) evidence (i.e., the MSS themselves; see step two below) over against *internal* evidence (i.e., considerations having to do with scribes or authors; see step three below), although there are a few notable exceptions. One is the so-called rigorous eclecticism.[3] This method relies almost exclusively on internal considerations and places little if any weight on external evidence, treating the MSS as little more than a storehouse of readings to be evaluated on other grounds.[4] On the other extreme is the majority text method. It seeks to eliminate entirely any appeal to internal evidence, arguing that at any given point a variant that is supported by a majority of the MSS ought to be accepted as original. This substitutes counting for reasoned criticism, and fails to realize that ten thousand copies of a mistake do not make it any less a mistake.[5]

What the majority text and the rigorous eclectic approaches have in common is a disregard for the history of the textual tradition. If, however, one takes the history of the text seriously, it becomes impossible to rely entirely upon either external or internal criteria alone. Instead, depending upon the facts in any given instance, a *reasoned* eclecticism applies a *combination* of internal and external considerations, evaluating the character of the variants in light of the MSS evidence and vice versa in order to obtain a balanced view of the matter and as a check upon purely subjective tendencies. This is the method and approach that will be presented below.[6]

---

3. Exemplified most notably by G. D. Kilpatrick and J. K. Elliott; see J. K. Elliott, "Keeping up with Recent Studies XV: New Testament Textual Criticism," *Expository Times* 99 (1987): 43–44.

4. See G. D. Fee, "Rigorous or Reasoned Eclecticism—Which?" in *Studies in New Testament Language and Text*, ed. J. K. Elliott (Leiden: Brill, 1976), 174–97.

5. For a bibliography and critique of this approach, see M. W. Holmes, "The 'Majority text debate': new form of an old issue," *Themelios* 8 (1983): 13–19.

6. The best introductory treatment of this approach is still that of Metzger, *Text*, 207–46.

The Evaluation of Variant Readings

The Fundamental Guideline

One overarching fundamental guideline governs all other considerations: *the variant most likely to be original is the one which best accounts for the existence of the others.* That is, when confronted with two or more variant readings in the text, one should ask, "Which one best explains, in terms of both external and internal evidence, the origin of the others?" It is important to emphasize that "best accounts for" is here defined in terms of *both* external and internal considerations, because *prerequisite to reaching a judgment about a variant is the reconstruction of its history.* Here both the majority text and rigorous eclectic approaches fall short in that they repeatedly contend for the originality of readings which cannot account for the historical (i.e., manuscript) evidence. Only the variant that can best account for all the evidence can seriously be considered as original.

The Basic Process

Within the framework established by the fundamental guideline several factors must be taken into consideration. Exactly which ones ought to be considered and how much weight is to be given to each depends upon the facts and circumstances in any given case. It may be helpful, therefore, to list the basic steps followed in the process of evaluating readings along with the various considerations which must be taken into account. The application and use of the steps will then be illustrated by several examples.

Step One: Organize the Data

Before attempting to evaluate a variant reading it is often helpful to organize the data provided by the textual apparatus. Whereas NA[26] indicates by means of its textual symbols whether a variant involves an addition (⌐), deletion (o o˅), transposition (⌐ . . . ˅), or substitution (⌐,⌐ . . . ˅), UBS[3] does not. On the other hand, whereas UBS[3] gives a very full listing of the evidence for each reading, NA[26], in order to save space, frequently lists only part of the evidence, leaving it to the reader to supply, with the help of the introduction to NA[26], whatever is lacking. But since few will have committed to memory all the information needed to do this mentally, it is best if one writes out as fully as possible the evidence for all the variants at a particular point in the text. Also, underlining or highlighting the differences often helps to clarify the issue or question to be resolved.

Often this step may be combined with step two below. Rather than repeating the evidence in the (somewhat arbitrary) order in which it appears in the apparatus (papyri, uncials, minuscules, lectionaries, versions, patristic citations), it is more helpful to categorize it according to its textual relationships (see step two, 3, and Table 1 below). A chart format (see Table 6 below) consisting of several rows across and six or more columns down is useful: in the first column are placed the variants, one per row, with one or more blank rows left between the variants. One could then use columns 2–5 to list for each variant the Alexandrian, Western, Byzantine, and other witnesses supporting it. The remaining columns could be used for notes or observations about internal considerations. The space under each variant provides room for notes on the dates of important witnesses (esp. early MSS and church fathers) or other comments. When completed, the chart should contain all the information reported in the apparatus in a reorganized and more informative format, along with a great deal of critical data not included in the apparatus. In short, a properly constructed chart will display virtually all the evidence needed to make a reasoned choice between the variants.

Step Two: Evaluate the External Evidence

There are four basic factors to consider when evaluating external evidence (i.e., evidence provided by the MSS and other witnesses).

1. *The Relative Date of the Witnesses.* The emphasis here falls primarily upon the earlier strata of MSS and citations (although it must be remembered that a late MS may preserve a very early form of the text; e.g., MS 1739 [10th cent. A.D.] preserves a text closely related to 𝔓[46] [ca. A.D. 200]). Does the earlier evidence support one variant more than the others? Are there some variants without any early support? Or do all the readings have early support? These are the kinds of questions to ask.

2. *The Geographic Distribution of the Witnesses.* Here the early

versions and patristic citations are particularly important, since the place of origin of many MSS is not known. Generally, the broader the geographic distribution of the supporting witnesses, the higher the probability that the variant may be original (assuming that remote witnesses are not otherwise related). It is also true, however, as in linguistics, that change often affects remote areas last, if at all; hence a true reading may be preserved in only a few witnesses from the fringes of the MSS tradition.

3. *The Genealogical Relationships between the MSS.* Most NT MSS tend to fall into one of three major text-types: (1) the Alexandrian, (2) the Western,[7] and (3) the Byzantine (or majority).[8] Hence it is necessary to determine whether the MSS supporting a variant represent a variety of text-types or are all from a single one, in which case it may be that a variant represents only a peculiarity of that text-type. And because MSS within the same text-type are genetically related, it is necessary to *weigh* rather than *count* the MSS evidence; i.e., once the reading of the text-type has been established, the addition of large numbers of additional witnesses of the same text-type does not appreciably affect matters.

Tables 1–5 present most of the major witnesses to the NT text arranged in lists according to text-type, insofar as it is known or can be determined. Dates of these (and other) witnesses are listed in NA[26] (Appendix I, 684–716, [for Greek MSS], or Introduction, 54*–62* [for early versions and church fathers]) and UBS[3] (Introduction, xiii–xl).

4. *The Relative Quality of the Witnesses.* This may well be the most difficult of the four external factors for beginners to master, and perhaps the most subjective. But it is an observable fact that certain MSS display fewer readings that are obviously secondary

---

7. The term "Western" is somewhat misleading. It was first applied to this particular textual tradition at a time when the only witnesses to it did have ties to the West, i.e., Rome, North Africa, and Gaul. Discoveries since then, however, have made it clear that this early textual tradition was widely disseminated throughout the Roman Empire, and may have originated in the East, perhaps in Egypt. The continued use of the term today is largely a matter of custom and convenience.

8. The so-called Caesarean text, together with some MSS labeled "pre-Caesarean," was for several decades thought to comprise a fourth text-type of the Gospels. This has recently been shown not to be the case. See B. M. Metzger, "The Caesarean Text of the Gospels," *Chapters in the History of New Testament Textual Criticism* (Leiden/Grand Rapids: Brill/Eerdmans, 1963), 42–72, and L. W. Hurtado, *Text-Critical Methodology and the Pre-Caesarean Text: Codex W in the Gospel of Mark* (Grand Rapids: Eerdmans, 1981).

Table 1 **Major Witnesses to the Gospels**

Alexandrian MSS[a]
  Primary Alexandrian 𝔓^{66} 𝔓^{75} ℵ (except John 1:1–8:38) B
  Secondary Alexandrian: C L/019 T W (Luke 1:1–8:12, John) Z Δ (Mark) Ξ 33
    892 sa bo
Western MSS: 𝔓^{45} (Matt.) ℵ (John 1:1–8:38) D/05 W (Mark 1:1–5:30) 0171
  it sy^s sy^c
Byzantine MSS: A E/07 F/09 G/011 H/013 K/017 M N P/024 R S U V W (Matt.,
  Luke 8:13–24:53) X Y Γ Δ (Matt., Luke, John) Θ (Matt., Luke, John) Λ
  Π Σ Φ Ω 047 050 055 063 064 0135 0211 700 1010 1424 (Matt., Luke, John)
  most minuscules
Other Important MSS: 𝔓^4 𝔓^{45} (Mark, Luke, John) 𝔓^{59} 𝔓^{60} W (Mark
  5:31–16:20) Θ (Mark) Ψ 067 070 083 0162 0233 f^1 f^{13} 28 157 565 579 1071 1241
  1424 (Mark) mae

[a]Labels used by other writers for the two subdivisions of this text-type ("primary" and
"secondary") include "neutral" and "Alexandrian" (Wescott and Hort); "Proto-Alexandrian"
and "Later Alexandrian" (Metzger, *Textual Commentary*); and "Alexandrian" and "Egyptian"
(Aland).

Table 2 **Major Witnesses to the Book of Acts**

Alexandrian MSS
  Primary Alexandrian: 𝔓^{74} ℵ A B 81
  Secondary Alexandrian: 𝔓^{45} C 33 (11:26–28:31) 104 453 945 1175 1739 1891
    2464
Western MSS: D/05 E/08 it^h sy^{hmg} mae Irenaeus Cyprian
Byzantine MSS: H/014 L/020 P/025 049 056 0142 6 33 (1:1–11:25) 189 383 424
  1241 most minuscules
Other Important MSS: 𝔓^{41} Ψ 36 323 326 614 1704 1884 2495

Table 3 **Major Witnesses to the Pauline Epistles (Including the
Book of Hebrews)**

Alexandrian MSS
  Primary Alexandrian: 𝔓^{46} ℵ B 1739
  Secondary Alexandrian: 𝔓^{11} 𝔓^{13} 𝔓^{16} 𝔓^{27} 𝔓^{32} 𝔓^{34} 𝔓^{40} 𝔓^{49} 𝔓^{61} 𝔓^{65} (?) A C H/015
    I 048 0243 33 81 104 326 1175 1506 1881
Western MSS: D/06 F/010 G/012 it
Byzantine MSS: K/018 L/020 049 056 0151 424* 945 most minuscules
Other Important MSS: 𝔓^{30} P/025 Ψ 075 0150 6 323 365 424^c 614 629 630 1241
  2464 2495

Table 4 **Major Witnesses to the Catholic Epistles**

Alexandrian MSS: 𝔓^{74} ℵ A B C Ψ 048 33 81 322 323 1241 1243 1739 1852 1881
  2464
Byzantine MSS: K/018 L/020 049 056 0142 most minuscules
Other Important MSS: 𝔓^{69} 𝔓^{72} 104 326 614 623 630 945 1505 1846 2298 2495

Table 5   **Major Witnesses to the Book of Revelation**

Alexandrian MSS
  Primary Alexandrian: A C 2053 2062 2344
  Secondary Alexandrian: $\mathfrak{P}$ [47] $\aleph$ 1006 1611 1678 1778 1841 1854 2020 2050
    2080 2329
Byzantine MSS
  Andreas MSS (= $\mathfrak{M}$ [A] in NA[26]): P/025 many minuscules
  Koine MSS (= $\mathfrak{M}$ [K] in NA[26]): 046 many minuscules
Other Important MSS: 051 052 2030 2351 2377

Note: The textual history of Revelation differs greatly from the rest of the NT. Though A and C are later witnesses than $\mathfrak{P}$ [47] and $\aleph$, both are of superior textual value. The Byzantine tradition has at least two major subdivisions: MSS that follow the text of Andreas of Caesarea's commentary on Revelation, and those that preserve a strictly Byzantine (Koine) text. For a brief overview, see Aland, *Text,* 242–43; for details see J. Schmid, *Studien zur Geschichte des griechischen Apokalypse-Textes,* 3 vols. (Munich: Karl Zink Verlag, 1955–56), and Z. C. Hodges and A. L. Farstad, *The Greek New Testament According to the Majority Text* (Nashville: Nelson, 1982) xxxii–xli, xlv–xlvi.

(conflations, stylistic improvements, harmonizations, etc.) or scribal slips than do other MSS, which suggests that they are the product of a more controlled copying process, and therefore may be judged more likely to preserve an uncontaminated form of the text.

Also, over time one will notice that certain combinations of witnesses and/or text-types tend to preserve the original text more often than others. Readings supported by both the Alexandrian and Western text-types generally will prove to be superior to other readings. An Alexandrian and Byzantine combination is nearly as good. Readings with Western and Byzantine support are very ancient but not often original. Variants supported by a combination of Western and "other" witnesses tend to be interesting rather than original. As for variants found in one text-type only, original readings frequently are preserved in the Alexandrian text-type alone; in fact, it is not uncommon for a small group of primary Alexandrian MSS to be right against all other witnesses (see, e.g., Col. 2:2 below). Only infrequently does the Western text-type alone preserve an original reading, and it is extremely rare (but not impossible) for the Byzantine alone to do so.

Step Three: Evaluate the Internal Evidence

Internal evidence is of two kinds: *transcriptional* (having to do with the habits and practices of scribes and editors) and *intrinsic* (having to do with the author's style and vocabulary). Each must be considered separately.

A. Transcriptional Considerations The aim here is to evaluate the readings in light of what is known about the process of transcription and the types of mistakes or alterations likely to have occurred during that process. These in turn may be further subdivided into two additional categories, unintentional and intentional. Certain aspects of transcribing a text written in *scriptio continua* (i.e., without break between letters or words) facilitated the commission of unintentional errors. It was an easy matter to lose one's place and thus either to omit (haplography) or duplicate (dittography) material by jumping (parablepsis, lit. "a looking beside") from the same letter or group of letters to another (homoioarcton, homoiomeson, or homoioteleuton, depending on whether the beginning, middle, or end of a word is involved; see John 5:44 below), or to confuse similarly appearing letters that may have been poorly or incompletely written (e.g., A/Δ/Λ, ΛΛ/M, Γ/Τ/Ι, etc.). Or, if a MS was the result of dictation, different letters that were pronounced alike may have been confused (e.g., ἔχομεν/ἔχωμεν at Rom. 5:1).

Under the heading of intentional changes come such common alterations as harmonization to parallel passages (see example on Luke 11:2, 4 and John 6:69 below; this could also happen unintentionally as well); substitution of more familiar words or synonyms for unusual or difficult terms (see example on Matt. 22:13 below); alteration of lexical forms or syntax to accord with Atticistic preferences; addition of understood pronouns or subjects, or of conjunctions, particles, etc.; or omission of material thought to be harsh, contrary to current usage or practice, or doctrinally offensive.

In short, the general tendency was towards smoothness, fullness, and clarity of expression. It follows, therefore, that the more difficult reading (more difficult, that is, in the sense that it is more likely to cause difficulty to a scribe) is more likely to be original, as is the shorter reading (assuming, of course, that it is not the result of homoioteleuton, a scribal tendency to abbreviate, etc.).

The line between intentional and unintentional changes is not always clear, but that is not particularly important. What is important is always to consider whether any of the variants at a given point may be accounted for on the basis of transcriptional considerations.

B. *Intrinsic Considerations* The aim here is to evaluate readings in light of what an author is most likely to have written. Factors to consider include the author's vocabulary and style, the flow of thought and logic of the immediate context (here exegesis may be decisive for the textual decision), congruence with the author's ideas or teachings, whether traditional material is being utilized, and, in the Gospels, the Aramaic background of Jesus' teachings.

Intrinsic considerations are often the most subjective kind of evidence the text critic must take into account, since at any particular point an author may have deviated from his usual style or lexical preference for the sake of variety, if nothing else. At times, however, intrinsic evidence can be decisive in judging between readings and for this reason must never be neglected (see, e.g., the discussion of 1 Thess. 2:7 below).

Step Four: Make a Decision

Much of the time all the lines of evidence will converge in support of one variant, and making a decision as to which variant most likely represents the original text will be relatively straightforward. At other times, however, the evidence will be split, sometimes quite evenly, between two or more variants. In these cases one must always keep in mind the fundamental guideline: the variant most likely to be original is the one which best accounts for, in terms of both external and internal considerations, the origin of the others. Careful reflection upon the competing variants in light of all the evidence will usually indicate which is more likely the original. To be sure, occasionally even the most expert critics are baffled or differ in opinion. Illustrating this are the dissenting notes in Metzger's *Textual Commentary* and the use of brackets by NA[26] and UBS[3] to mark material whose presence or position in the text is disputed.

By now it should be clear that textual criticism is an art as well as a science. Like other historical disciplines it resists being reduced to a mechanical application of any one rule or set of rules. Each new variant confronts the critic with a potentially unique set of circumstances and data, and must be approached on that basis. Thus it is no surprise that two instances of variation may offer variants having identical external attestation and yet be evaluated quite differently on the basis of other considerations. As A. E. Housman so aptly and colorfully expressed it,

> A textual critic engaged upon his business is not at all like New-ton investigating the motions of the planets: he is much more like a dog hunting for fleas. If a dog hunted for fleas on mathematical principles, basing his researches on statistics of area and popula-tion, he would never catch a flea except by accident. They require to be treated as individuals; and every problem which presents itself to the textual critic must be regarded as possibly unique.[9]

The Evaluation of Variant Readings: Selected Examples

The following section attempts to illustrate, by means of a discussion of selected variant readings, the principles outlined above. Not every point touched on earlier could be mentioned here, of course, but the range and variety of the chosen examples should suffice to give one a feel for how textual critics go about the business of applying these principles to specific problems.

Due to space considerations only one example of the chart format suggested under step one (see above) could be given (see table 6 below). The reader, however, may find it helpful, and is encouraged, to construct such a chart for each of the other exam-ples in the course of working through the ensuing discussion. Sigla used are those found in NA[26] (see Introduction, 44*–66*).

Luke 11:2, 4

What are the opening and closing words of the Lord's Prayer in Luke's Gospel? The MSS offer the following possibilities:

11:2 πάτεϱ   𝔓[75] ℵ B f[1] 700 pc vg sy[s] Marcion Tertullian Origen
      πάτεϱ ἡμῶν L pc
      πάτεϱ ἡμῶν ὁ ἐν τοῖς οὐϱανοῖς A C D K P W X Δ Θ Π Ψ f[13]
        28 565 892 1010 1071 1241 𝔐 it sy[c,p,h] co

---

9. A. E. Housman, "The Application of Thought to Textual Criticism," in *Selected Prose*, ed. J. Carter (Cambridge: Cambridge University Press, 1961), 132–33.

11:4   πειρασμόν 𝔭⁷⁵ ℵ*,² B L f¹ 700 pc vg sy^s sa bo^pt Marcion
        Tertullian Origen
        πειρασμὸν ἀλλὰ ῥῦσαι ἡμᾶς ἀπὸ τοῦ πονηροῦ (ℵ¹) A C D K
        W X Δ Θ Π Ψ f¹³ 28 33 565 892 1010 1071 1241 𝔐 it
        sy^{c,p,h} bo^pt

The MS support for the two sets of variants is so similar that they may be evaluated as a unit. In numerical terms the support for the longer reading is overwhelming. When the evidence is weighed, however, rather than counted, the situation is rather different. In view of the conjunction of Western and Byzantine support, the longer reading clearly is an early one, but 𝔭⁷⁵ and the patristic citations show that the shorter reading is even earlier (see table 1 above). The longer reading is supported by representatives of the secondary Alexandrian, Western, and Byzantine textual traditions, the shorter largely by primary Alexandrian witnesses and, significantly, the Vulgate and Sinaitic Syriac. The geographic distribution of the witnesses for each is roughly similar; the shorter reading, however, has the edge in terms of relative quality. Overall the external evidence favors the shorter reading.

As for internal evidence, the key consideration in this instance is transcriptional in nature. Given that liturgical use was made of the Matthean form of the prayer (see Matt. 6:9–15), is a scribe more likely to have shortened the longer reading (thereby creating a discrepancy), or added to the shorter one in order to harmonize it to the much more familiar Matthean version? The answer is clear: if the longer reading were original, it is virtually inconceivable that a scribe would cut out such well-known phrases, whereas if the shorter reading is original, it is easy to account for the rise of the longer reading as the result of inadvertent or deliberate assimilation to the better known form of the prayer.

In short, the convergence of both external and internal considerations in favor of the shorter reading demonstrates conclusively that it preserves the original text of the Lucan form of the Lord's Prayer.

John 6:69

The difference between the New King James and the New International versions of John 6:69—". . . You are the Christ, the Son of the living God" *vs.* ". . . you are the Holy One of God"—only hint at the extent of variation in this text (see table 6). The textual evidence reads as follows:

(1) ὁ Χριστὸς ὁ υἱὸς τοῦ Θεοῦ τοῦ ζῶντος K (Δ) Θ^c Π Ψ 0250 *f*¹³ 28 700 892 1071 1241 𝕸 it^{mss} sy^{p,h} bo^{mss}

(2) ὁ Χριστὸς ὁ υἱὸς τοῦ Θεοῦ C³ Θ *f*¹ 33 565 *pc* it^{mss} sy^s

(3) ὁ υἱὸς τοῦ θεοῦ it^b sy^c

(4) ὁ Χριστός Tertullian

(5) ὁ Χριστὸς ὁ ἅγιος τοῦ θεοῦ 𝔓⁶⁶ sa^{mss} ac² bo

(6) ὁ ἅγιος τοῦ θεοῦ 𝔓⁷⁵ ℵ B C* D L W sa^{ms} pbo

An initial assessment suggests (barring some consideration to the contrary) that readings (2), (3), (4), and (5) may be set aside at once on the basis of their slim external attestation alone; that they appear upon further investigation to be the result of harmonization to or conflation with parallel passages (John 11:27, 1:49, and Mark 8:29, respectively) clinches the case against them. Readings (1), which has good Byzantine and some versional and secondary Alexandrian support, and (6), which has support from primary Alexandrian and Western witnesses, require further attention.

Both readings have parallels elsewhere in the Gospel accounts: (1) parallels Matthew 16:16, the disciple's confession at Caesarea Philippi, the synoptic episode parallel to John 6:60–71, while (6) parallels Mark 1:24/Luke 4:34, where an unclean spirit about to be cast out acknowledges that Jesus is "the Holy One of God." Conceivably either one could be explained as the result of assimilation to the parallel passage. It seems far more likely, however, that scribes would harmonize (6) to Matthew 16:16, and thereby remove a discrepancy between the two parallel episodes, than that they would create a discrepancy by replacing (1) with words spoken elsewhere only by an unclean spirit. Thus one may conclude that transcriptional considerations favor (6) as the more difficult reading.

The same may be said for intrinsic considerations. In verse 69 Peter says "we have come to know," or "we have recognized the truth" (πεπιστεύκαμεν), implying a new depth of insight on the disciples' part. Yet the essence of the other variants here—that Jesus is Messiah and Son of God—was already confessed as

Table 6   **Textual Variations of John 6:69**

Variant	Alexandrian	West.	Byzantine	Other	Notes
ὁ Χριστὸς ὁ υἱὸς τοῦ θεου τοῦ ζῶντος	892 bo^mss	it^mss	K Δ Θ^c Π 700 𝔐 sy^h	Ψ 0250 f^19 28 1071 1241 sy^p	good Byzantine, some versional support; 892 = secondary Alexandrian
	892 = 9th		9–11th cent.; sy^h = 616	8–13th cent. sy^p = 5th?	
	= Matt. 16:16 (Caesarea Philippi), same incident as John 6:60–71; removes discrepancy; assimilation to parallel?				
ὁ Χριστὸς ὁ υἱὸς τοῦ θεοῦ	33	it^mss sy^s	Θ* 1010	f^1 565	1) scattered external support
	9th	sy=4th	9th, 12th	12th, 9th	2) harmonized to John 11:27
ὁ υἱὸς τοῦ θεοῦ		it^b sy^c			1) external evidence very slim
		5th?			2) harmonized to John 1:49?
ὁ Χριστὸς		Tertullian			confusion with Mark 8:29?
		3rd cent.			
ὁ Χριστός ὁ ἅγιος τοῦ θεοῦ	𝔓^66 (!) coptic vss.				early expansion of next variant? cf. Mark 8:29
	𝔓^66 = ca. 200				
ὁ ἅγιος τοῦ θεοῦ	𝔓^75 B C L W	ℵ D			very strong primary Alexandrian MSS with good Western support
	3rd 5th 5th 4th 8th	4th 5th			
	= Mark 1:24/Luke 4:34, confession of unclean spirit; would scribe attribute that to disciples? More difficult reading. New information about Jesus at this point; sets up John 10:36; 17:19.				

early as 1:41 and 1:49. Not only is (6), however, quite appropriate as the disciples' response to the events recorded in John 6; it also sets up, in a typically Johannine way, 10:36 (the Father sanctified [ἡγίασεν] and sent Jesus into the world) and 17:19 (Jesus sanctifies [ἁγιάζω] himself for the disciples' sake). Of all the variants it best fits both the immediate context and the structural development of the book as a whole.

Thus all three lines of evidence—external, transcriptional, and intrinsic—come together in support of (6), and it is not surprising to find that the UBS editorial committee assigned an [A] rating (= "virtually certain") to their choice of ὁ ἅγιος τοῦ θεοῦ as the original text of John 6:69.

John 5:44

Though much less complex than the last example, this variant is of interest because of the similar alignment of the MS evidence. Consideration of other factors, however, leads to a different conclusion. In the phrase καὶ τὴν δόξαν τὴν παρὰ τοῦ μόνου θεοῦ οὐ ζητεῖτε ("yet you do not seek the praise that comes from the only God") one finds these variants:

τοῦ μόνου 𝔓⁶⁶ 𝔓⁷⁵ B W itᵃ, ⁽ᵇ⁾sa ac² pbo boᵖᵗ

τοῦ μόνου θεοῦ ℵ A D K L Δ Θ Π Ψ 063 0210 f^1 f^{13} 28 33 565 700
892 1071 1241 𝔐 it vg syᶜ,ᵖ,ʰ,ᵖᵃˡ boᵐˢˢ

While the primary Alexandrian support for the shorter reading is early and very impressive, internal considerations suggest that in this instance it is also wrong. First, θεοῦ appears to be required by the context, a point confirmed by the observation that John nowhere else calls God ὁ μόνος. Second, the accidental omission of $\overline{\Theta Y}$ (the customary contraction of θεοῦ) from the sequence TOYMONOY$\overline{\Theta Y}$OY seems more likely than its insertion. Thus both intrinsic and transcriptional considerations favor θεοῦ, which also has substantial external support (ℵ, secondary Alexandrian, Western, and Byzantine; see table 1 above). It seems relatively certain, therefore, that here the longer reading is original, rather than the shorter.

Colossians 2:2

At Colossians 2:2 one finds what appears at first to be a bewildering profusion of endings to the phrase εἰς ἐπίγνωσιν τοῦ μυστηρίου. As listed by NA²⁶ they are:

(1) τοῦ θεοῦ Χριστοῦ 𝔓⁴⁶ B vgᵐˢ Clementᴬˡᵉˣ Hilary

(2) τοῦ θεοῦ D¹ H P 1881 2464 *pc* saᵐˢ

(3)   τοῦ Χριστοῦ   81 1241ˢ (1739) *pc* b Fulgentius

(4)   τοῦ θεοῦ ὅ ἐστιν Χριστός   D* a vgᵐˢˢ Augustine

(5)   τοῦ θεοῦ τοῦ ἐν Χριστῷ   33 Ambrosiaster

(6)   τοῦ θεοῦ πατρὸς Χριστοῦ   ℵ 048

(7)   τοῦ θεοῦ πατρὸς τοῦ Χριστοῦ   A C 1175 *pc* (f m vgˢᵗ syᴾ) saᵐˢˢ
       bo

(8)   τοῦ θεοῦ καὶ πατρὸς τοῦ Χριστοῦ   ℵ² L Ψ 365 945 *pc* vgᵐˢ

(9)   τοῦ θεοῦ πατρὸς καὶ τοῦ Χριστοῦ   0208 *pc*

(10)   τοῦ θεοῦ καὶ πατρὸς καὶ τοῦ Χριστοῦ   D² K 104 181 326 614
       2495 𝔐 syʰ**

The application of the basic guideline, however, quickly reduces the number of variants worthy of serious consideration to just two. For although (10) receives the support of by far the largest number of MSS, they are all relatively late. In view of this it must be judged to be a conflation of (8) and (9), which are expanded forms of (7), which in turn appears to be an expanded form of (6).

As for the other readings, (1) is quite ambiguous; it could mean "the mystery of God Christ," "the mystery of God's Christ," or "God's mystery, that is, of Christ." Readings (2), (3), (4), and (5), apart from their generally slender external support, are all easily explained as attempts to clarify (1), while if any of them were original, the existence of the other four is inexplicable.

Thus the "bewildering profusion" of variants is quickly reduced to just two, (1) and (6). As for choosing between them, (6) is also easily explained as another attempt to clarify (1), whereas if (6) were original, it becomes difficult, if not impossible, to account for the rise of (1), (2), (3), (4), or (5). Clearly (1) is able to account for all the rest of a way none of the others can. Furthermore, its external support (early primary Alexandrian; see table 3 above) is quite strong, particularly when one adds to it the indirect testimony of those MSS supporting readings (2)–(5) which, by attempting to explain (1), testify to its existence. It seems clear, therefore, that the text of Colossians 2:2 originally read εἰς ἐπίγνωσιν τοῦ μυστηρίου τοῦ θεοῦ, Χριστοῦ.

1 Thessalonians 2:7

In 1 Thessalonians 2:7 did Paul write ἐγενήθημεν νήπιοι ("we were babes") or ἐγενήθημεν ἤπιοι ("we were gentle")? In this instance neither external nor transcriptional factors are decisive, and a final decision will turn on intrinsic considerations. The manuscript evidence looks like this:

νήπιοι 𝔓 65 ℵ* B C* D* F G I Ψ* 104* 326c   451 1962 2495 *pc* it vgww
  sams bo ClementAlex

ἤπιοι ℵc A C2 D2 K P Ψc 33 81 104c 326* 614 629 630 1241 1739 1881
  𝔐 vgst (sy) samss

While at first glance the external evidence (see table 3 above) seems to favor νήπιοι (𝔓 65 ℵ B D it Clement is a strong Alexandrian–Western combination), the Alexandrian (A 33 81 1739) and versional (sy sa) support for ἤπιοι is substantial, and the oldest evidence for each is equally early (the ancestor of 1739 is at least as early as 𝔓 65). Moreover, in this instance the difference in external support is less significant than usual in light of the very slight transcriptional difference between the two readings.

As for transcriptional considerations, it is easy to see how either reading could give rise to the other, either by haplography (accidental omission of one of a pair of letters or sequence of letters) or dittography (repetition of one or more letters). If dictation was part of the copying process, the pronunciation of the two would have been almost indistinguishable. Thus either reading can account for the other, but on transcriptional grounds alone it cannot be determined which is original.

Turning to intrinsic considerations, three points may be made in favor of νήπιοι. First, νήπιος is a typically Pauline word; he is responsible for eleven of its fifteen occurrences in the NT, while ἤπιος occurs elsewhere only at 2 Timothy 2:24. Second, in 2:3–6 Paul defends himself against the charge of using flattery and guile to his advantage, against which νήπιος, suggesting a certain innocence and guilelessness, is a more appropriate response than ἤπιος. Third, the violent shift of metaphor from "babe" to "nurse" certainly makes νήπιος the more difficult reading.

On the other hand, Paul elsewhere never applies νήπιος to himself, only to his converts. And since it is the more familiar word, scribes would be more likely to substitute it for the less familiar ἤπιος (as in fact a few [D F G] did at 2 Tim. 2:24) than vice versa. Second, the clause in which [ν]ηπιος occurs is a response not to 2:3–6 but 2:7a: "As apostles of Christ," Paul writes, "we could have 'thrown our weight around'," to which the logical response is surely "instead, we were *gentle*." Moreover, only ἤπιος fits the particular cultural background against which Paul is writing,[10] and sets up the following comparison, "like (ὡς) a nurse taking care of her children."

Finally, "the category 'more difficult reading' is relative, and a point is sometimes reached when a reading must be judged to be so difficult that it can have arisen only by accident in transcription."[11] That appears to be the case here. Even if the external evidence is held to favor νήπιοι, the ease with which it could have arisen by dittography and the intrinsic sense of the immediate context, together with the cultural context, are decisive in favor of ἤπιοι.

Matthew 22:13

Three forms of the king's instructions to his servants are found in the MSS at this point:

(1) δήσαντες αὐτοῦ πόδας καὶ χεῖρας ἐκβάλετε αὐτὸν εἰς ℵ B L
     Θ 085 f[1.(13)] 700 892 pc lat (sy[p]) co

(2) ἄρατε αὐτὸν ποδῶν καὶ χειρῶν καὶ βάλετε αὐτὸν εἰς D it
     (sy[s,c]) Irenaeus Lucifer of Calaris

(3) δήσαντες αὐτοῦ πόδας καὶ χεῖρας ἄρατε αὐτὸν καὶ ἐκβάλετε
     αὐτὸν εἰς C (M) W (Φ) 0138 (565 1241 1424) 𝔐 f (sy[h])

Variant (3), the Byzantine reading, is easily accounted for as a combination of (1) and (2), whereas it is not possible to derive both (1) and (2) from (3), as a little experimentation will demonstrate; hence it may be set aside as a clever conflation.

The difference between (1) and (2) are (a) δέω (+ αὐτοῦ πόδας

---

10. See A. J. Malherbe, " 'Gentle As A Nurse': The Cynic Background to I Thess ii," *Novum Testamentum* 12 (1970): 203–17.
11. Metzger, *Text*, 209.

καὶ χεῖρας) *vs.* αἴρω (+ αὐτὸν ποδῶν καὶ χειρῶν, which is idiomatically correct with this verb); (b) ἐκβάλλω *vs.* βάλλω; and (c) subordination (participle . . . finite verb) *vs.* parataxis (finite verb . . . καὶ . . . finite verb). In this instance transcriptional considerations are of little help in choosing between the two variants, since the differences are obviously not accidental. It is just possible that αἴρω ("seize") has been deliberately substituted for δέω ("bind") because it was thought to be more suited to the setting (why bind someone just to toss them out of the banquet hall?), but this is too slim a point to carry much weight. Intrinsic factors are also indecisive. On the basis of usage, all four verbs under evaluation may be said to be equally Matthean (δέω occurs 10 times, αἴρω 19, βάλλω 34, and ἐκβάλλω 28). Also, while Matthew generally prefers subordination to parataxis, this can be turned around to favor (2) as the less common construction (and thus more likely to be altered).

Hence it is necessary to make the decision solely on external grounds. Here Westcott and Hort's dictum—knowledge of documents should precede judgment upon readings—comes into play. The Western textual tradition, and particularly D, its leading witness, exhibits a decided tendency towards substitutions and revisions (of which the above variant is typical) which almost always prove to be secondary rather than original. On the other hand, the Alexandrian text-type manifests a consistent freedom from these types of secondary alterations. In instances like this, when a decision must be made on purely external grounds, one is justified in preferring the Alexandrian reading and adopting (1) as the text of 22:13.

Acts 16:4

Alexandrian	Western
ὡς δὲ διεπορεύοντο τὰς πόλεις	διερχόμενοι δὲ τὰς πόλεις ἐκήρυσσον [καὶ
παρεδίδοσαν αὐτοῖς	παρεδίδοσαν αὐτοῖς—D only] μετὰ πάσης παρρησίας τὸν κύριον Ἰησοῦν Χριστὸν ἅμα παραδιδόντες καὶ
φυλάσσειν τὰ δόγματα	τὰς ἐντολὰς

τὰ κεκριμένα ὑπὸ τῶν

ἀποστόλων καὶ πρεσβυτέρων   ἀποστόλων καὶ πρεσβυτέρων. . .

---

text: 𝔓⁴⁵ 𝔓⁷⁴ ℵ A B C 33 1739 𝔐   *text:* D (sy^hmg Ephraem)

The Western text may be translated (with the differences italicized): "And *while going* through the cities *they preached* [*and delivered to them*] *with all boldness the Lord Jesus Christ, at the same time delivering also the commandments* of the apostles. . . ."

The variants in this verse exemplify an issue that confronts the textual critic throughout Acts, namely, that in the early church the text of this book circulated in two forms, Alexandrian and Western, which differ in both length (the latter is about 8.5 percent longer) and character, the Western generally being the more picturesque, detailed, and tendentious of the two. A good example of the tendentious character of the Western textual tradition may be found in the following example.

Acts 3:17

Alexandrian	**Western**
Καὶ νῦν, ἀδελφοί,	Καὶ νῦν, ἄνδρες ἀδελφοί,
οἶδα ὅτι	ἐπιστάμεθα ὅτι ὑμεῖς μὲν
κατὰ ἄγνοιαν	κατὰ ἄγνοιαν
ἐπράξατε . . . ¹⁸ ὁ δὲ θεός . . .	ἐπράξατε πονηρόν . . . ¹⁸ὁ δὲ θεός . . .

---

text: ⁷⁴ ℵ A B C 1739 𝔐   *text:* D (E h mae)

The Western text may be paraphrased as follows: "And now, brothers, *we* [the apostles of Christ] *know* that *you* [the Jews], *on the one hand,* did *a wicked thing* in ignorance . . . *but, on the other hand,* God . . . [fulfilled his purpose]." The point of these differences is apparent: the distinction between Jew and Christian is sharpened, the disparity between the Jews' actions and God's purpose is emphasized more strongly, and the Jews' role in the death of Jesus is, despite their ignorance, explicitly labeled a crime.[12]

How are these variants to be evaluated? Though numerous hypotheses have been offered to explain the differences between the origins of the two forms of the text,[13] nothing proposed to date has gained anything approaching general assent. There has emerged, however, what may be termed a "working consensus," perhaps best exemplified by the work of the UBS Editorial Committee. In view of the current situation, the Committee

> proceeded in an eclectic fashion, holding that neither the Alexandrian nor the Western group of witnesses always preserves the original text, but that in order to attain the earliest text one must compare the two divergent traditions point by point and in each case select the reading which commends itself in the light of transcriptional and intrinsic probabilities.
>
> In reviewing the work of the Committee on the book of Acts as a whole, one observes that more often than not the shorter, Alexandrian text was preferred. At the same time the Committee judged that some of the information incorporated in certain Western expansions may well be factually accurate, though not deriving from the original author of Acts.[14]

In the light of these comments it is no surprise to observe that virtually without exception today the Alexandrian reading is the preferred text in both 16:4 and 3:17, the Western text (both here and in general) being viewed as the result of later editorial revision and expansion. In the meantime the matter of the origin and relationship of the two forms of the text of Acts remains an open question.[15]

The preceding examples should serve (1) to illustrate the application of the primary guideline and basic process outlined

---

12. See E. J. Epp, *The Theological Tendency of Codex Bezae Cantabrigiensis in Acts* (Cambridge: Cambridge University Press, 1966), 41ff.

13. For a concise survey see Metzger, *Commentary,* 261–72.

14. Metzger, *Commentary,* 271–72.

15. E.g., the venerable theory that both forms are the work of the author, who produced two editions of the book, has recently been revived in a brief but provocative and persuasive article by M.-E. Boismard ("The Text of Acts: A Problem of Literary Criticism?" in *New Testament Textual Criticism: Its Significance for Exegesis. Essays in Honour of Bruce M. Metzger.* eds. E. J. Epp and G. D. Fee [Oxford: Oxford University Press, 1981], 147–57).

above; (2) to demonstrate that no one MS or textual tradition is always right; and (3) to make clear that no one rule, consideration, group of MSS, etc., can be followed or applied to textual problems in a mechanical or thoughtless fashion. To quote Housman again, textual criticism

> is purely a matter of reason and of common sense. . . . [it] is not a branch of mathematics, nor indeed an exact science at all. It deals with a matter not rigid and constant, like lines and numbers, but fluid and variable; namely the frailties and aberrations of the human mind, and of its insubordinate servants, the human fingers. It therefore is not susceptible of hard-and-fast rules. It would be much easier if it were; and that is why people try to pretend that it is . . . Of course you can have hard-and-fast rules if you like, but then you will have false rules, and they will lead you wrong; because their simplicity will render them inapplicable to problems which are not simple, but complicated by the play of personality.[16]

Every textual problem must be approached on its own terms; all the critic knows about MSS, about scribes, about the author, must be brought to bear on it. Above all, the fundamental guidelines must be kept in mind: Which variant best accounts for the origin of the others? The variant which, after thoughtful consideration of all the evidence, best satisfies this question will almost invariably best represent the original text.

---

16. Housman, "Thought," 132.

3

New Testament Greek Grammatical Analysis
Scot McKnight

The Significance of Greek Syntax for New Testament Exegesis

Saint Theresa of the Child Jesus once wishfully claimed, "If I had been a priest, I should have made a thorough study of Hebrew and Greek so as to understand the thought of God as he has vouchsafed to express it in our language."[1] As then, so today: the privilege is ours to learn to read the Greek New Testament; but, unlike St. Theresa's day, the privilege is not restricted by gender. Learning Greek today, however fruitful for exegetical precision, personal development, and ministry enrichment,[2]

---

1. From M. Zerwick and M. Grosvenor, *A Grammatical Analysis of the Greek New Testament*, 2 vols. (Rome: Biblical Institute Press, 1979), copyright page.
2. In 1918, J. Gresham Machen wrote: "Every scientific student of the New Testament without exception knows that Greek is really necessary to his work: the real question is only as to whether our ministry should be manned by scientific students" ("The Minister and His Greek Testament," in J. H. Skilton, *Studying the New Testament Today. Vol. 1: The New Testament Student* [Philadelphia: Presbyterian and Reformed, 1974], 154). See also A. T. Robertson, *The Minister and His Greek New Testament* (Nashville: Broadman, 1977), esp. 15–28; J. Piper, "Brothers, Bitzer Was a Banker!" *The Standard* (June 1983): 18–19; B. B. Warfield, "The Religious Life of Theological Students," in *Selected Shorter Writings of Benjamin B. Warfield–I*, comp. J. E. Meeter (Nutley, N. J.: Presbyterian and Reformed, 1970), 411–25.

may not be so simple. Thus a few introductory comments ought to be made before commencing.

Rarely has so much been expected of so few. Those in ministry are expected to be competent in church history, systematic theology, ethics, apologetics, contemporary social analysis, Christian education, missions, evangelism, homiletics, and psychology. At the same time, they are expected to master at least two archaic languages—and these, it is often claimed, must be reduced in palatable form for the person on the street! Furthermore, one must frankly admit that the typical preparation a student receives today in secondary education and college is not conducive to the technical language of grammarians.[3] Learning Greek is significant for exegesis and is a privilege—but it is not easy and this ought to be kept in mind.[4] However, I believe that Greek can be mastered by the average student if that student develops a disciplined habit.[5] Exasperation and pain, with discipline, can give birth to a settled contentment.[6]

First, this essay discusses five important elements of syntax[7] which have been chosen because they demonstrate the significance of Greek syntax for exegesis and theology. Though other features of Greek syntax could have been examined, the student will avoid many pitfalls in preparing texts if these five elements are grasped. Second, this essay outlines a method for deepening one's knowledge of Greek grammar through diagramming. The

---

3. This deficiency in preparation has been traced in many recent critiques of American society. See, e.g., M. J. Adler, *Reforming Education. The Schooling of a People and their Education beyond Schooling* (Boulder, Colo.: Westview, 1977); A. Bloom, *The Closing of the American Mind* (New York: Simon & Schuster, 1987); E. D. Hirsch, Jr., *Cultural Literacy: What Every American Needs to Know* (Boston: Houghton Mifflin, 1987).

4. See also J. H. Greenlee, "The Importance of Syntax for the Proper Understanding of the Sacred Text of the New Testament," *Evangelical Quarterly* 44 (1972): 131–46.

5. See the story A. T. Robertson tells of John Brown of Haddington in *Minister*, 103–8.

6. In my first year of teaching a struggling student handed me the following humorous poem on classical and Hellenistic Greek:

> Greek is a language,
> At least it used to be.
> It killed off all the Greeks
> And now it's killing me.
> All have died who ever spoke it.
> All have died who ever wrote it.
> All will die who ever learn it.
> Blessed death, they surely earn it!

7. A simple introduction to the categories and terms of syntax is J. H. Greenlee, *A Concise Exegetical Grammar of New Testament Greek*, 5th rev. ed. (Grand Rapids: Eerdmans, 1986).

essay is written for Greek exegesis students; therefore, it assumes that students have worked through an elementary grammar and have an adequate grasp of morphology, vocabulary, and the rudiments of syntax. But what is syntax?

Syntax

Syntax deals with the relationships of words to one another; however, these relationships are not governed by ideal "grammar laws." Syntactical grammars categorize and describe relationships that have been observed as consistent. For instance, grammars define a genitive absolute as a substantive and a participle in the genitive case that have no relationship to the main sentence (hence, "absolute"). This definition holds true only in a general way, for often NT writers, especially Matthew and Mark, do not use the construction as stated, as Matthew 1:18 illustrates. It reads μνηστευθείσης τῆς μητρὸς αὐτοῦ Μαρίας τῷ Ἰωσήφ, πρὶν ἢ συνελθεῖν αὐτοὺς εὑρέθη ἐν γαστρὶ ἔχουσα ἐκ πνεύματος ἁγίου ("When his mother Mary had been betrothed to Joseph, before they came together she was found to be with child by the Holy Spirit"). The "subject" of the genitive absolute clause (Μαρίας) is also the subject of the main verb (εὑρέθη) and therefore the clause is not truly "absolute."[8] This illustrates for us the "descriptive" rather than "prescriptive" nature of NT Greek syntax,[9] which clearly varies by individual author.[10]

---

8. Another defective use may be seen at Matthew 17:14 where Matthew omits the substantive altogether (ἐλθόντων without a substantive). Further examples may be found in N. Turner, *Syntax* (Edinburgh: T. & T. Clark, 1963), 322–23; F. Blass and A. Debrunner, *A Greek Grammar of the New Testament and Other Early Christian Literature*, trans. and rev. by R. W. Funk (Chicago: University of Chicago Press, 1961), § 423. The following are other standard grammars: J. H. Moulton, W. F. Howard, and N. Turner, *A Grammar of New Testament Greek*, 4 vols. (Edinburgh: T. & T. Clark, 1908–76); Vol. I, *Prolegomena*, by J. H. Moulton (3d ed., 1908); Vol. II, *Accidence and Word-Formation*, by W. F. Howard (1920); Vol. III, *Syntax*, by N. Turner (1963); Vol. IV, *Style*, by N. Turner (1976); A. T. Robertson, *A Grammar of the Greek New Testament in the Light of Historical Research* (Nashville, Tenn.: Broadman, 1934); C. F. D. Moule, *An Idiom Book of New Testament Greek*, 2d ed. (Cambridge: Cambridge University Press, 1963); M. Zerwick, *Biblical Greek Illustrated by Examples*, trans. J. P. Smith (Rome: Biblical Institute Press, 1963). A useful volume on the verb is E. D. Burton, *Syntax of the Moods and Tenses of the New Testament Greek*, 3d ed. (Chicago: University of Chicago Press, 1898). The standard grammar of classical Greek is H. W. Smyth, *Greek Grammar*, rev. G. M. Messing (Cambridge: Harvard University Press, 1956).

9. Scholars have long debated the nature of NT Greek; for this discussion, see esp. the grammars of Zerwick, *Biblical Greek*, §§ 480–94; Turner, *Syntax*; idem, "Biblical Greek—the

In the following discussion of various aspects of syntax, only a few examples will be given; further discussions can be found through the footnotes.

Genitive Case

Of particular concern for exegesis is the genitive case because its function is to specify some relationship of a substantive in the genitive to a substantive or verb.[11] As relationships are multiple, so also are the kinds of genitives and, therefore, particular care must be exercised in determining the nuance of the genitive. Notice the string of genitives Paul uses in Colossians 1:5–6: ἐν τῷ λόγῳ τῆς ἀληθείας τοῦ εὐαγγελίου τοῦ παρόντος εἰς ὑμᾶς ("in the word of truth of the gospel which came to you"). If τῷ λόγῳ is taken as a noun of action, τῆς ἀληθείας could be an objective genitive ("preaching the truth"). Or, is the genitive an epexegetic ("the Word, i.e., the truth") or qualitative ("true message") genitive? Is the second genitive, τοῦ εὐαγγελίου, the object of τῷ λόγῳ ("preaching the gospel") or is it epexegetic ("the true message, i.e., the gospel")? This illustrates the possibilites that the exegete encounters when seeking to unravel the possible relationships expressed by the genitive case. If one does not understand how the genitive is used, it will be nearly impossible to secure a confident interpretation. Consequently, one of the features of Greek syntax that needs thorough study is the genitive case. A few examples of the value of understanding the genitive follow.

Because the Semitic languages frequently influenced NT syntax, the genitive is often used as a simple adjective; this use has been called the Hebrew or descriptive genitive (also attributive genitive, genitive of quality, genitive of definition). When Paul perceived the propensity of the "old man" to sin and its utter wretchedness, he asked, τίς με ῥύσεται ἐκ τοῦ σώματος τοῦ

Peculiar Language of a Peculiar People," *Studia Evangelica* 7 (1982): 505–12; M. Silva, "Bilingualism and the Character of Palestinian Greek," *Biblica* 61 (1980): 198–219; G. H. R. Horsley, "Divergent Views on the Nature of the Greek of the Bible," *Biblica* 65 (1984): 393–404.

10. It is not possible to sketch here the various styles of NT authors; on this, see Turner, *Style*.

11. The adnominal genitive describes the relation of a substantive in the genitive to another noun; the adverbial genitive describes the relation of a substantive in the genitive to a verb. A list of uses, with many examples, appears in Blass and Debrunner, *Grammar*, §§ 162–86; Turner, *Syntax*, 207–19, 231–36.

θανάτου τούτου ("Who will deliver me from this body of death?" Rom. 7:24). Paul used the qualitative genitive τοῦ θανάτου here to describe the kind of σῶμα in view, namely, a mortal body, one that dies.[12] Thus, the body Paul had in view is characterized by mortality. In contrast, it is the Spirit of God who regenerates unto life (immortality, Rom. 8:2).

Allied with this use is the epexegetic genitive, a genitive which restates a noun with which it is used. In John 2:21 we read ἐκεῖνος δὲ ἔλεγεν περὶ τοῦ ναοῦ τοῦ σώματος αὐτοῦ ("Now he [Jesus] was speaking of the temple of his body"). In this sentence the second genitive, τοῦ σώματος, modifies τοῦ ναοῦ by restating it; that is, "of the temple, which is his body". Jesus is described here as speaking of his body in the figure of a temple, an image with great significance.

Students generally find it difficult to develop a sensitivity for the subjective and objective genitives; these are genitives modifying a so-called noun of action. (Nouns of action often terminate in –τηρ, –της, –σις, –τις, –μος, –εια, –α, or –η.) Thus the subjective genitive functions as a subject of a noun which itself functions as a verb; conversely, the objective genitive functions as the object of a noun which functions as a verb. Furthermore, the context determines the direction of the action and, admittedly, context is not always conclusive. A clear example of the objective genitive (the noun is active and the genitive which modifies it receives the action of that noun) is found in Romans 10:2: ὅτι ζῆλον θεοῦ ἔχουσιν ("that they have a zeal of God"). This should be construed as "they seek after God," with θεοῦ functioning as the object of ζῆλον.[13] A more interesting example is τοῦ Χριστοῦ in 2 Corinthians 5:14. Does ἡ γὰρ ἀγάπη τοῦ Χριστοῦ συνέχει denote "Christ's love for me" (subjective genitive) or "my love for Christ" (objective genitive)? The context suggests clearly the former because it speaks of the Christ-event, namely, Christ died for his people.[14] The implications of this exegetical decision are

---

12. For further examples, see Turner, *Syntax,* 212–14; Blass and Debrunner, *Grammar,* § 165; Zerwick, *Biblical Greek,* §§ 40–41. An extensive discussion of the various forms of the adjective genitive may be found in S. E. Porter, "The Adjectival Attributive Genitive in the New Testament: A Grammatical Study," *Trinity Journal* 4 (1983): 3–17.

13. See C. E. B. Cranfield, *The Epistle to the Romans,* International Critical Commentary, 2 vols. (Edinburgh: T. & T. Clark, 1979), 2:513–14.

14. On this, see R. P. Martin, *2 Corinthians,* Word Biblical Commentary, Vol. 40 (Waco, Tex.: Word, 1986), 127–28. In the examples given in the text, whereas the "love" of Christ is

obvious because now the motivation for preaching in Paul's mind is ultimately rooted, not in his affections for God (however true and strong they may be), but in God's active love for him in Christ.[15]

Genitives governed by prepositions are not so difficult to categorize since they are, in effect, determined by the preposition. Thus, Matthew tells us something about the nature of God's Word through various prepositions: ἵνα πληρωθῇ τὸ ῥηθὲν ὑπὸ κυρίου διὰ τοῦ προφήτου λέγοντος (Matt. 1:22). Whereas it was spoken by (ὑπό) the Lord, he did so through (διά) a prophet; it is God's Word given through a human being.[16]

Article

A second element of Greek syntax yielding valuable insights for exegesis is the article. The article is used to indicate definiteness or to designate a generic idea, while its absence (anarthrous) usually means indefiniteness, though an anarthrous noun can be definite in meaning as well. But for exegesis, three particular uses of the article have been given special prominence.

Granville Sharp's Rule, formulated originally in 1798, specifies that when two nouns of the same case are connected by καί, a single article before the first noun denotes conceptual unity with the second noun, whereas the repetition of the article denotes particularity.[17] An example of conceptual unity occurs in Titus 2:13 (τοῦ μεγάλου θεοῦ καὶ σωτῆρος ἡμῶν Ἰησοῦ Χριστοῦ; "the great God and our Savior, Jesus Christ") where the single article (τοῦ) almost certainly demonstrates that the author thought of Christ as deity. By using one article in Revelation 1:5,

---

clearly an action, "zeal" is not so clear. Grammarians often define "objective" in a wider sense than simply the "object of a noun that functions verbally." See Blass and Debrunner, *Grammar*, § 163.

15. Zerwick, *Biblical Greek*, §§ 36–39, has classified some of these as general genitives. For a similar view, see Turner, *Syntax*, 210–12.

16. For further analysis of prepositions, see M. J. Harris, "Prepositions and Theology in the Greek New Testament," in *The New International Dictionary of New Testament Theology*, ed. Colin Brown, 3 vols. (Grand Rapids: Zondervan, 1975), 3:1171–1215.

17. The full rule is cited in Robertson, *Minister*, 62. Sharp, however, did not claim any application of this rule to plural nouns or proper names. Furthermore, Sharp's rule does not mean that each noun refers to the same object, i.e., when Matthew uses one article for the Pharisees and Sadducees, as in Matthew 3:7 (τῶν Φαρισαίων καὶ Σαδδουκαίων), that does not mean that he is referring to the same group. Rather, Matthew intends to depict the group together, however different they were in reality.

the seer unites the one who loves us with the one who frees us from our sins (τῷ ἀγαπῶντι ἡμᾶς καὶ λύσαντι ἡμᾶς), the love of Christ being the propelling force of his redemptive work.[18] An example of a repeated article to denote particularity can be found at Revelation 1:8 (Ἐγώ εἰμι τὸ ἄλφα καὶ τὸ ὦ): Jesus is both the beginning and the end. At times, a single preposition has the same unifying force (Matt. 3:11 [ἐν πνεύματι ἁγίῳ καὶ πυρί; "by the Holy Spirit and fire"]). The importance of this single preposition is that Matthew does not intend his readers to think of two baptisms, one in the Holy Spirit and one in fire; rather he depicts one baptism that both regenerates and purges or judges.[19]

Even more discussion has grown around E. C. Colwell's Rule.[20] Colwell concluded that "definite predicate nouns . . . regularly take the article" in a copulative sentence. He then inferred four rules: (1) "definite predicate nouns regularly have the article if they follow the copula"; (2) "definite nouns which precede the verb usually lack the article"; (3) "proper names regularly lack the article in the predicate"; (4) "predicate nominatives in relative clauses regularly follow the verb whether or not they have the article."[21] The implications of these observations are particularly notable in Mark 15:39 where Mark records the centurion confessing Jesus as God's Son, but with an anarthrous noun: οὗτος ὁ ἄνθρωπος υἱὸς θεοῦ ἦν. Did Mark mean to suggest, because the noun was anarthrous, that Jesus was just a Son of God? Does he mean that Jesus is one among many? The implication of Colwell's investigation is that anarthrous nouns that precede the copula are often definite in meaning; that is, υἱός can be definite in meaning (and probably is because of Mark 1:1). Thus, it can be concluded with absolute certainty that Mark does not necessarily say that Jesus is simply one son among many. The same is true of John 1:1: θεὸς ἦν ὁ λόγος. θεὸς is

---

18. On this see further in Turner, *Syntax*, 181–82; Moule, *Idiom*, 181–82, 109–10; Zerwick, *Biblical Greek*, §§ 184–85; Blass and Debrunner, *Grammar*, § 276. A full discussion of Titus 2:13 can be found in M. J. Harris, "Titus 2:13 and the Deity of Christ," in *Pauline Studies*, eds. D. A. Hagner and M. J. Harris (Grand Rapids: Eerdmans, 1980), 262–77.

19. On Matthew 3:11, see J. D. G. Dunn, *Baptism in the Holy Spirit* (Philadelphia: Westminster, 1970), 8–22, esp. 10–13; further examples can be found in Harris, "Prepositions," 3:1178.

20. E. C. Colwell, "A Definite Rule for the Use of the Article in the Greek New Testament," *JBL* 52 (1933): 12–21; see also Turner, *Syntax*, 182–84; Zerwick, *Biblical Greek*, §§ 172–75; Moule, *Idiom*, 115–16; D. A. Carson, *Exegetical Fallacies* (Grand Rapids: Baker, 1984), 86–88.

21. Colwell, "Definite," 20.

anarthrous because it precedes the copula ἦν and ὁ λόγος is articular because it follows the copula. It must be noted that Colwell's rule, however valuable it may be, does not demand that anarthrous nouns preceding the copula are necessarily definite. What can be concluded, however, is that anarthrous nouns may be anarthrous only because of word order, i.e., anarthrous nouns are not necessarily indefinite in meaning.

A final matter regarding the article is Apollonius' canon, namely, that two nouns in regimen (a noun with a dependent genitive) are either both arthrous or both anarthrous.[22] Thus, when a noun is connected with a noun in the genitive, either both have an article or neither has one. For example, Paul follows this "rule" in his usage of the Spirit of God. When the governing noun (*nomen regens*) is articular, the dependent noun in the genitive (*nomens rectum*) is also articular: ἐν τῷ πνεύματι τοῦ θεοῦ ἡμῶν (1 Cor. 6:11); when the governing noun is anarthrous, so also is the dependent noun: ἐν πνεύματι θεοῦ (1 Cor. 12:3). But the fact is that this is not a "law" either. Thus, in Romans 3:25 we read εἰς ἔνδειξιν τῆς δικαιοσύνης αὐτοῦ ("to show his righteousness") when it perhaps should have been either εἰς τὴν ἔνδειξιν τῆς δικαιοσύνης αὐτοῦ or εἰς ἔνδειξιν δικαιοσύνης αὐτοῦ. Many exceptions have been noted and various explanations offered.[23] The basic explanation takes two factors into account: (1) the *governing* noun may be anarthrous without necessitating the omission of the article in the *governed* noun; (2) the article can be omitted in the case of proper names and national appellations.

Voice

Because the middle voice was losing ground in Hellenistic Greek, its presence in the NT calls the interpreter to attention. The middle is used to express the participation of the subject in the action of the verb. Thus, when Paul describes the gospel with a present middle participle in Colossians 1:6 (καρποφορούμενον, "bearing fruit"), he does so to indicate the innate productivity of the gospel. God's work is done, not simply because of human

---

22. See Turner, *Syntax*, 180; Moule, *Idiom*, 114–15.
23. See esp. S. D. Hull, "Exceptions to Apollonius' Canon in the New Testament: A Grammatical Study," *Trinity Journal*, n.s., 7 (1986): 3–16.

efforts, but because the gospel is inherently effective.[24] And, at 1 Corinthians 6:11, Paul's statement to the Corinthians, ἀλλὰ ἀπελούσασθε ("you were washed"), suggests decisive participation by the Corinthains: "you got yourselves washed." Whether or not the reflexive sense is found in the NT is another matter. As C. F. D. Moule remarks, "it is far from easy to come down from the fence with much decisiveness on either side in an exegetical problem if it depends on the voice."[25] And one thing is clear: in the NT the middle voice is never unambiguously reflexive. This urges the exegete to use caution when seeking to draw fine lines, particularly as pertains to the so-called cessation of tongues mentioned by Paul in 1 Corinthians 13:8.[26]

NT exegetes draw attention to a usage of the passive called the "theological" or "divine" passive. NT writers, especially when reporting a saying of Jesus, often avoid mentioning God by turning an expression into the passive voice. Thus, in Matthew 5:4 we read ὅτι αὐτοὶ παρακληθήσονται, "because they will be comforted." Rather than saying, "because God will comfort them," Matthew omits "God" out of reverence for him and a passive construction emerges.[27] What the interpreter needs to avoid is thinking that the comfort just occurs; rather, God's merciful favor is in view.

Tense

Unlike English tense, Greek tense refers to "kind of action as depicted by the author" and not primarily to time. "The original function of the so-called tense stems of the verb in Indo-European languages was not that of levels of time (present, past, future) but that of *Aktionsarten* (kinds of action) or aspects (points of view)."[28] A proper understanding of what

---

24. On the middle, see Moule, *Idiom*, 24–26; Turner, *Syntax*, 53–57.
25. *Idiom*, 24.
26. See Carson, *Exegetical Fallacies*, 77–79.
27. Two further examples can be seen at Luke 12:7 (ἠρίθμηνται, "God has counted") and Mark 2:5 (ἀφίενται, "God has forgiven"). On this, see Zerwick, *Biblical Greek*, § 236; J. Jeremias, *New Testament Theology: The Proclamation of Jesus*, trans. J. Bowden (New York: Scribner's, 1971), 9–14, who cites many examples. However, one must not take it to be an instance of irreverence when God is the subject of an active verb.
28. Blass and Debrunner, *Grammar*, § 318. It is not clear whether Blass means "or" in the sense of "in addition to" or that *Aktionsart* is another way of saying "point of view." In the light of the definitions of the various *Aktionsarten* in § 318.1–5, it appears that the latter is the

the Greek tense does and what it does not do is essential for exegesis.[29]

First, Greek tense traditionally concerns *kind of action* (*Aktionsart*): continuous (present, imperfect tenses), completed (perfect, pluperfect) and unspecified (aorist). (The future tense is the Greek tense that primarily concerns time). Second, and more importantly, Greek tense primarily is concerned with kind of action *from the author's standpoint* (aspect). In modern discussions, much is being made of the distinction between traditional understandings of *Aktionsart* and modern views of aspect, the former referring to reality (how an action occurred in reality) and the latter to depicted action (how the author presents that action).[30] What is significant to observe is that Greek tense concerns a *depiction* of action, however that action may have occurred in reality. Zerwick clearly observes that "the use of the 'tenses' is determined not so much by the objective reality . . . as by the speaker's needs."[31] Third, time is a concern only in the indicative mood and then it is often secondary; in the other moods, the factor of time is almost absent and is relative to its context.[32] These three observations have led some modern grammarians to the following categorical understanding of aspects (formally, tenses); there is (1) the imperfective aspect (present and imperfect—in the indicative mood "true tenses"); (2) the perfective aspect (perfect, pluperfect, and future perfect); and (3) the aoristic aspect (aorist in each mood). In addition, the future is a true "tense" in that it concerns primarily time.[33] Thus, the traditional categories of *Aktionsart* are being clarified in that the emphasis is being given to their aspectual or depictional nature, with the aorist receiving particular attention.[34]

case. Observe his emphasis on "is conceived as." Though his definitions are sound, the same cannot always be said of explanations of the examples.

29. For some typical fallacies, see Carson *Exegetical Fallacies*, 69–80. See also R. J. Erickson, "*OIDA* and *GINŌSKŌ* and Verbal Aspect in Pauline Usage," *Westminster Theological Journal* 44 (1982): 110–22.

30. An excellent presentation, with many nuanced examples, is K. L. McKay, "Syntax in Exegesis," *Tyndale Bulletin* 23 (1981): 39–57; idem, "On the Perfect and Other Aspects in New Testament Greek," *Novum Testamentum* 23 (1981): 289–329.

31. *Biblical Greek*, § 241.

32. See Zerwick, *Biblical Greek*, § 240; Turner, *Syntax*, 59–60; Blass and Debrunner, *Grammar*, § 318.

33. McKay refers to the future tense as "defective"; see "Perfect," 290.

34. F. Stagg observed that "departure from the aorist is exegetically more significant than the presence of the aorist" ("The Abused Aorist," *Journal of Biblical Literature* 91 [1972]: 231).

Perhaps the clearest illustration of this nature of Greek tense (aspect) is the so-called historical present, by which the author depicts an action as in process when that action has already occurred. This usage appears approximately 150 times in Mark (e.g., λέγει in Mark 1:14 [the parallel at Luke 5:14 is an aorist], and 2:5 [the parallels at Matt. 9:2 and Luke 5:20 are aorists]).[35] The point is that, though the action may have occurred in the past, the author does not depict that action in the past; instead, he chooses to depict that action as in process, perhaps to add life to the narrative, to emphasize a following statement, or to effect a literary and geographical change.[36] To explain these instances "historically" confuses reality (how it happened) with depiction (how the author presents it). The interchange between Peter and Jesus recorded in Matthew 18:21–22 illustrates the importance of this distinction. Whereas Peter's question is introduced with the aorist tense (εἶπεν), Jesus' response, which makes the following words emphatic and continually applicable, is introduced with the present tense (λέγει), though Jesus' statement was undoubtedly also made in the past.

Aorist Tense

Certainly the aorist tense has been the most misunderstood of all the elements of Greek syntax. In 1972, Frank Stagg chronicled a widespread "abuse of the aorist" and his evaluation still holds: a great deal of meaning has been extracted from the aorist tense that it is not intended to serve. Much of this abuse relates to a fundamental misperception of the depictional nature of the Greek aorist tense (i.e., its aspectual nature). The aorist tense, in other words, is used to depict an action *without reference to how that action took place*. In other words, it is concerned not with *how* something took place, but *that* it took place.[37] For instance, Jesus Christ may have been sacrificed once for all *in reality* (see Heb.

---

35. For more, see Turner, *Syntax*, 60–62; Blass and Debrunner, *Grammar*, § 321.
36. See R. Buth, "Mark's Use of the Historical Present," *Notes on Translation* 65 (1977): 7–13; S. H. Levinsohn, "Preliminary Observations on the Use of the Historic Present in Mark," *Notes on Translation* 65 (1977): 13–28.
37. R. W. Funk stated, "whatever its actual duration, the act or series of acts is conceived as a whole" (*A Beginning-Intermediate Grammar of Hellenistic Greek*, 2d ed., 3 vols. [Missoula, Mont.: Scholars, 1973], § 788). See further in Stagg, "Abused Aorist," 222–23.

9:26, 28), but that perfective notion is not denoted by the aorist tense at 1 Corinthians 5:7 (ἐτύθη). Paul simply notes *that* Christ was sacrificed, not *how* the oblation took place or whether its effects are permanent.[38]

The aorist is constative (or complexive, global) unless the context demands otherwise. The constative aorist is used to describe action represented as a whole, without reference to progress or completion.[39] An example may be found in Colossians 1:7 where Paul says, καθὼς ἐμάθετε ἀπὸ Ἐπαφρᾶ τοῦ ἀγαπητοῦ συνδούλου ἡμῶν ("just as you learned from Epaphras, our dear fellow servant"). The Colossians undoubtedly listened to Epaphras instruct them many times, perhaps for months on regular occasions. Thus, Paul could have easily chosen the imperfect ἐμανθάνετε to depict this continual process. Instead, he chose the aorist because he wanted to depict the action without reference to *how* it took place but *that* it took place. The importance of this observation for exegesis is that we cannot conclude from the aorist tense that the Colossians only learned about the gospel on one occasion. Paul's concern is neither how often they learned nor for how long they listened.

It is also important not to misinterpret aorist commands, as in Romans 6:13: ἀλλὰ παραστήσατε ἑαυτοὺς τῷ θεῷ ὡσεὶ ἐκ νεκρῶν ζῶντας καὶ τὰ μέλη ὑμῶν ὅπλα δικαιοσύνης τῷ θεῷ ("but present yourselves to God as those alive from the dead and your members as instruments of righteousness to God"). Does Paul's use of the aorist here suggest that one can make a single offering and be done with it? Does Paul suggest that one can reach a new level of Christian existence by a comprehensive, single self-sacrifice? Not at all. The aorist tense is chosen for exactly the opposite reason, namely, Paul does not want to depict *how* or how many times that sacrifice will take place. Rather, he sums up, with a constative aorist, Christian living as sacrifice. Furthermore, the present prohibition in 6:13 (μηδὲ παριστάνετε, "do not continue presenting") that precedes the aorist command clearly

---

38. Cf. G. D. Fee who infers this once-for-all point from the aorist in 1 Cor. 5:7 (*The First Epistle to the Corinthians*, New International Commentary [Grand Rapids: Eerdmans, 1987], 217 n. 14).

39. On this, see Blass and Debrunner, *Grammar*, § 332 (though the editors here assume incorrectly that the action is already completed; it may be and it may not be); Zerwick, *Biblical Greek*, §§ 253–55; Turner, *Syntax*, 71–72.

suggests that repeated sacrifices could be the reality envisaged. The aorist tense then is used to depict an action without reference to its completion or process.[40]

Some other uses of the aorist are at least disputable when analyzed from the perspective of aspect. In fact, many of the other categories of the aorist are determined more by vocabulary and context than by the aorist itself. Thus, probably too much is made of the ingressive (or inchoative, inceptive) aorist. In almost every instance the ingressive nature of these verbs is related more to the kind of action inherent in the verb itself or the mood of that verb than in the aorist. The ingressive category is often used to describe the genus of aorist commands and prohibitions. Thus, N. Turner says, "Somewhat peremptory and categorical, they [aorist imperatives] tend to be ingressive, giving either a command to commence some action or a prohibition against commencing it. On the other hand, present imperatives give a command to do something constantly, to continue to do it; or else a prohibition against its continuance, an interruption of action already begun."[41]

What needs to be observed is that all commands and prohibitions are ingressive by nature, whether they are aorist or present, because one must somehow begin the action commanded or stop an action prohibited. In other words, while it may be realistic (and homiletically potent) to say that the aorist imperatives of James 4:9 are ingressive (ταλαιπωρήσατε καὶ πενθήσατε καὶ κλαύσατε, "be wretched, mourn and weep"), the aorist tense does not convey that meaning. Rather, the aorist serves to specify *that* they were to do these things, not *when* or *how*.[42] With imperatives it is more accurate to speak of the aorist being used to express categorically *that* something must be done, whereas the present imperative expresses the author's depiction of the action in which someone is to participate in either a durative or iterative manner.

---

40. The older commentary of W. Sanday and A. C. Headlam, *The Epistle to the Romans*, International Critical Commentary (Edinburgh: T. & T. Clark, 1902), 161, is misleading here in translating the aorist " 'dedicate by one decisive act, one resolute effort.' " More accurate is Blass and Debrunner, *Grammar*, § 337.1.

41. *Syntax*, 74–75.

42. Turner, *Syntax*, 76, translated these imperatives in the following manner: "start to be wretched and mourn and weep."

The culminative or perfective aorist is slightly different since Hellenistic Greek saw the gradual replacement of the perfect tense with the aorist. Again, however, what appears to be perfective in force is more often determined by the meaning of the verb and how English idiom translates that verb than by a "use" of the aorist tense.[43] When Mark records Jesus quoting Psalm 22:2 (LXX 21:2) from the cross (Mark 15:34), the aorist tense εἰς τί ἐγκατέλιπές με is often translated as an English perfect: "Why have you abandoned me [and left me in this condition]?" This could be accurate, but the author may have nothing more in mind than "Why did you desert me?" with no concern for abiding results—in which case the aorist is not a culminative but a constative. One can at least ask why the author chose the aorist rather than the perfect in this instance. Again, as stated earlier, the aorist tense is constative unless it can be clearly proven otherwise.

The proleptic aorist describes the use of the aorist for an action that is yet future. Thus, Galatians 5:4 reads κατηργήθητε ἀπὸ Χριστοῦ, οἵτινες ἐν νόμῳ δικαιοῦσθε ("whoever seeks to be justified by law will be separated from Christ"). Here future consequences are drawn out without reference to kind of action prior to the conditions being met. This aorist seems to be used for dramatic effect and/or certainty of result but it seems restricted to contingencies or conditional type constructions (e.g., John 15:6, 8).[44]

These are but a few important syntactical and grammatical issues that exercise great influence in exegesis. Students of the Greek New Testament will need to learn as fully as possible the standard categories that are used in grammars and commentaries. Once these categories are learned, exegesis becomes an operation that can be performed with considerable precision and accuracy.

It was mentioned above that students entering seminaries today often have received inadequate preparation for the complexity of technical discussions about grammar. One of the most

---

43. So also Turner, *Syntax*, 72; Moule, *Idiom*, 11.
44. See Zerwick, *Biblical Greek*, §§ 257–58; Turner, *Syntax*, 74. For a similar caution regarding gnomic aorists, see Moule, *Idiom*, 12–13; Zerwick, *Biblical Greek*, § 256; see also the cautions of Turner, *Syntax*, 73–74.

proven methods for eliminating such a deficiency and mastering Greek syntax is to diagram Greek sentences.

Diagramming Greek Sentences

The goal of diagramming is simple: to identify and display the grammatical function of each word in a sentence. Until one can display (or identify) the grammatical function of each word, it is unlikely that the grammar has been grasped.[45]

Rule #1

Place all conjunctions and particles in the left margin. Particles and conjunctions are to be placed in the margin at the left since they identify the various relationships of sentences and words.

Rule #2

Identify the kind of sentence and place each word in its slot. Greek sentences can be identified by the verb, conditional particle, or question mark and are of the following types: transitive (a verb that has an object), intransitive (a verb with no object), passive (a verb whose subject receives the action of the verb), copulative (a verb of being: εἰμί, γίνομαι), conditional (a sentence with a protasis [εἰ, ἐάν] and an apodosis), discourse (a sentence with a verb of saying or thinking, often introduced by dependent or recitative ὅτι), and interrogative (a question).

Each sentence is to be diagrammed in the following word order: (1) subject, (2) verb, (3) direct object, and/or (4) indirect object. This implies that many words will be dislocated from their present context and relocated in one of these slots. These four slots are to be kept on the same line of the diagram though it must be observed that not every sentence necessarily contains words that occupy each slot.

After any particle or conjunction, the *subject* of the verb is the

---

45. A more complete survey of diagramming can be found in G. D. Fee, *New Testament Exegesis: A Handbook for Students and Pastors* (Philadelphia: Westminster, 1983), 60–77.

first word on the main line; if the subject is implied, construct the subject (either in Greek or English) and place in brackets, as is done in the example below. (When an article is used, place it immediately before the word with which it is used.) At times the subject may be a noun clause (e.g., Matt. 18:5).

[ἐγώ] ἀνεθέμην τὸ εὐαγγέλιον αὐτοῖς (Gal. 2:2).

"[I] set before them the gospel."

The *verb* of the sentence is the second word on the main line; if the verb has a negative, place it immediately before the verb.

[ἐγώ] **ἀνεθέμην** τὸ εὐαγγέλιον αὐτοῖς (Gal. 2:2).

The *direct object* occupies the third slot on the main line; this word is often in the accusative case. Because Greek syntax is complex, other grammatical features can also appear in this slot. Object infinitives and clauses that function as objects (e.g., direct discourse beginning with recitative ὅτι, substantival participles) can also take this slot. In the case of a double accusative (Mark 6:34; Acts 13:5), the second accusative follows the first.

[ἐγώ] ἀνεθέμην **τὸ εὐαγγέλιον** αὐτοῖς (Gal. 2:2).

The *indirect object* follows the direct object on the main line. Again, one cannot simplistically reduce the indirect object to a dative (indirect object) noun.

[ἐγώ] ἀνεθέμην τὸ εὐαγγέλιον **αὐτοῖς** (Gal. 2:2).

Rule #3

Place subordinate elements under the word being modified and indent two spaces. Grammatical features that are not placed in one of the above slots need to be subordinated to one of those slots by dropping one line and indenting two spaces. Thus, if a word or set of words is not a subject, verb, object, or indirect object, they modify one of those categories. (Typical modifiers, which may subordinate or coordinate, include prepositional phrases, adverbial and adjectival participles, adverbs, adjectives, relative clauses, genitive modifiers, etc.) In the following example (table 7), the relative pronoun ὅ corresponds to its antecedent, the noun εὐαγγέλιον, and is therefore coordinate (see Rule #4), whereas the prepositional phrase ἐν τοῖς ἔθνεσιν is adverbial and therefore subordinate to the verb κηρύσσω.

Table 7   **Diagram of Galatians 2:2b**

[ἐγώ] ἀνεθέμην τὸ εὐαγγέλιον αὐτοῖς
    ὃ [ἐγώ] κηρύσσω
        ἐν τοῖς ἔθνεσιν

"[I] set before them the gospel
    that I preach
        among the Gentiles."

Rule #4

Line up coordinate elements under the word with which they are coordinate. Coordinate features, regardless of the slot they occupy, should be lined up vertically. In Galatians 2:2 the verbs are coordinate because they have the same grammatical function in their respective sentences; the prepositional phrases, κατὰ ἀποκάλυψιν and ἐν τοῖς ἔθνεσιν, are subordinate to the verbs ἀνέβην and κηρύσσω because they modify those verbs; the relative clause ὃ [ἐγώ] κηρύσσω clarifies by restatement εὐαγγέλιον. Notice, furthermore, that relative clauses become new sentences at the appropriate modification point (see table 8).

Table 8   **Diagram of Galatians 2:2a, b**

δὲ [ἐγώ] ἀνέβην
    κατὰ ἀποκάλυψιν
καὶ [ἐγώ] ἀνεθέμην τὸ εὐαγγέλιον αὐτοῖς
    ὃ [ἐγώ] κηρύσσω
        ἐν τοῖς ἔθνεσιν

"But [I] went up
    according to a revelation
and [I] placed before them the gospel
    that I preach
        among the Gentiles."

Miscellaneous Rules

Copulative sentences can be diagrammed as follows:

δὲ ὁ θεὸς ἐστιν εἷς (Gal. 3:20).
"But God is one."

Here the subject is ὁ θεὸς and the predicate is εἷς with the copula ἐστίν. Frequently the copula is omitted and must be reconstructed (e.g., Gal. 3:21: ὁ οὖν νόμος [ἐστίν] κατὰ τῶν ἐπαγγελιῶν; "Therefore, is the law contrary to the promises?"). On other occasions it is more complex, as illustrated from Galatians 3:10.

γὰρ (ὅσοι εἰσιν ἐξ ἔργων) εἰσίν ὑπὸ κατάραν (Gal. 3:10)
νόμου
"For (whoever is of the works of the law) is under a curse."

In this sentence the subject of the copula is a relative clause (the words within the parentheses) with the descriptive genitive νόμου modifying the noun ἔργων; further, the predicate of both copulas is a prepositional phrase (ἐξ ἔργων, ὑπὸ κατάραν).

Conditions can be diagrammed in two different ways. If one chooses to begin with the dependent clause (the protasis), the diagram in table 9 of a passive verb sentence in Galatians 3:21 is suggested.

Table 9   **Diagram of Galatians 3:21b**

γὰρ εἰ νόμος ἐδόθη
   ⌐ ὁ δυνάμενος ζωοποιῆσαι
   ↖ ἡ δικαιοσύνη ἂν ἦν ἐκ νόμου
         ὄντως
"For if a law had been given,
   ⌐ that was able to produce life
   ↖ righteousness would have been of the law."
       truly

This "unreal" condition, noted by ἂν in the apodosis, begins with a simple protasis with a passive verb; the noun is modified by an adjectival participle which itself is completed by an aorist infinitive. The apodosis, indicated by the arrow, is a simple copulative sentence with an adverb modifying the verb.

If one chooses to begin with the independent clause (apodosis), the scheme in table 10 may be used, with the protasis diagrammed as a subordinate clause.

Table 10   **Alternative Diagram of Galatians 3:21b**

γὰρ ἡ δικαιοσύνη ἂν ἦν ἐκ νόμου
      ὄντως
      εἰ νόμος ἐδόθη
      ὁ δυνάμενος ζωοποιῆσαι

Table 11 illustrates how a sentence may be diagrammed when it contains *indirect* or *direct discourse,* as in Galatians 2:14.

Table 11   **Diagram of Galatians 2:14b**

[ἐγώ] εἶπον [ὅτι] τῷ Κηφᾷ
 ἔμπροσθεν πάντων
  εἰ σὺ ζῇς. . . .
[I] said to Cephas
 before everyone,
  "If you live. . . ."

Paul here reports what he said to Cephas at Antioch. The subject is implied by the verb; the object of the verb εἶπον is recitative ὅτι but, since it has been omitted, it has been reconstructed; the indirect object is τῷ Κηφᾷ; an adverbial modifier, which explains where Paul made his stunning observation, is subordinated to the verb. The content of ὅτι is then unrolled in direct discourse (εἰ σὺ ζῇς . . .), diagrammed in coordination with ὅτι.

Vocatives, since they are not truly part of the sentence, are to be on a line by themselves. *Genitive absolutes,* so common in narratives, are to be diagrammed as subject and verb on a separate line above the main line (as if it were a separate sentence).

Diagramming is a tedious and exacting exercise. Its difficulty is outstripped only by the reward of a more precise understanding of the text. It is often the case that diagramming forces us to identify grammar that would not otherwise have been examined.

Galatians 3:1–5

The following diagram of Galatians 3:1–5 (table 12) illustrates diagramming and provides an opportunity to observe the type of grammatical observations that can be gleaned from diagramming. The rules oulined above are applied to each of the sentences in Galatians 3:1–5; if the student works carefully with this outline, the rules will be seen. (If needed, the student ought to consult a standard translation.)

The purpose of diagramming, again, is to identify and specify the grammatical function of each word. It can be seen, however, that diagramming involves decisions about syntax and exegeti-

Table 12   Diagram of Galatians 3:1–5

3:1	Ὦ ἀνόητοι Γαλάται
	τίς ἐβάσκανεν ὑμᾶς
	οἷς Ἰησοῦς Χριστὸς προεγράφη
	ἐσταυρωμένος κατ᾽ ὀφθαλμοὺς;
3:2	[ἐγώ] θέλω μαθεῖν τοῦτο
	μόνον ἀφ᾽ ὑμῶν
	[ὑμεῖς]ἐλάβετε τὸ πνεῦμα
	ἐξ ἔργων
	νόμου
ἢ	ἐξ ἀκοῆς
	πίστεως;
3:3	[ὑμεῖς]ἐστε ἀνόητοί;
	οὕτως
	[ὑμεῖς]ἐπιτελεῖσθε;
	νῦν
	σαρκὶ
	ἐναρξάμενοι
	πνεύματι
3:4	[ὑμεῖς]ἐπάθετε τοσαῦτα;
	εἰκῇ
	(εἴ γε καὶ εἰκῇ.)
3:5 οὖν	(ὁ ἐπιχορηγῶν τὸ πνεῦμα ὑμῖν
καὶ	ἐνεργῶν δυνάμεις [ἐνεργεῖ]
	ἐν ὑμῖν) ἐξ ἔργων
	νόμου
ἢ	ἐξ ἀκοῆς
	πίστεως;

cal options. The more the student diagrams the more adept he or she becomes at it.

Concluding Exhortation

Not enough can be said nor can one urge students sufficiently about the importance of mastering the fundamentals of Greek grammar if proficiency and accuracy in interpretation are the goal. Major NT exegetical tools assume competency in reading Greek and proponents of competing theological views often appeal to points of grammar and syntax for their conclusions. What can be done to learn Greek adequately?

At our seminary I have begun a "Ten Minute Society." This "Society" is a voluntary organization of students who have committed themselves to reading the Greek NT for ten minutes a day, five days a week. Membership lasts three years and—to avoid any external pressure—we never meet. This exegesis teacher believes that if students will discipline their schedule to include habitual reading of the Greek NT for ten minutes a day for three years that that habit will become a permanent acquisition. And competency in reading Greek is a skill that the church can ill afford to lose. Μακάριος ὁ ὑπομείνας εἰς τὸ τέλος.[46]

46. I am grateful to my colleagues, M. J. Harris, D. A. Carson, and D. J. Moo, for their comments on an earlier draft of this essay. In addition, Cindy Robinson, one of our Greek exegesis students, offered helpful insights from a student's perspective; her suggestions have improved the essay at numerous points.

4

New Testament Word Analysis
Darrell L. Bock

Watching a building under construction fascinates people. After the edifice has been constructed piece by piece, it eventually reveals a master plan. Similarly, words—the building blocks of Scripture—reveal mind-changing concepts about God and his world. The construction of words determines not only the meaning of the parts but also shapes the concepts of the whole. Studying the words of the NT involves investigating the most basic components that lead to exegetical and theological discovery. When one examines the words in the NT, one is looking at the units that form the starting point for exegetical and theological discovery. There is something exciting about understanding not only what is before the student of Scripture but in determining how that understanding is present.

Unfortunately, there often is a lack of total agreement about the nature of the message. What can get in the way of agreement? How is the interpreter to hurdle the obstacles that obscure the view of the building? This essay will attempt to explain what hinders our understanding of the meaning of words and how words should be handled exegetically. In thinking through word analysis, one should first consider several fundamental questions: What are the basic rules of word study? What obstacles impede an understanding of the meaning of words? These two questions form the first and second sections of this study.

In the third major section we will overview the diachronic and synchronic approaches to word study. The fourth and final section will detail the stages of word analysis, including a list of common errors that often accompany the study of words. A proper method may not remove all the ambiguity and debate—after all, humans are finite creatures—but it should allow exegetes to understand why the building looks the way it does and to articulate clearly their understanding to others so that together they can discuss and benefit from each other's insights and observations on the Scriptures.

Fundamental Rules of Word Study

In thinking about words and exegesis, there are three fundamental rules that should have general assent:

1. *The exegete must initially pursue the meaning intended by the author for his original audience.*[1] Communication fundamentally involves the transfer of an idea from one mind to another. In biblical exegesis the interpreter's goal is to understand what the original author said through the terms

---

1. This is the *initial* goal of the exegete. The exegete is preoccupied with the message of the human author. Initially the goal is to understand the message as set forth in the setting in which the author operated. The process of correlating that message with other biblical texts, either earlier or later ones, is the task of a subsequent theological process. In this latter phase one wrestles with concepts like the "progress of revelation," the "fuller sense" that God intended, the use and application of the OT in the NT, and the personal application of the text. All of these involve subsequent reflection beyond the initial exegetical concern with the message of a given document in a given setting. E. D. Hirsch presents a fine discussion and defense of authorial intention in *Validity in Interpretation* (New Haven: Yale University Press, 1967). For a fine caveat in regard to authorial intention, see J. P. Louw, *Semantics of New Testament Greek* (Philadelphia/Chico: Fortress/Scholars, 1982), 48. The complex issue of *sensus plenior* is handled nicely by D. J. Moo, "The Problem of Sensus Plenior," in *Hermeneutics, Authority, and Canon*, ed. D. A. Carson and J. Woodbridge (Grand Rapids: Zondervan, 1986), 179–211, 397–405.

In speaking of authorial intention, one does not try to reproduce what the author must have been thinking at a given point or why he wrote. Rather, the interpreter's goal is to ascertain what the writer wanted to communicate through the terms he chose for his message. Speaking about an author's intention is more appropriate than speaking about the meaning of the text, since words do not carry meaning autonomously and their meaning can be variously construed when detached from their original setting. The concern of the exegete is the meaning of the author's mind.

he used. One needs to recognize that words do not automatically have meaning. They receive their meaning from
the author who produced the words.

Another point emerges from this consideration. To communicate, the message must be potentially shareable with
the audience. It must relate to a category of meaning that
they can perceive—or else the message is incomprehensi-
ble. This observation does not deny that an author can
communicate new sense in the words that he uses. It does
suggest, however, that when the author intends new
meaning, he will signal it so that the audience can grasp
the new force of the term.[2]

2. *To establish the precise meaning of a word, one must recognize its
possible range of meanings.* Often an interpreter simply assumes that a word has a certain meaning. However, the
meaning of terms can change—from situation to situation,
from person to person. Therefore, the exegete must exercise care in studying the words that compose the message
of Scripture.

3. *Words operate in a context and receive meaning from that context.* This point is crucial. Words as separate, isolated en-
tities do not provide the key to the meaning of Scripture.
Instead, words *in relationship* to other words form the basis
of the concepts that represent the message of a text. Thus
the major concern of the exegete in determining the meaning of a word is the setting of the word in its verse, paragraph, and book.

These three fundamentals provide a solid foundation for lexical analysis—a crucial discipline that the exegete must master in
order to interpret the Word of God correctly.

---

2. This means that in historically sensitive exegesis one will not use later NT passages to
determine the referents of OT passages. Since meaning can emerge in a variety of ways
when one introduces the factor of the passage of time, going to later revelation at this stage
of the exegetical-interpretive process would possibly cloud the force of the original message,
if not obscure it altogether. For this complex area see D. L. Bock, "Evangelicals and the Use
of the Old Testament of the New," *Bibliotheca Sacra* 142 (1985): 209–23, 306–18, which surveys
and evaluates four models offered by evangelicals to deal with this particularly difficult
issue.

The Complexities of Meaning

The Meaning of Meaning

Formally speaking, meaning and the study of words are bound together with the formal and broader discipline of semantics.[3] Semantics is the study of "signification" or "meaning." It can offer to the interpreter many insights regarding the issue of method. The goal of this discipline at the lexical level is to examine how meaning is communicated through words.

In semantics one of the problems of lexical meaning is, in fact, determining what one means by speaking about a word's meaning![4] Semanticists have produced as many as twenty-five possible senses for meaning; but a few distinctions are extremely significant for exegesis and indicate the need for careful analysis. A list of these distinctions follows.

1. *Entailment meaning* pertains to a word or idea that implies some type of conclusion not explicit in the term or context. For example, a passage that shows Jesus engaged in an activity that only God can perform entails the idea that Jesus is divine, even though that specific theological assertion is not explicitly made in the text.
2. *Emotive meaning* applies to the use of a term that carries emotional force.
3. *Significance meaning* refers to a term or concept that takes on new meaning when brought into a context different from the original one (e.g., the NT use of the OT).
4. *Encyclopedic meaning* denotes all the possible meanings that a term may have. One generates such a list from a

---

3. See J. Barr, *The Semantics of Biblical Language* (Oxford: Oxford University Press, 1961), 1; A. Thiselton, "Semantics and New Testament Interpretation," in *New Testament Interpretation*, ed. I. H. Marshall (Grand Rapids: Eerdmans, 1977), 75–104, esp. 75; M. Silva, *Biblical Words and Their Meaning: An Introduction to Lexical Semantics* (Grand Rapids: Zondervan, 1983). For an excellent study of all aspects of semantics as it applies to NT word studies, see J. P. Louw, *Semantics of New Testament Greek*. This study addresses meaning as it is related to words, sentences, and paragraphs. For the broader discipline of semantics, see S. Ullmann, *The Principles of Semantics*, 2d ed. (Oxford: Blackwells, 1957), 1–137, 197–258; idem, *Semantics: An Introduction to the Science of Meaning* (Oxford: Blackwells, 1962).

4. G. B. Caird, *The Language and Imagery of the Bible* (Philadelphia: Westminster, 1980), 37–61.

dictionary or lexicon.[5] This range of possible meanings allows for a variety of possible interpretations, as well as misinterpretations.

5. *Grammatical meaning* refers to the grammatical role of a term, such as the categories that one learns in an intermediate Greek grammar course. Some interpreters use this limited area of meaning to secure meaning, when in fact often all it does is limit the possible meanings. For example, ἀκούσας in Ephesians 1:15 is a temporal circumstantial participle. Thus it means, "when I heard."

6. *Figurative meaning* indicates the use of a term because of the association it makes, not because of the term's sense and referent are directly applied. For example, when Jesus speaks of faith that can "move mountains," he is not referring to the use of earth-moving equipment but to faith that can do marvelous things. Many exegetical debates turn on whether a term is literal or figurative, which is always an appropriate question to consider. Usually an understanding of genre, idiom, and authorial style can help in interpreting figures.

These senses of meaning can be significant in assessing the force of a given term, and must receive attention in thinking through the study of a term. However, they are not as central to the study of a term as the three basic elements of a word.

The Three Elements of a Word

Words are basically made up of three elements that contribute most directly to their intended meaning: *sign, sense,* and *referent.* In reality a word is a symbol that communicates meaning within

---

5. In a normal lexicon the meanings of a word are simply listed along with passages that reflect a particular meaning. They can also be charted semantically in relation to the term's "field of meaning," where the senses are charted as categories of meaning that a word may have and are placed alongside other terms that can be associated with that category of meaning (see Thiselton, "Semantics," 91, where he charts out the word πνεῦμα; see also Louw, *Semantics,* 60–66). Words that address the same conceptual area are said to share the same semantic domain. A semantic domain lexicon examines words according to conceptual groupings. See J. P. Louw and E. A. Nida, eds., *Greek-English Lexicon of the New Testament based on Semantic Domains* (New York: United Bible Societies, 1988). For another excellent treatment of the various relationships among words, see Silva, *Biblical Words,* 118–35.

a given culture or subculture.[6] A word does not *have* meaning; it is *assigned* meaning through cultural convention and usage.

The first element of a word is the *sign*, the collection of symbols that comprise a word. For example, the English word "paraclete" is made up of nine alphabetic symbols. These symbols allow us to identify and pronounce the word. If we know the symbols and the coding patterns of the language, then we can understand the meaning.

The second element of a word is *sense*, which is the content associated with the symbol.[7] The sense of a word is closely related to the lexical definition of the word. However, the concept referred to by the sense of the term need not precisely identify the actual referent. For example, paraclete means "comforter," which by itself is ambiguous in English, since it could refer specifically either to an object similar to a quilt or to a sympathetic encourager. The ambiguity results because terms vary in their level of "specificity and vagueness." Some senses are specific; others relative. Sense gets one closer to the meaning of a text, but it does not always specify that meaning. The context in which the word appears will help us not only to determine the term's sense, but also, hopefully, its referent. Nonetheless, once the general content of the term is clear, one begins to know the general sense of the passage.

The third element of a word is *referent*. The referent is the actual thing denoted by the term. In John 14–16, for example, the referent of "paraclete" is clearly neither a human sympathetic figure nor a blanket; rather the term refers specifically to the Holy Spirit. This clearly demonstrates that a knowledge of the referent produces specificity and clarity in exegesis.

The complex nature of a word's meaning and its various elements require that the exegete exercise great care in approaching the study of words. Once the exegete has grasped the fundamentals of word study, the meaning of meaning, and the basic elements of a word, then he or she can proceed with care and precision in the actual procedure of word analysis.

---

6. This point is illustrated by the existence of different languages and alphabets, which are simply different symbolic systems for representing concepts in words.

7. Silva, *Biblical Words*, 101–3.

Diachronic and Synchronic Word Analysis

Word meanings can be examined in two ways. First, words can be studied historically by examining how they have been used in the past and how they have changed in meaning through time. This is called *diachronic word analysis,* the approach of *TDNT* and *NIDNTT.*[8] These two reference tools examine a word's use beginning with the classical Greek period and continuing through the NT or even the patristic period. Examining words in this way indicates the possible senses that a term may have.

Second, words can also be studied within a given period (e.g., the intertestamental period, or pre-A.D. 70), or within the writings of a specific author (e.g., Paul, John, Matthew, Philo, or Josephus). This is called *synchronic word analysis.* This is perhaps the most crucial phase of lexical analysis since the meaning of a word in its specific context, either temporal or literary, is the major concern of the exegete.

The following sections present an example of both the diachronic and synchronic processes used for NT word analysis.

A Basic Procedure for NT Word Analysis

Getting Started: Selection of Terms

Several options are available when selecting terms for closer analysis. First, one could choose to study any words whose English definition is unclear. Second, words that have apparent synonyms and antonyms make good candidates. Third, words that are used rarely or only once (hapax legomena) are also good candidates, especially if they appear to carry conceptual weight

---

8. *Theological Dictionary of the New Testament,* ed. G. Kittel and G. Friedrich, trans. G. W. Bromiley, 10 vols. (Grand Rapids: Eerdmans, 1964–76), abbrev. *TDNT,* and *The New International Dictionary of New Testament Theology,* ed. C. Brown, 4 vols. (Grand Rapids: Zondervan, 1975–85), abbrev. *NIDNTT.* The difference in these tools is that *TDNT* lists individual lexical terms tied to a specific root form, while *NIDNTT* organizes words according to concepts, groups of similar lexical terms, or synonyms that may not necessarily share the same root form. While *TDNT* provides fuller historical information, *NIDNTT* traces concepts better since it explicitly associates related terms. For a critique of *TDNT,* see J. Barr, *Semantics,* 21–45, 206–62.

in a passage. Fourth, figures make a good choice, since their precise meaning is often not transparent. The most crucial words, however, are those terms that are either repeated or that bear the conceptual weight of a passage. One must understand these to ascertain the meaning of a passage.

An expositor should learn how to spot the key terms in a given passage. If a personal reading of the text does not reveal these key terms, then the use of lexically sensitive commentaries on the Greek text can often help to locate them. Another way to discover these key terms is by comparing different English translations. If the translations render the original Greek text with clearly distinct English terms, then perhaps those terms that differ merit closer examination.

Four Stages of Word Study

A diachronic word study includes four distinct stages, each of which utilizes a certain tool or set of tools.[9] The examination of terms used during the classical Greek period (900 B.C.–330 B.C.) requires the use of the Liddel-Scott-Jones lexicon.[10] Next one enters the Hellenistic or koine period (330 B.C.–A.D. 330). Here one will consider three groups of material: the LXX, popular nonbiblical sources, and the NT. A study of the Septuagint (LXX) will involve the use of the concordance of Hatch and Redpath.[11] An examination of terms in nonbiblical sources of the koine period involves using both LSJ and the volume of Moulton

---

9. A fifth step could be added that studies the use of NT terms in Christian patristic literature. For this latter step, use G. W. H. Lampe, *A Patristic Greek Lexicon* (Oxford: Clarendon, 1961–68), which gives one access to the use of terms in the writings of the church fathers. The most complete collection of Greek patristic texts is J.-P. Migne, *Patrologia Graeca*, 161 vols. (New York: Adlers, 1965–1971). Many of these texts have been translated and can be located in other series. A possible sixth step could examine the use of related terms in Jewish or rabbinic literature (e.g., Hebrew or Aramaic equivalents). For this step, judiciously use H. L. Strack and P. Billerbeck, *Kommentar zum Neuen Testament aus Talmud und Midrasch*, 6 vols. (Munchen: Beck, 1921–61). See also M. Jastrow, *A Dictionary of the Targumim, the Talmud Babli and Yerushalmi, and the Midrashic Literature* (London: Judaica, 1971).

10. H. G. Liddell and R. Scott, *A Greek-English Lexicon: A New Edition Revised and Augmented Throughout with Supplement*, rev. H. S. Jones and R. McKenzie, 9th ed. (Oxford: Oxford University Press, 1924–40; Supplement, 1968). Hereafter abbreviated as LSJ.

11. E. Hatch and H. A. Redpath, *A Concordance to the Septuagint and the Other Greek Versions of the Old Testament (Including the Apocryphal Books)*, 2 vols. (1897; reprint, Graz: Akademische Druck–u. Verlagsanstalt, 1975; reprint, Grand Rapids: Baker, 1983).

and Milligan.[12] The study of terms in the NT will involve the use of a NT concordance, the most up-to-date being the work produced by Bachmann and Slaby.[13]

Practically speaking, the best way to proceed is to take a sheet of paper and record the results of the study in these four periods, which will ultimately help to organize one's thoughts and formulate one's conclusions about the data. For exegesis, the most significant results will emerge as one moves closer to the text in question, with primary consideration being given to context and authorial intention.[14]

The following sections illustrate the four stages of a word study, using the Greek noun ἀρραβών as an example.

Classical Usage

The diachronic study begins with the data in LSJ. The goal at this level is to establish the various senses the term has and to date them by determining if in fact they are classical or koine uses. As a general rule, classical usage occurs before about 300 B.C. One should examine the entry in LSJ to determine the distinct definitions of the word. For ἀρραβών, the basic definitions are: (1) earnest-money, caution-money; (2) pledge, earnest; and (3) present, bribe.[15] The examples in the writings of Isaeus[16] and Aristotle show that ἀρραβών is a commercial term that refers to the initial payment in a series of payments. Classical sources to which LSJ refers may be checked in *The Loeb Classical Library* (LCL).[17]

The study of a word's usage in the classical period yields a

---

12. J. H. Moulton and G. Milligan, *The Vocabulary of the Greek New Testament* (Grand Rapids: Eerdmans, 1974).

13. H. Bachmann and H. Slaby, eds., *Computer-Konkordanz zum Novum Testamentum Graece* (New York: W. de Gruyter, 1980). Another concordance that could be used is that by W. F. Moulton and A. S. Geden, *Concordance to the Greek Testament*, 5th ed. (Edinburgh: T. & T. Clark, 1897; supplement, 1977), a work based on the 1881 text of Westcott and Hort. Major advantages of the *Computer-Konkordanz* include not only its use of the most recent Greek text but also the larger context it provides for each word it cites. Advanced students will profit by using the *Vollständige Konkordanz zum griechischen Neuen Testament*, ed. K. Aland, 2 vols. (Berlin: Walter de Gruyter, 1978, 1983), a multivolume tool that offers complete word statistics.

14. It should be stressed that in lexical matters evidence for usage is weighed, not counted. Thus a word whose meaning is uncertain will not necessarily reflect the most popular sense; and the context will always be the most important factor.

15. LSJ, 246.

16. LSJ cites Isaeus 8.20; however, the term of the entry is not found in this section but in 8.23.

17. *The Loeb Classical Library* (Cambridge, Mass.: Harvard University Press) is an extensive collection (approx. 450 vols.) of both Greek and Latin texts with English translations.

base from which to draw possible meanings. Only in the case of rarely used words, however, does it have significant importance, though the examples may illustrate the force of the term.

Hellenistic Biblical Usage (LXX)

In this particular step, one studies the use of Greek terms in the LXX, the Greek translation of the Hebrew Old Testament.[18] Here the study becomes more interesting and complicated: more interesting, because one of the objectives of this step is to determine possible religious or theological meanings for terms in the LXX; more complicated, because this step involves a knowledge of Hebrew.

This particular step, however, is not free from potential errors. One common error is simply to discover the Hebrew word behind the Greek translation in the LXX, and then determine the translation of the Hebrew word to get the Greek idea. This procedure ignores three important facts. First, words in languages do not overlap exactly in meaning.[19] Second, the LXX is often a paraphrase and not a word-for-word rendering of the Hebrew.[20] In fact, in some places the exact wording of the LXX is very uncertain. Third, often a particular Greek term was chosen not because the translator was attempting to render a specific Hebrew term, but because of the way the passage had been traditionally read and translated. These facts should warn the exegete against hastily concluding that a term has picked up its Greek sense from the Hebrew or that a term indicates technical Hebraic usage. The words may be used in a similar manner, but that does not mean they carry exactly the same sense.

Once the exegete has generated a list of Hebrew words that the Greek LXX terms translate, then he should study the mean-

---

18. For a helpful presentation on the value of the LXX for biblical studies, see F. W. Danker, "The Use of the Septuagint," in his *Multipurpose Tools for Bible Study*, 3d ed. (St. Louis: Concordia, 1970), 81–95.

19. For example, English has one word for "history," while German has two, "Geschichte" and "Historie." To equate either of the German words with the English is to lose some of the precision in the German terminology. The problems in this area are detailed by Silva, *Biblical Words*, 52–73.

20. In fact, the translation quality of the LXX varies from book to book. For details, see J. Roberts, *The Old Testament Text and the History of the Ancient Versions* (Cardiff: University of Wales Press, 1951), 172–87. For a recent overview of Septuagintal studies, see E. Tov, "Jewish Greek Scriptures," in *Early Judaism and its Modern Interpreters*, ed. R. Kraft and G. W. E. Nickelsburg (Philadelphia: Fortress, 1986), 223–37.

ings of those Hebrew terms in a Hebrew lexicon and, if possible, a theological dictionary for biblical Hebrew words.[21]

Looking up ἀρραβών in the LXX reveals that this term occurs only in Genesis 38:17, 18 and 20,[22] the passage about Tamar and Judah. In these verses the meaning of ἀρραβών clearly is "pledge," since an object was given to Tamar as a guarantee. The term as used here indicates a "business" deal; though no money was exchanged, a family seal, cord, and staff were. A glance at the Hebrew term עֵרָבוֹן which is translated "pledge" (NIV), shows that the LXX term is merely a transliteration of the Hebrew term. It is a "loanword," that is, a borrowed word.

Hellenistic Nonbiblical Usage

When we move to this period, we begin to cross from diachronic analysis to synchronic analysis. The objective in this phase of study is to trace the variety of meanings a given term has within the time period of 330 B.C. to A.D. 100. Actually, the koine period extends beyond this later date, but when studying NT usage the student need not move beyond the period of the NT writings.

A significant resource for the study of Hellenistic Greek words in nonbiblical sources is the volume by Moulton and Milligan.[23] This tool illustrates the use of koine Greek words as found in papyri and epigraphical remains. Some examples are left untranslated, but fortunately, most examples are translated or summarized, as well as dated. Some examples postdate the NT period and should be excluded. However, many excellent examples occur that vividly illustrate the everyday usage of many terms.[24]

---

21. F. Brown, S. R. Driver, and C. A. Briggs, eds., *A Hebrew and English Lexicon of the Old Testament* (Oxford: Clarendon Press, 1907); L. Koehler and W. Baumgartner, eds., *Lexicon in Veteris Testamenti Libros*, 2d ed. (Leiden: Brill, 1958). The latter volume is undergoing a complete revision under a new name (*Hebräisches und aramäisches Lexikon zum Alten Testament*, 3 vols. [Leiden: Brill, 1967, 1974, 1983]). The student should also consult the ongoing work of G. J. Botterweck and H. Ringgren, eds., *Theological Dictionary of the Old Testament*, (Grand Rapids: Eerdmans, 1974–), of which five volumes have been published (twelve volumes are projected).

22. Hatch and Redpath, *Concordance to the Septuagint*, 160.

23. See n. 12. This work is somewhat dated (1932); however, it is in the process of being updated by a working group of the Society of Biblical Literature (SBL), but it is uncertain when the update will be produced.

24. Moulton and Milligan contains only a small sampling of all of the occurrences of a given word, so it should not be regarded as providing an exhaustive treatment of terms in this period.

A quick look at ἀρραβών in Moulton and Milligan discloses several important items.[25] First, the entry notes that the term is a Semitic loanword, an observation we made earlier after comparing the LXX term with the Hebrew term that it translated. Second, the entry gives alternate spellings of the term. Third, according to several helpful examples, ἀρραβών is used for a deposit of 1000 drachmae for the purchase of a cow, a deposit of 160 drachmae for a land purchase, and a downpayment of 8 drachmae for the services of a mouse catcher. These examples clearly indicate the use of ἀρραβών as a commercial term. A note to the entry says, "The above vernacular usage amply confirms the NT sense of an 'earnest,' or a part given in advance of what will be bestowed fully afterwards, in 2 Cor 1[22], 5[5], Eph 1[14]."[26] In this entry, they have not only defined the NT term with "earnest" but have also paraphrased it with "a part given in advance of what will be bestowed fully afterwards."[27]

In some cases, the study of terms in the koine period will surface new meanings. Usually, however, the koine sources will supply information about the common understanding of terms in the period contemporary to the NT writings.

Hellenistic Biblical Usage (NT)

The objective of this phase of word study is to determine the meaning of a term in the NT. There are a variety of ways to do this. First, one can study the use of a term author by author, creating lists for each writer of the NT material. This approach allows the student to make valuable biblical-theological observations by observing each author's distinctive treatment of terms. Second, the use of a term can be studied within a specific genre (i.e., within the Gospels, Pauline Epistles, Apocalypse, etc.). The value of this division is that one can examine how genre may affect the use of certain terms and images. Third, one can also study the use of a term by proceeding through the text in chronological order. This process is perhaps

---

25. Moulton and Milligan, *Vocabulary*, 79.
26. Ibid.
27. The entry includes several intriguing later examples. One example relates ἀρραβών to "purchasing a wife." A second example speaks of the engagement ring as an ἀρραβών. Again, the picture of an object as a pledge is very clear here.

less helpful in the Gospels, since these documents in their final written form portray events that occurred considerably earlier. But in Paul or in the general Epistles this third approach can help trace the development of a writer's theology or the theology of the early church. (Here "development" may simply mean the introduction of a new topic that naturally produced new associations.)

Now what does one find about ἀρραβών?[28] It occurs only three times in the NT, all in Pauline letters. Its use in 2 Corinthians 1:22; 5:5; and Ephesians 1:14 show that it is related both to the Holy Spirit and to the idea of sealing. According to 2 Corinthians 1:22, God "put his Spirit in our hearts as a deposit [ἀρραβών], guaranteeing what is to come." In 2 Corinthians 5:5 Paul states that God "has given us the Spirit as a deposit [ἀρραβών], guaranteeing what is to come." Ephesians 1:13–14 says that believers "were marked in him with a seal, the promised Holy Spirit, who is a deposit [ἀρραβών] guaranteeing our inheritance until the redemption of those who are God's possession. . . ." Thus the gift of God's Spirit to believers not only indicates God's ownership (seal) of them, but also a pledge of his future inheritance for them. Clearly, for Paul the Spirit is a pledge, a promise of more to come.

This concludes the basic four-step process. A question that the exegete might now ask, however, is "Which tools should I own?" Ideally, all the tools that have been mentioned should be owned. But at a minimum, one should own the Bauer lexicon, a Greek NT concordance, and either *TDNT* or *NIDNTT*. The advantages of *TDNT* are that its articles offer a full array of ancient references, often cite portions of the pertinent ancient texts, and frequently include notes about the exegetical possibilities in a given passage. *NIDNTT* has the advantage of examining concepts, of being more up to date in its discussion and method, and of being more succinct. Also, the one-volume abridgement of *TDNT*, called "little Kittel," is helpful as a quick reference guide and gateway to the larger *TDNT*.[29]

---

28. Bachmann and Slaby, *Computer-Konkordanz*, 222.
29. "Little Kittel" (Grand Rapids: Eerdmans, 1985), prepared by G. Bromiley, is the one-volume abridged edition of *TDNT*.

Avoiding Errors: Common Fallacies Made in Word Analysis

Before turning to the final step of the procedure, one additional issue needs attention: to note the common fallacies made in the word-study process.[30] Several of the most common fallacies are listed in the following paragraphs.

The *etymological fallacy*, also known as the "root fallacy," assumes that the meaning of a word is governed by the meaning of its root or roots.[31] Also, it may assume that what a word originally meant is what a later author meant by the term. Though the sense may be related, it is not certain that an author cites a term with a knowledge of the meaning of its component parts. Thus it is best not to appeal to etymology unless contextual factors make it clear the author is aware of this meaning.

Illegitimate totality transfer assumes that a word carries all of its senses in any one passage. It could be called "meaning overload." However, linguists agree that the "correct meaning of any term is that which contributes the least to the total context."[32] One of the implications of this error is that technical meanings or unusual meanings for terms need to be determined contextually rather than imported from other contexts. It is best not to give a term a specific nuance in a given context unless double entendre is clearly signaled by context, authorial style, or genre.

Another error is the problem of *semantic anachronism*, in which a late meaning of a word is read back into an earlier term. What often contributes to this error is the way that the church today uses biblical terminology. Often a technical meaning will develop for a term that is more specific than ancient usage. A simple example of this is the term "salvation," which in the popular modern church almost always means justification. In the NT, however, the term can refer to justification, sanctification, glorification, or to all of these together. Another example of this problem is when appeal is made to later Jewish or Greek

---

30. For a more comprehensive discussion of fallacies, see D. A. Carson, *Exegetical Fallacies* (Grand Rapids: Baker, 1984), 25–66. He notes sixteen such fallacies. This essay shall note only the more common errors.

31. See Louw, *Semantics*, 23–31; Silva, *Biblical Words*, 35–51; Barr, *Semantics*, 107–60.

32. E. A. Nida, "The Implications of Contemporary Linguistics for Biblical Scholarship," *Journal of Biblical Literature* 91 (1972): 86; Louw, *Semantics*, 51–52.

materials to support a first-century meaning for a term that lacks attestation for that sense in earlier sources. Obviously keeping a careful eye on the dates of sources guards against this error.

Semantic obsolescence is when one assigns to a term an early meaning that is no longer used. In NT word study this would be the same as giving a classical Greek meaning to a first-century koine Greek term. An English illustration can suffice. One reason why the KJV is difficult to read in places is because some meanings of its terms have fallen out of use since A.D. 1611. The term may exist but it no longer carries the meaning it once had.

The *prescriptive fallacy* argues that a word has only one meaning and means the same thing in every passage. For example, if a word has the meaning "X" in 13 out of 14 occurrences, then it must mean "X" in the disputed case. But word meanings are determined by context, not word counts.[33]

The *word-idea fallacy* assumes that the study of a term is the study of an idea. But the study of a concept is broader than word study, and many terms can be related to a single concept. For example, if one studies the concept of Jesus as King, one is not limited to those texts where the term "king" (Gk. βασιλεύς) appears. Other relevant terms for study might include "rule," "reign," "kingdom," etc.

The *referential fallacy* limits meaning only to a specific referent. However, in contexts where principles are given, where commands are offered, where figures are used, or where abstractions are expressed, it is faulty to limit the meaning to a single referent. In such cases, the specific referent of a term is not the only object to which the passage can be related.[34]

When the OT prophets, for example, characterized the return from exile as a "new exodus," they applied an earlier image of the OT to their own experience. When the NT authors cited OT passages that originally referred to Yahweh and applied them to

---

33. This raises a key issue that often complicates exegesis, especially for the beginning student. One does not establish a meaning merely by showing that a term's sense is contextually possible. Often commentators think their work is done when they have shown that a context could support the defended sense. However, the sense that should be chosen is the one that is the most likely among the options. Often a context can support a variety of senses, but the meaning is the one that fits the context the most naturally and with the least amount of contextual strain.

34. This fallacy is the most abstract of the ones mentioned and is difficult to explain briefly. For a more detailed discussion, see Silva, *Biblical Words*, 103–8.

Jesus, they avoided the referential fallacy by interpreting the OT in the light of activities that Jesus performed. It should be noted, however, that as one moves beyond the original referents to which an author refers, the interpreter is moving beyond the technical realm of exegesis, whose goal is to recover the original intention of the author.

Verbal parallelomania refers to the practice of some biblical exegetes who claim that the presence of the same term in several different contexts automatically indicates conceptual parallelism, borrowing of terms, or literary dependency. Admittedly, many ancient cultures used similar terms in vaguely similar contexts, and the Greek religious world used terms that also appear in the NT. However, Philo's use of the term *logos* does not mean that it has the same sense for him as it does for the apostle John. Only careful, comparative study of all relevant texts will establish the veracity of possible parallels, borrowings, or literary dependencies.

Perhaps the most serious error is the *selective evidence fallacy* wherein one cites only the evidence that favors the interpretation one wants to defend. Certainly, unintentional errors in judgment do occur sometimes. However, the intentional avoidance of certain facts will always result in inaccurate and biased conclusions.

These nine fallacies present a cross section of some of the obstacles that can hinder the exegete in determining the meaning of words. At one time or another every exegete trips over one or more of these obstacles while engaged in the enterprise of interpretation. This is why dialogue with other reference works is an essential part of the process. Thus we include one final step in the analysis of words: comparing the results of our study with the results obtained by other biblical scholars.

Checking Other Authorities: BAGD,[35] TDNT, NIDNTT

A check of these sources shows that our analysis of ἀρραβών agrees with that of others. For example, the *TDNT* article says

---

35. *BAGD* is the abbreviation for W. Bauer, *A Greek-English Lexicon of the New Testament and Other Christian Literature,* trans. W. F. Arndt and F. W. Gingrich, rev. ed. F. W. Gingrich and F. W. Danker (Chicago: University of Chicago Press, 1979).

that ἀρραβών "always implies an act which engages to something bigger."[36] Thus the Spirit is "the guarantee of their full future possession of salvation,"[37] an excellent description of the contextual force of the term ἀρραβών. *NIDNTT* agrees with this description but also notes that since the Spirit is a gracious gift from God, one should not speak of God as our debtor.[38] This is one instance in which the image differs from its daily use. *BAGD* defines ἀρραβών as a "first installment," "deposit," "down payment," and "pledge." It is a commercial or legal term that denotes "pay[ing] part of the purchase price in advance, and so secures a legal claim to the article in question, or makes a contract valid."[39]

This concludes the final step of the process of word analysis. Thus the use of a term has been traced through various periods (diachronic word analysis), as well as the NT period (synchronic word analysis).

Lexical analysis is demanding but necessary. Through lexical study the barriers that hinder one's understanding of the meaning of terms are often overcome or significantly lowered. The exegete who strives to understand the basic rules of word study, who grasps the complexities of meaning, who appropriates and implements sound methodology, and who avoids the common fallacies made in word study will be able to achieve a high level of accuracy in interpreting words, the building blocks of Scripture.

---

36. *TDNT,* 1:475
37. Ibid.
38. *NIDNTT,* 2:39–40.
39. *BAGD,* 109.

5

Sociology and New Testament Exegesis

Thomas E. Schmidt

Sometimes I am afraid that we are finding enormously complicated ways of stating the obvious." With this statement a scholar involved in the integration of sociology and New Testament studies began a presentation at a recent national meeting of the Society for Biblical Literature. Using illustrations from the Gospels, he explained ways that primitive peoples react to those who pose a threat to their own group. He concluded that Jesus' opponents accused him of being demon-possessed as an expression of their perception of Jesus as a threat to them.

To say the least, I was not impressed by the method that led to such an obvious result. It seemed that the session was an excellent example of the tongue-in-cheek caution with which it began. This and a number of similar instances lead me to suspect that the marriage of sociology and NT studies is not a match made in heaven. There is a danger that those on the New Testament side of the arrangement are "marrying for money"; that is, they are trying to legitimate the inexact, debate-ridden field of exegesis by giving it the appearance of scientific precision. It certainly sounds better in many social and intellectual circles to say "I apply social-scientific methodology to ancient religious texts" than to say "I study the Bible." Of course, impurity of motives can be a two-way street: in conservative evangelical circles, the acceptability of those two statements would be reversed.

But leaving aside motives, another fundamental question must be asked before the conservative evangelical will venture to dip so much as a little toe in the waters of social-scientific method. It is this: If sociological analysis is given to the explanation of cause and effect in group behavior, is there room for the impact of ideas, or more importantly, the God of the Bible, on human phenomena?

In their collection of date and analysis, sociologists attempt to avoid questions of true and false, good and evil, inspired and uninspired, supernatural and natural. Sociology attempts, in its purest form, simply to understand what people do. Occasionally, this understanding allows predictions of what people are likely to do under certain circumstances. On rare occasions sociologists will venture so far as to reveal approval or disapproval of phenomena, but this comes close enough to value judgment to prove distasteful to most in the field. A biologist, after all, does not comment on the right of one microorganism to devour another. Likewise, a scientific view of human behavior should refrain from such judgements, since "right" and "wrong" are themselves determined by the forces of societal development.

The word "determine" becomes the key and provokes more questions. Does one's environment determine one's behavior? Does it make any sense to speak of human choice if even minute details of behavior are environmentally determined? Is the word "God" merely a convenient term for mysterious determining forces that work upon us to conform us to the group in which we find ourselves placed? Or is there a "Being" outside the environment who is actually effecting phenomena within it? And the inevitable question: Can one who believes in such a "Being" use sociological method, even selectively, without being affected adversely by its apparent skepticism about human choice, the sovereignty of God, and the reality of good and evil?

This is not the proper context for a detailed exploration of these questions,[1] but I pose them at the outset for two reasons.

---

1. A number of helpful treatments of the tension between sociology and theology are available. I recommend R. Perkins and B. Sayers, "Between Alienation and Anomie: The Integration of Sociology and Christianity," *Christian Scholar's Review* 17 (December 1987):

First, the conservative reader may come to this chapter already armed with these questions, and should know that I have faced them. Second, the conservative reader who has not yet posed these questions will be led inevitably to them as he or she encounters the increasingly widespread employment of social-scientific method, and he or she may be better equipped to handle the trauma if the questions are asked from the outset. The last question—Should conservatives employ this method?— is perhaps the most pertinent here. The very existence of this chapter suggests that the answer is at least a qualified "yes." In spite of the limitations of the method and the dangers it poses to orthodox belief, there are benefits unique to the social-scientific method that warrant exploration of its findings. Put more simply and positively, social-scientific method can increase our understanding of the biblical world and thus enable us to interpret the message of the Scriptures with greater accuracy and clarity.

Social Description, Sociological Clarification, and Sociological Analysis

The uninitiated reader may assume that any title containing the words "social" or "sociological" along with some reference to the New Testament will be relevant. But depending on which book or article one picks up first, the material may appear either surprisingly familiar or hopelessly intimidating. A continuum of material ranges from what scholars used to call "New Testament background" or "historical criticism"[2] to highly technical studies employing terms entirely foreign to nonsociologists (and even, I have discovered, to some sociologists!). Three points along this continuum might be isolated in order to help orient a person who comes to the material with a traditional theological training. The reader should be aware that, although the works cited here are fairly distinct, a given book or article may cover the entire continuum.

122–142; T. F. Best, "The Sociological Study of the New Testament: Promise and Peril of a New Discipline," *Scottish Journal of Theology* 36 (1983): 181–194; and D. Tidball, *The Social Context of the New Testament* (Grand Rapids: Zondervan, 1984), 11–22.

2. Consider, for example, the chapters on historical criticism in G. E. Ladd, *The New Testament and Criticism* (Grand Rapids: Eerdmans, 1967), and in J. H. Hayes and C. R. Holladay, *Biblical Exegesis: A Beginner's Handbook* (Atlanta: John Knox, 1982).

Social description, the first point along the continuum, is a fitting designation for works supplying data about the NT world. Descriptions of geography, economic life, religious practices, daily life, and the political scene fall into this category. Ten years ago *The New Testament Environment* was published.[3] More recently, a very similar book, *The New Testament in Its Social Environment*[4] has been written. This later work gives less attention to religious practices and political history and more to descriptions of daily life, but otherwise the shift is more one of terminology than substance. The data are often merely reorganized into new categories. More substantial shifts are likely to occur in the next ten to twenty years, however, as sociologists and theologians reach consensus in areas they are now exploring and as sociological terminology becomes more familiar. As these conditions are met, books dealing with social description will become less recognizable by today's standards. They will move further in the direction of interpretation of data and will employ the technical vocabulary of sociology. Almost gone are the days when NT background merely provided illustration (e.g., "Here is what a Jewish tentmaker might have looked like standing in front of a public building in Corinth"). Almost here are the days when, for many, "background" has become "foreground," i.e., the proper interpretive mechanism for understanding a text (e.g., "Here is the function of an itinerant, marginal artisan in the transformation from cult to religion").

Sociological clarification is the midpoint on the continuum from the familiar to the unfamiliar. In this category are a large number of books and articles written since the late 1970s which attempt to distill some of the more technical work of sociologists in order to encourage biblical scholars to look at the Scriptures in new ways. They use technical language, but they carefully explain the terms and show how they enlighten the text. They usually begin with a history of sociological work on the NT and a defense of its ability to "explain" rather than to "explain away" the early Christian phenomenon. Whereas social description at-

---

3. E. Lohse, *The New Testament Environment,* trans. J. E. Steely (Nashville: Abingdon, 1976).

4. J. E. Stambaugh and D. L. Balch, *The New Testament in Its Social Environment* (Philadelphia: Westminster, 1986). See also R. M. Grant, *Early Christianity and Society* (New York: Harper & Row, 1977).

tempts a translation in the reader's own language, sociological clarification attempts a glossary of the new language. There is no standard organization of the material, since the authors are choosing subject matter for clarification from among numerous possibilities. This makes it difficult to summarize these treatments; but perhaps I can whet the reader's appetite by relaying an example.

H. C. Kee discussed the increasing organization or "institutionalization" of the church through the NT period and beyond.[5] He asked whether this should be described as *secularization* (the church accommodating itself increasingly to the surrounding culture) or *sacralization* (the church expressing its commitment in a more ordered manner). Kee argued for the latter, and explained that an important part of this process is the production of a *myth*, a story or symbolic account of the important truths of the movement. This way of viewing the developments in the first-century church is helpful in several ways. It views the increasing institutionalization of the church and the production of literature as necessary and constructive for the growth of the movement. It shows the integral relation between increased organization in the church and literary activity. And while it acknowledges parallels between Christianity and other religious movements in these particulars, it does so without casting a shadow over the legitimacy of Christian truth claims.

This last point is relevant to so much of the discussion of sociology that it demands further clarification here. The point is that, if Christianity is true, we should expect a perfectly loving, empathetic God to accommodate himself to human expectations and forms. We should expect, therefore, to see numerous parallels and similarities to other religious phenomena. This is certainly true of the ministry of Jesus. He heals, exorcises, and performs miracles over nature: all amazing enough, but all within the parameters of expectation for a prophet or messiah at that time. Does the fact that he failed to demonstrate advanced scientific knowledge, to predict the discovery of the New World,

---

5. *Christian Origins in Sociological Perspective* (Philadelphia: Westminster, 1980), 40–45, 99–106. I regret that space does not allow further examples. An outstanding survey is B. Malina, *The New Testament World: Insights from Social Anthropology* (Atlanta: John Knox, 1981); see also A. Malherbe, *Social Aspects of Early Christianity* (Philadelphia: Westminster, 1983) and D. Tidball, *Social Context*.

or to fly, compromise his uniqueness or the claim that he is divine? No. In taking on human flesh, the Son took on sociological as well as physical attributes, and they formed boundaries for his ministry.[6] Similarly, the whole of the early Christian phenomenon very naturally took on many of the attributes of other religious movements. This neither compromises its uniqueness nor diminishes the role of God's Spirit in guiding believers. If the faith is true and God's Spirit is in control, the uniqueness is to be sought in the power evident in transformed lives and not in the particular forms of expression that those lives embody. Such forms will vary as the Spirit works in different social contexts. God was incarnate in completely human form, Jesus, and now he works through his completely human body, the church.

At the far end of the continuum in terms of familiarity to the uninitiated reader is *sociological analysis*. In this category are articles (and, increasingly, whole books) that take as a starting point a sociological perspective and the methods and vocabulary of the social sciences. The approach is confusing at several levels. For one thing, there are at least four perspectives from which to begin a sociological analysis,[7] and an author rarely reveals, much less explains, which one he is employing. Like a biblical exegete who assumes that his readers will recognize that he is employing a form-critical approach rather than a source-critical approach, so a sociologist will assume that his readers will recognize him as a structural functionalist rather than a symbolic interactionist. That is the generous view: at times it appears that the experienced exegete who is a novice sociologist simply adopts a particular perspective without knowing that it is subject to dispute. Further confusion is caused by reliance on third- or fourth-hand authority. Consider, for example, the exegete-sociologist who documents his application of theory to the NT text by making reference to a sociological study of cult development in colonial Melanesia. Such a study in turn relies upon the perspective and methodology of a theoretical sociologist which in itself may be subject to dis-

---

6. For a lucid attempt to show Jesus operating within the "constraints" of history, see A. E. Harvey, *Jesus and the Constraints of History* (Philadelphia: Westminster, 1982), esp. 1–10.

7. Malina (*Insights*, 18–24) offers an introduction to these different approaches. A more detailed and very helpful explanation is offered by J. H. Elliot in "Social-Scientific Criticism of the New Testament and its Social World: More on Methods and Models," *Semeia* 35 (1986): 1–26.

pute.[8] Every connection is subject to debate. And to complicate matters further, a few works by NT sociologists are reaching "standard" status, and are now being quoted as authoritative in their own right. These are the attendant frustrations of a pioneering discipline. The field is so new and moving so quickly that college sociology majors have little advantage over theologians. For now, the prudent approach is to familiarize oneself with the literature, watch for an emerging consensus in areas of debate, and keep a critical eye open for helpful insights.

The Model in Sociological Theory

Having surveyed the kinds of material being produced by those attempting to integrate sociology and theology, it will be useful to take a closer look at sociological method applied to specific questions. The common method of the sociologist is to construct a model to clarify the data by showing similarities among properties.[9] The hope is that less familiar material will make more sense when its similarity to more familiar material is shown. How is this done? Let us suppose that you want to do a study of fish fossils. You might begin by drawing a "model" fish: long body, bony mouth, lidless eyes, gills, dorsal fin, ventral fin, tail fin. Now, whenever you discover evidence of a fish, you would compare it to your model. If you find only part of a fish, you may be able to reconstruct it based on your modern model. If you are not sure about the remains, you may either adjust the model or discard the remains as "non-fish." The trick, of course, is to construct a model sufficiently detailed and specific to provide plenty of meaningful material for comparison but general enough to allow for differences from modern fish. Too much detail, and there is a

---

8. The important studies of millenarian cults often used for comparative purposes are K. Burridge, *New Heaven, New Earth* (Oxford: Oxford University Press, 1969); N. Cohn, *The Pursuit of the Millenium* (New York: Harper & Row, 1961); Y. Talmon, "Pursuit of the Millenium: The Relation Between Religious and Social Change," *Archives Européennes de Sociologie* 3 (1962): 125–148; and P. Worsley, *The Trumpet Shall Sound*, 2d ed. (New York: Schocken, 1968). Foundational works include P. L. Berger, *The Sacred Canopy: Elements of a Sociological Theory of Religion* (Garden City, N.Y.: Doubleday, 1967); P. L. Berger and T. Luckmann, *The Social Construction of Reality: A Treatise in the Sociology of Knowledge* (Garden City, N.Y.: Doubleday, 1966); and M. Weber, *Sociology of Religion* (Boston: Beacon, 1963).

9. J. H. Elliot ("Methods and Models," 3–9) offers further clarification concerning the definition and use of models.

risk either that the fish fossil won't fit the model or that the researcher will try to force it to fit: "My model fish has vertical
stripes; therefore, all ancient fish had vertical stripes." Too little
detail, and the researcher risks insignificant observations: "Evi-
dently, both the modern fish and the ancient fish spent a great
deal of time in a watery environment." The balance between
complexity and generality is difficult to achieve; but the ichthyolo-
gist, at least, has the advantage of visual observation.

The sociologist must substitute words for observable data,
and, as any writer knows, the price of accuracy may be too high.
Elliot diagrams a model for the portrayal of ancient Palestinian
society which contains no less than eleven (subdivided!) foci of
control connected by no less than thirty-three arrows (of varying
size) indicating inter-foci influence.[10] The other extreme is illustrated by the statement of P. Worsley that millenarian movements (like early Christianity) begin where there is "a situation
of dissatisfaction with existing social relations and of yearnings
for a happier life."[11] We are forced to ask when such conditions
are *not* present, and such a model appears to be hopelessly
general. With these cautions in mind, let us take a closer look at
the contribution of sociological analysis in two related areas: the
socioeconomic circumstances of early believers and the propagation of the movement toward the end of the first century.

The Social Level of the First Christians

A significant contribution of sociological study has been to
warn readers of ancient texts against reading with a modern
bias. It is common, for example, for us to think of poverty and
wealth in terms of "class" distinctions (i.e., lower, middle, upper) and to define "class" in terms of levels of income (e.g., less
than 50% of median income per annum equals poverty). But in
the New Testament world, classes as we know them were not
recognizable, and social levels were not measurable in terms of
income. When people at that time thought of a poor person,
they thought of one who had lost his/her livelihood (e.g., a

---

10. Ibid., 14.
11. P. Worsley, *Trumpet*, 243.

widow or cripple), not of one who had a low income (e.g., a day laborer or peasant).[12] The discussion of socioeconomic circumstances, then, revolves around terms like "rank," "status," and "level."

Actually two fairly distinct discussions are taking place in the scholarly community: one regarding the Palestinian community and the other regarding the Pauline community. In the former case, discussion revolves around the social level of the audiences of Jesus, his first followers, and the Jerusalem church. The Gospels provide the primary evidence, although debate continues about how to use the teachings of Jesus to supplement the sketchy biographical material in these books. In the latter case, discussion has centered on the Corinthian church, and a combination of biblical and extrabiblical literary material along with archaeological data have made up the primary evidence.

K. Kautsky, a Marxist writing in 1908, had a far-reaching impact when he described the first generation of believers as part of an ignorant and oppressed proletariat.[13] F. C. Grant confirmed this picture in some detail in his standard work.[14] In their characterizations of the time period surrounding the ministry of Jesus, they claimed conditions of overwhelming taxation, overpopulation, natural disasters, armed conflict, and the rapidly increasing polarization of classes. This social description, based on the most tenuous evidence,[15] has produced a popular picture of Palestine in which Jesus lead a lean and tattered group of followers through a parched land seething with unrest.

---

12. Malina, *Insights,* 84–85.

13. K. Kautsky, *The Foundations of Christianity,* trans. H. F. Mins (New York: Russell & Russell, 1953).

14. *The Economic Background of the Gospels* (Oxford: Oxford University Press, 1926).

15. For example, Grant (*Economic Background,* 105) makes the preposterous claim that Jews were paying close to half of their income in taxes. Most of this percentage is based on the Jewish tithe and offering system, which was voluntary and ignored by the majority of the population; the rest is based on Roman taxes, which applied primarily to landowners and merchants. Amazingly, Grant's estimate still finds its way into the secondary literature, and at times Grant is the sole source at key points in the construction of an argument. See, for example, J. G. Gager, *Kingdom and Community: The Social World of Early Christianity* (Englewood Cliffs, N.J.: Prentice Hall, 1975), 24 n. 19; D. Mealand, *Poverty and Expectation in the Gospels* (London: SPCK, 1980), 8 n. 28; P. Davids, *The Epistle of James* (Grand Rapids: Eerdmans, 1982), 32 n. 105; P. U. Maynard-Reid, *Poverty and Wealth in James* (Maryknoll, N.Y.: Orbis, 1987), 15 n. 7; D. E. Oakman, *Jesus and the Economic Questions of His Day* (Lewiston, N.Y.: Edwin Mellen, 1986), 71 n. 125. The refutation of this estimate and the other elements of this view of the Palestinian economic picture is contained in the first chapter of my *Hostility to Wealth in the Synoptic Gospels* (Sheffield: JSOT, 1987).

More recently, sociologists have appropriated the work of form critics to apply Jesus's teachings to the same picture. According to a highly influential work of G. Theissen, the early believers projected their frustrations back into the words of the founder of the movement:

> To work off their aggression, in vivid imaginary pictures they depicted the fearful end of the rich and the good fortune of the poor in the world to come (Luke 16.19–31). This is the way that the deprived have always consoled themselves.[16]

Similarly, J. G. Gager asserted that

> . . . the economic pronouncements in early Christian literature reveal . . . the economic status of believers. . . . They reflect the fact that early believers came primarily from disadvantaged groups."[17]

The description of incipient Christianity advanced by Marxists and social gospel theorists in the early part of the century has more recently been supplemented by the work of form and redaction critics[18] and then set under the interpretive grid of a sociological model to fill in gaps in the evidence. The model that has been used most widely is that of the "millenarian movement." This model, developed by studies of cult activity in primitive cultures,[19] contains the following basic features: (1) a primitive, agrarian group is confronted suddenly by a dominant colonial power; (2) a prophet (or "charismatic leader") appears to give voice to the hopes of the oppressed for a reversal of the social order during an imminent, earthly period of bliss (the millenium) for the elect; and (3) a cult forms around this charismatic leader.

At first glance, the beginnings of Christianity look very much like this model, and together with the higher critical material

---

16. G. Theissen, *Sociology of Early Palestinian Christianity*, trans. J. Bowden (Philadelphia: Fortress, 1978), 13.

17. Gager, *Kingdom*, 24.

18. The most important example of the use of form and redaction criticism in support of this view is Mealand's *Poverty and Expectation in the Gospels* (n. 15 above). In *Hostility to Wealth in the Synoptic Gospels* (n. 15 above), I attempt to argue (against Mealand et. al.) at least for consistency and integrity, if not authenticity, of the Gospel pronouncements on wealth.

19. See note 8 above.

and the popular social description, it is not surprising that the coherence between this model and the Gospels has only recently been challenged. But on closer inspection, serious doubts begin to arise about the fit between the facts and the model. First-century Palestine was not a primitive economy. The Romans and other imperial nations had been a fact of life as dominant colonial powers for hundreds of years. Strong evidence suggests that the area was politically and economically stable during the decades surrounding Jesus's ministry. Also, it is an oversimplification to contend that Jesus called for a reversal of the social order.

But some of the strongest evidence calling for a reevaluation of the model stems from work done on the Pauline community, where a new consensus emerging in the mid-1980s argued that "a Pauline congregation generally reflected a fair cross-section of urban society."[20] The usual proof-text suggesting economically poor believers ("not many of you were . . . powerful, not many were of noble birth," 1 Cor. 1:26) was questioned increasingly by sociologists and others who saw contrary evidence in the literary level of New Testament writings,[21] the issues discussed in the texts,[22] and the positions and names of individuals.[23] True, not many were powerful or of noble birth, but those "not many" were apparently very important. Furthermore, a person could fit that description, which would amount to low rank, but still possess high status (e.g., as a synagogue ruler, 1 Cor. 1:14; see Acts 18:8). And a wealthy freedman or merchant would possess neither rank nor status, but he might aspire to it (and receive Paul's censure for his pretensions; 1 Cor. 4:10).

This new view of Paul's community as reflecting a broad social base should influence the model used to clarify the level of the Palestinian community. The literary level and social level of its leadership is similar, the strong interest in the use of wealth presupposes an audience wealthy enough to be concerned, and

---

20. W. Meeks, *The First Urban Christians* (New Haven: Yale, 1983), 73; cf. Malherbe, *Social Aspects*, 118–121; G. Theissen, *The Social Setting of Pauline Christianity*, trans. J. H. Schütz (Philadelphia: Westminster, 1982), 70–73.

21. Malherbe, *Aspects*, 30–45.

22. Meeks, *Urban*, 63–72.

23. E. A. Judge, *The Social Pattern of Christian Groups in the First Century* (London: Tyndale, 1960), and *Rank and Status in the World of the Caesars and St. Paul* (Christchurch, New Zealand: n.p. 1982); cf. Meeks, *Urban*, 55–63.

the variety of social levels of those with whom Jesus has contact may indicate greater diversity than the older view portrayed.[24]

The Advance of Christianity in the First Century

Another important sociological model which builds on the discussion of social levels considers the roles of *relative deprivation* and *cognitive dissonance* in the origin and propagation of the Christian message. Use of the former term represents a modification of the earlier view that early believers were attracted to the movement because they were deprived. Relative deprivation means that they *felt* deprived; that is, their encounter with the powerful colonial force caused them to perceive new expectations without the means to satisfy them.[25] Even a well-to-do Palestinian Jew would lack Roman rank and might lack status (e.g., a tax collector), and his relative deprivation would make him ripe for millenarian activity. This adjustment of the model appears to account for the broader-based constituency of the ministry of Jesus evident in the Gospels, and I will consider it further below. For now it is useful to bring us back to the model of millenarian cult formation outlined earlier, namely, "deprived" people gather around the charismatic leader who promises the millenium.

A problem arises with the millenarian model at this point, because another distinctive of the movements is that they are short-lived. This is due to the obvious fact that the millenium fails to arrive and eventually even the prophet dies. The cult suffers, or, in psychological terms, its members experience *cognitive dissonance:* the trauma of unmet expectations. But why in the

---

24. See E. A. Judge, "The Early Christians as a Scholastic Community," *Journal of Religious History* 1 (1960): 4–15, 125–37, for the interesting thesis that Jesus and his followers were more of a scholastic community in the rabbinic tradition than a millenarian movement (cf. Tidball, *Social Context*, 37–40). It is possible that the community (esp. "the poor among the saints in Jerusalem" mentioned in Romans 15:26) was actually a group within the group existing for the purpose of study and prayer. This provocative possibility and its relation to Essene and pagan practices is developed by B. J. Capper, "PANTA KOINA: A Study of Earliest Christian Community of Goods in its Hellenistic and Jewish Contexts" (Ph.D. diss., Cambridge University, 1985).

25. Gager (*Kingdom,* 25–28) applies relative deprivation theory to incipient Christianity.

case of Christianity does the group survive and in fact begin energetic missionary activity just at the point of disappointed hopes regarding the imminent millenium? The theory explained by Gager is that cognitive dissonance creates pressure on the group to resolve the tension without abandoning belief.[26] Making converts quickly reinforces the individual's sense of personal and group legitimacy. The more people that can be persuaded to believe, the more likely that the belief is valid.

The weaknesses of relative deprivation and cognitive dissonance theory as applied to incipient Christianity may be due, ironically, to ethnocentrism on the part of the theorists. D. F. Aberle explained that relative deprivation must involve *legitimate* expectation on the part of the "deprived" group.[27] It is difficult to establish legitimacy of expectation, especially across cultures and centuries, and the imposition of modern American standards of status expectation on first-century Jews violates a cardinal rule of sociology. Of course the Jews of Jesus's day wanted to improve their lot, cast off Roman dominance, and receive God's promises, but how can we measure the distance for them between desires, predictions, and standards? Malina has challenged the applicability to Christian origins of cognitive dissonance theory by arguing that Gager is imposing upon the ancient phenomenon modern standards of what makes for dissonance.[28] For us, external verifying evidence causes us to shift belief systems. We apply inductive scientific method and adjust under the pressure of new data. For the ancients, a simple logical consistency of the fundamental tenets of the belief system was all that was required. External evidence was potentially deceptive and therefore irrelevant. Contradictions were only apparent and so did not require adjustment or abandonment of the belief system. More specifically, the kingdom was coming "soon," and that was good enough. The fact

26. Ibid., 37–49.
27. D. F. Aberle, "A Note on Relative Deprivation Theory As Applied to Millenarian and Other Cult Movements," in *Millenial Dreams in Action: Studies in Revolutionary Religious Movements*, ed. S. L. Thrupp (New York: Schocken 1970), 209–214. Gager (*Kingdom*, 59 n. 33) cites Aberle but does not discuss legitimacy of expectation.
28. B. Malina, "Normative Dissonance and Christian Origins," *Semeia* 35 (1986): 35–55. D. Tidball (*Social Context*, 61–64) also offers a critique of the cognitive dissonance explanation on the grounds that Christianity was a missionary religion before Jesus's death and that believers understood the delay of Jesus's return before it became a firm expectation. In my opinion, these arguments rely too heavily on internal evidence to carry much weight in the current debate among sociologists.

that Christians were willing to live with diversity and paradox—
even, if you will, with a measure of confusion—explains why
they succeeded where other more rigid, isolated groups failed.

Integrating Sociology and Theology

By means of this survey of recent contributions I have attempted to give the reader a sense of the possibilities and attendant frustrations of this major new movement in the study of the
New Testament. Some readers may find the survey too critical,
others too sympathetic. In any case, there can be no doubt that,
for the traditionally trained exegete, sociological method appears to be a strange bedfellow. Yet several basic principles of
integration outlined below will suggest the potential usefulness
and legitimacy of sociological method for NT studies.

1. *Sociological method will increase the accuracy with which exegetes view the biblical world.* The sociologist working with the
New Testament is interested primarily in what the text meant to
its original audience. He is on guard against reading his modern word definitions or his cultural bias into the text. Even
where he is mistaken in his application of models, his commitment to the biblical point of view will give new impetus to
cautious and thorough portrayals of the ancient world. Malina,
for example, offers fresh perspectives on the concepts of honor,
personality, possessions, and purity in the New Testament
world.[29] D. L. Balch has contributed a dramatic new perspective
on the address to women in 1 Peter 3:1–6, contending that the
instruction is meant to protect converts from criticism commonly levelled against female members of new religious movements.[30] Theissen has advanced the intriguing thesis that opposition to Paul was due to his failure to follow the pattern of a
charismatic leader.[31] In some cases, ideas and insights such as
these may have been reached without the benefit of sociological
method, but there can be no doubt that the method has offered

---

29. *Insights.*
30. D. L. Balch, *Let Wives Be Submissive: The Domestic Code in 1 Peter* (Chico, Calif.: Scholars, 1981).
31. G. Theissen, *Setting,* 48–54.

a fresh approach toward a more thorough understanding of the New Testament.

2. *Sociological method does not involve evaluation of the truth, historicity, or veracity of the text.* This is difficult for some to acknowledge. Early twentieth-century liberalism provided a major impetus for the application of sociology to theology, and even now Marxists and others with left-wing political perspectives find the approach useful to further their agendas. Modern university professors sometimes use sociological terminology to debunk Christian truth claims. But all of these are examples of bad sociology, not proof that sociology is bad. The objective sociologist describes, as accurately as possible, how groups behave. To the extent that he does his job well, he avoids an assessment of how they *ought* to behave and whether their beliefs are *true*. A Christian sociologist who studies modern cults obviously must distinguish between the beliefs he holds and the beliefs he describes in his research, but so must an atheist who studies Christianity. Both attempt to do accurate work.

3. *Sociological method does not require the conclusion that human behavior is determined solely by social factors.* What the sociologist describes as "social determinants" are not necessarily the ultimate determinants. The problem of sorting out ultimate determinants is analogous to the tension between free will and predestination. Descriptions of group activity may be a way of speaking, on the human plane, about how God works his will in the world. Furthermore, the conclusion that a particular group is likely to act in a certain way does not mean that all individuals within the group will act that way. With that understanding, sociology remains descriptive with regard to individual action: we can say "this happened," even "this happened, as it usually does," but never "this had to happen."[32]

4. *Sociology does not preclude the uniqueness of Christianity.* Any comparative study of religion will bring about a crisis of faith as a believer encounters for the first time beliefs and practices, even apologetic methods, that look very much like his own. Since the

---

32. See C. S. Evans, "Must Sociology Presuppose Determinism?" in *The Sociological Perspective: A Value-Committed Introduction,* ed. M. R. Leming, R. G. DeVries, and B. F. J. Furnish (Grand Rapids: Zondervan, 1989), 45–59.

sociologist makes a living out of the portrayal of parallel or comparable phenomena, his discipline is naturally suspect. Perhaps the scarcity of competent Christian sociologists is caused not by the discipline destroying the faith of those who approach it, but by the fearful faithful avoiding the discipline.

As I explained in an earlier paragraph, uniqueness is to be sought in the power that transforms lives, not in the forms of expression peculiar to Christian tradition. Certainly Christianity has unique features, most notably the incarnation, which offer substance to the claim that the Christian faith is profound and worthy of serious consideration as preferable to other belief systems. But the crisis of particularism is caused not by comparisons of myths (or doctrines) but by comparisons of the human practices that grow out of them. Indeed, this is more properly, or at least more commonly, the domain of sociology. Still, the believer must ask, If God's Spirit is guiding the church, shouldn't Christian practice be different, and not be lumped together with the morass of human religious activity? Again, I stress two factors: first, that the Spirit of a perfect God, a God of incarnation, will accommodate himself to human forms; and second, that each *individual* will or will not yield himself to the Spirit's control. And at that point, behaviors and comparisons of groups are not at issue. Obedience is at issue, and obedience is unique enough.

The Use of Sociology in Exegesis

Having come to grips with the challenges of integration between disciplines, the student is faced with the question of application. How does one "do" sociological analysis without the benefit of extensive training? Mastery of more traditional approaches to exegesis requires a great deal of expertise and practice, as the rest of this volume attests. Yet here is a distinct approach with its own vocabulary and in-house squabbles among scholars over appropriate mechanisms for analysis. It may be more fair, then, to speak of promise and peril than to pronounce judgment. In any case, several practical steps can and should be taken by students of Scripture in order to profit from this increasingly influential approach.

1. *Become familiar with the terminology and significant contributions of the field.* This essay is merely introductory. I have designed the notes to serve as a select bibliography, and I recommend that the reader learn the vocabulary and insights of sociological method directly from these major recent contributors. More specifically, I recommend (in order of preference) the books by Malina, Malherbe, Kee, and Tidball as introductions to the method; the book by Gager (and the critiques by Malina and Schmidt) as an influential example of sociological analysis; and the books by Meeks and Theissen as specific contributions on the Pauline community. The books by Berger and Burridge, and the article by Elliot, are important for methodological background. Remember that it is well worth the time to build an understanding of the underlying theory if one is to keep a critical eye on the ever-increasing derivative material, which is often written by authors who are trained in theology but formally uneducated in sociology. Unfortunately, not one book is available to explain all facets of this enterprise, but it may be too early to produce one with any claim to comprehensiveness. On the other hand, there should be no substitute for discerning appreciation of the contributions of these many authors through direct encounter with their works.

2. *Become familiar with intertestamental and classical literature.* This recommendation pertains to the best and worst of sociological method. The greatest contribution that this literature can make is to give us new insights into the world of the NT, and these terribly neglected sources offer a wealth of material for comparative studies. They encourage us to see that world more fully. The greatest danger of sociological method is that an inaccurate or anachronistic model, imposed on the ancient data, can actually distort rather than clarify the text. This is especially dangerous when the sociologist concentrates on a particular situation as a response to an *immediate* cause. Familiarity with the ideological background and foreground of NT material is a useful guard against this danger.

3. *Ask "sociological" questions as a normal part of the analysis of a text.* Gradually, a sensitivity will build toward the difference between our world and the biblical world, and the student will

begin to construct a more accurate picture of both. These relatively simple questions include:

> How would a person at that time hear this word, phrase, or
> proposition?
>
> What does the author take for granted that his audience will
> understand?
>
> What will be the affect on the world of the original audience if
> it responds to the author?

Such questions, persistently and carefully asked, will serve as
checks to the tendency to read modern word meanings and
cultural bias into the text. An honest look at any passage in the
NT with these questions in mind, whether in preparation for a
scholarly article or a Sunday school class, will lead to new insight and to new humility.

My friend and former colleague, R. G. DeVries, of St. Olaf College, provided valuable
criticisms of the first draft of this chapter which helped me to avoid cross-disciplinary
gaffers.

6

New Testament Theological Analysis
L. D. Hurst

Dogmatism: A Refuge for the Lazy Mind

Samuel Johnson, the great eighteenth-century lexicographer, was once asked to define the word "patriotism." "Patriotism," he replied, "is the last refuge of the scoundrel." While I do not know if he was correct on the subject of scoundrels and patriots, I have no doubt that his famous dictum could be borrowed and applied, in a modified form, to those who aspire to the task of NT theology. "Dogmatism is the first refuge of the lazy mind" is a statement which might well stand at the head of every course of lectures on the subject.

Lest I be misunderstood, however, I should hasten to point out that by "dogmatism" I do not mean "dogmatics." Dogmatics is the valuable discipline in which Christians attempt to make sense of the historic Christian faith in the context of the modern world. By dogmatism I mean what Webster's *New World Dictionary*[1] means by it: "dogmatic assertion of opinion, usually without reference to evidence."

In this essay I will maintain that NT theology is a discipline

---

1. *Webster's New World Dictionary of the American Language* (New York: World, 1962), 431.

wholly concerned with evidence. However, it is not always practiced that way. "Liberal" NT theologians often come to the text
with a belief that it could be nothing more than a disconnected
series of culturally-bound statements that have no more divine
revelatory value than the *New York Times*. "Conservatives," on
the other hand, often come to the Bible convinced that they
know already what it is going to say. Do they not know its
author personally? Has he not spoken to them in their life? And
is not the Bible also his word to them? Thus for many the Bible
becomes a single book, written by one author—God. And although the backgrounds, personalities, and special interests of
its human authors are often acknowledged with enthusiasm, the
divine element tends to predominate, to the point that the human authors recede into the background. These are extremes,
and there are many grades of variation between them.

Every NT theologian certainly has the option to come to the
material affirming it to be any kind of literature he or she likes—
whether a random collection of human opinions or the very Word
of God. But does this give him or her the right as well to come to
the text having predetermined what it must or must not mean on
any given subject? Absolutely not! NT theology is, first and last, a
historical and scientific discipline.[2] Its function is descriptive
rather than prescriptive, and hence it must be kept totally distinct
from both systematic theology and apologetics. It does not claim
to make Christianity either logical or credible.[3] Of course, the NT
theologian's labor may turn out to be useful to dogmaticians or
apologists. It will be their raw material. But ultimately the task
involves objective observation rather than prescription. Conservative scholars will probably never wish to draw a complete line
between description and prescription, since once the original
meaning of a biblical author is ascertained, it often becomes for
them authoritative and transcultural.[4] But ultimately how the

---

2. This raises the enormous question of the nature of NT theology itself, particularly
with regard to the role of history in the discipline. See R. Morgan, *The Nature of New
Testament Theology* (London: SCM, 1973); H. Boers, *What Is New Testament Theology?* (Philadelphia: Fortress, 1979); K. Stendahl, "Biblical Theology, Contemporary," in *The Interpreter's
Dictionary of the Bible*, ed. G. A. Buttrick (Nashville: Abingdon, 1962), 1:418–32.

3. See G. B. Caird, *New Testament Theology*, completed and ed. L. D. Hurst (Oxford:
Clarendon Press, forthcoming), chap. 1.

4. See J. D. G. Dunn, "The Task of New Testament Theology," in *New Testament Theology
in Dialogue: Christology and Ministry*, ed. J. D. G. Dunn and J. P. Mackey (Philadelphia:
Westminster, 1987), 3.

meaning of the text is to be applied today is a topic which belongs more to the realm of systematic theology than biblical theology.

Troubled Waters: Problems of a New Testament Theologian

NT theology is both a many splendored and a many troubled thing. Its splendors are obvious. It seeks to understand the earliest documents of the world's largest religion. But its troubles are also numerous. In fact, at the outset the interpreter faces a hydra-headed set of problems. There is no way all of these can be treated in a single essay, but some of the more significant of them may be delineated here.

1. The Culture Gap.

The cultures of the first and twentieth centuries are widely different, and often the cultural context of a given biblical author or document may be lost to us. As historians, we may attempt to recreate the ancient culture with all of the investigative tools at our disposal. But in the end we must admit that it may not always be possible to know completely what it was like to be an inhabitant of the first-century world. When Paul said that a prophesying woman ought to have a veil on her head "because of the angels" (1 Cor. 11:10), or when Jesus appeared to commend an unprofitable steward for his shrewdness (Luke 16:8), it is very difficult to know precisely what they were talking about. But is it impossible? Dennis Nineham said it is; for Nineham the gap is so wide that one cannot re-create the ancient situation today, and thus objective analysis of the NT is also impossible. The interpreter will always read his or her concerns into the text. Thus Nineham took delight in quoting the well-known epigram of Louis MacNeice:

> These dead are dead
> .   .   .   .
> and how one can imagine oneself among them I do not know;

It was all so unimaginably different
And all so long ago.[5]

The Oxford scholar G. B. Caird[6] argued differently. For him it was possible to re-create the past. In fact, Caird argued that NT theology is involved precisely with what Nineham claimed to be impossible: bringing dead people back to life. In this case the task of the NT theologian is similar to the mythical experience of Odysseus, who, in order to gain a forecast of his own destiny, had to descend to the underworld to interview the dead prophet Teiresias (Homer, *Odyssey* ix). But all that remained was a shade—a pale outline of his former self. Thus Odysseus's guide instructed him to kill a sheep and pour its blood into the shadowy outline of the dead man in order to reanimate him. The NT theologian, Caird continued, must do something similar, only in this case it must be his or her *own* blood—the blood of hard work, sympathy, and imagination. The problem with this analogy, of course, is that any theologian who attempts such a transfusion must be of the same "blood type" as the dead person, that is, he or she must understand that person's categories. And in the case of those aspiring to write an entire work comprising all of the NT writers, in which about ten authors must be "brought to life," the interpreter needs to be a universal donor! From this parallel it is clear that for Caird the modern interpreter must seek to understand what the ancient author said to his own day if his words are going to be relevant to us today.[7]

Conservative scholars at this point may leap into the discussion, insisting that the writers are already alive. Like Enoch, they died, but are "still speaking" (Heb. 11:4). The words of the NT writers are the Word of God, and that Word is always living and active (Heb. 4:12). And such a position is, of course, intellec-

5. D. E. Nineham, *The Use and Abuse of the Bible* (London: Macmillan, 1976), 24.
6. Caird, *New Testament Theology.*
7. For conservative views on the hermeneutical question of the original intentionality of the text and the authority of later meanings it is given, see, e.g., E. Johnson, "Author's Intention and Biblical Interpretation," 402–9, and the responses of E. D. Radmacher and W. C. Kaiser, Jr., 433–47, in *Hermeneutics, Inerrancy, and the Bible,* ed. E. D. Radmacher and R. D. Preus (Grand Rapids: Zondervan, 1984). For a nonconservative view, see W. J. Houston, " 'Today in Your Hearing': Some Comments on the Christological Use of the Old Testament," in *The Glory of Christ in the New Testament: Studies in Christology in Memory of George Bradford Caird,* ed. L. D. Hurst and N. T. Wright (Oxford: Clarendon Press, 1987), 37–47.

tually acceptable. But the writers were also human beings. As far as we know, Enoch himself did not write anything; thus the author of Hebrews is engaging in metaphor. Those who did put pen to paper had special interests, loves, hates, anxieties, biases, pressures, personal problems, and areas of uncertainty which were not apparently eliminated by an overruling divine control. To deny this is to "docetize" the Bible, to turn its writers into mere ciphers, not human beings. Thus the sensitive NT theologian will be aware of the culture gap, the problems it poses, and the dangers of assuming too easy a transcription of the ancient world to the modern.

2. The Hermeneutical Circle.

This idea, usually associated with Rudolf Bultmann,[8] is a corollary of the above problem. Simply put, it maintains that while the interpreter is working on the text, the text is working on the interpreter. Hence one can never completely get away from one's own presuppositions, and purely objective exegesis is impossible. Conservatives generally reject this view.[9] In fairness to both sides of the continuing debate, we may concede that Bultmann was correct to draw attention to our tendency to bring our own biases to the text, but also that Caird was right to remind us that through hard work—that is, by studying the original languages, cultures, and mind-sets of the NT writers, combined with a share of sympathy and simple common sense—we may recreate their situation with a relatively high degree of accuracy.

3. Incomplete Evidence.

In many ways the NT is like an enormous jigsaw puzzle, with a number of missing pieces. The apostle Jude had intended to send his readers an epistle about "our common salvation" (Jude 3), but

---

8. See Bultmann's famous essay, "Is Exegesis Without Presuppositions Possible?" in *Existence and Faith* (London: Collins Fontana, 1964), 342–51. A recent excellent treatment of the whole question is that of G. N. Stanton, "Presuppositions in New Testament Criticism," in *New Testament Interpretation: Essays on Principles and Methods,* ed. I. H. Marshall (Grand Rapids: Eerdmans, 1977), 60–71.

9. Cf., e.g., the NT theologies of Donald Guthrie and Rudolf Bultmann. To read these two books together is to wonder if they are talking about the same subject.

never did. Paul wrote one or more letters to the church at Corinth which have been lost, as was a letter from the church at Laodicea. Luke mentioned other Gospels which had been written before him (Luke 1:1–4). Have they survived? John told us that there were many other things that Jesus did which were never recorded (John 21:25). A collection of the sayings of Jesus, usually known by the designation Q, may have circulated independently of the Gospels, and is now lost. Certain facts surrounding the Epistle to the Hebrews (e.g., its authorship, recipients, date and circumstances) have utterly eluded historical inquiry.

We have no idea, furthermore, who founded the churches at Rome or Alexandria, nor do we know much about the great "bridge" church at Syrian Antioch or of those churches of the Lycus Valley (see Rev. 1–3). The Book of Acts leaves out some important aspects of Paul's life, such as his letters, which in turn raises the question of what else Luke may have left out of his account.[10] Reading some of the letters of Paul (e.g., Galatians, 1 and 2 Corinthians) is sometimes like listening to only one end of a telephone conversation. And, had the church at Corinth not been abusing the Lord's Supper (1 Cor. 11:17–34), we would never have known that the Last Supper was intended by Jesus to be the Lord's Supper, perpetuated in the practice of Christians other than the Twelve.

Thus the NT writings have an occasional quality which cannot be avoided.[11] Why some things were preserved, and others were not, is an unanswered question with which the NT theologian must soon learn to live, however unhappy he or she may feel. The real question, however, is this: Do we have enough pieces of the puzzle to assemble it? Do we have a picture on the puzzle box to help us know where to insert the pieces? Those who see the puzzle as hopelessly fragmented and incomplete will tend to downplay any idea of the unity of the Bible as a divine revelation for all ages. For them it is "simply a sequence of occasional statements."[12] Others will see in the NT a coherent

---

10. On the problem of Luke's apparent omissions, see D. Guthrie, *New Testament Introduction*, 3d ed. (Downers Grove, Ill.: Inter-Varsity, 1970), 354–63.

11. This is rarely questioned for most NT books. For an attempt to show the occasional nature of even Romans and Galatians, see J. C. Beker, *Paul the Apostle: The Triumph of God in Life and Thought* (Philadelphia: Fortress, 1980), 23–131.

12. The phrase is Dunn's from his "The Task of New Testament Theology," 9.

and recognizable picture which God himself has taken a hand in preserving. In such a scenario enough pieces of the puzzle remain to enable us to reconstruct, if not the whole picture, enough of the picture to see what—or who—is being portrayed.

4. Unity and Diversity.

This in some ways derives from the problem of incomplete evidence. Is the theology of the NT writers essentially the same? Or is there an impossibly wide diversity of opinion within the NT, even on central issues such as Christology, soteriology and eschatology? Again, some scholars would deny that there even is such a thing as NT theology—only NT *theologies*. Those who approach this question from a more conservative angle, on the other hand, will tend to see an essential unity among the NT writers, and sometimes this even extends to minute points of detail. Here writers such as J. D. G. Dunn[13] and B. D. Chilton[14] have done a considerable service by showing how a writer may maintain both elements—unity and diversity. Dunn sees diversity *within* the unity, and vice versa. He has not escaped criticism, however, mostly from those on the more conservative end of the spectrum;[15] for some to talk of unity and diversity is theological "double-talk," with diversity meaning contradiction. The NT, it is said, cannot contradict itself.[16] But this can degenerate into an extremely narrow understanding of diversity, and it underscores how subjective the modern discipline of NT theology can be, even among writers who by other canons might be considered conservative. There is an element of imagination—dare one say "art"?—which must be brought to the task. How the stress between the two elements—the unity and the diversity—is to be distributed will ultimately depend upon the good sense, not to mention the total theological vision, of the interpreter. What one person sees as a contradiction might appear to another as a variant facet of the

---

13. J. D. G. Dunn, *Unity and Diversity in the New Testament: An Inquiry into the Character of Earliest Christianity* (Philadelphia: Westminster, 1977).

14. B. D. Chilton, *Beginning New Testament Study* (Grand Rapids: Eerdmans, 1987), 172–92.

15. See, e.g., D. A. Carson, "Unity and Diversity in the New Testament: The Possibility of Systematic Theology," in *Scripture and Truth*, ed. D. A. Carson and J. D. Woodbridge (Grand Rapids: Zondervan, 1983), 65–95.

16. For a number of discussions of this view, see the numerous articles found in *Hermeneutics, Inerrancy, and the Bible*.

same theological truth. In any case, we will probably not be far from wrong to see the NT as something like an elaborate score of music, replete with melodies and countermelodies, which were never meant to be played in unison.[17]

5. The Question of Development.

Did the theology of the NT "develop"? This will be a question which is largely decided by one's own background and presuppositions. Those who tend to downplay any elements of unity and divine revelation in the NT will see much progression of thought from the earliest period of the early church to the time of the Gospel of John. Those who view the NT writings as divinely inspired will tend to downplay the idea that its writers, or Jesus himself,[18] could have developed in their thinking, since development means change, and God does not change. "Jesus Christ is the same yesterday and today and forever" (Heb. 13:8). NT theology is therefore essentially the same from the earliest writers to the latest.

Here the Christian needs to consider carefully how he or she understands the way in which God reveals himself in history. And, in terms of revelation, there is no reason to fear the idea of growth or development. Even the most conservative scholar will admit that there is a phenomenon known as "progressive revelation" in the OT. Why he or she ultimately could not commit to the belief, in theory at least, that the same kind of thing happened in the NT is not immediately clear to the neutral observer. To be sure, one is dealing with a much shorter period of time; and certainly the Christian believes that God's final word to the human race has come in Jesus (see Heb. 1:1–2). But must one thereby also insist that it was all revealed at the moment of Jesus' resurrection and the coming of the Spirit at Pentecost? Reasonable interpreters

---

17. The idea of the Bible as a piece of music is often employed both by noninerrantists and inerrantists. For example, Caird, a noninerrantist, used this idea to illustrate the theological diversity within the NT (*New Testament Theology*, chap. 1), whereas J. G. Davis used it to indicate a "divinely inspired and inerrant theological symphony," in which there is "a perfect harmony because its author was none other than God himself" ("The Unity of the Bible," in *Hermeneutics, Inerrancy, and the Bible*, 641, 655).

18. But cf. evangelical scholar J. R. Michaels, in *Servant and Son: Jesus in Parable and Gospel* (Atlanta: John Knox, 1981), 163–66, who argued that Jesus decided to enlarge his mission to include the Gentiles only after the faith of the Syro-Phoenician woman surprised him.

will have to say no.[19] In the realm of Christology, for instance, they will point to reasons for saying that the NT shows a logical development. Luke's perception of Christ's person appears to be "lower" or more "functional" than John's. The same may be said of Luke's Christology in relation to Mark's—an important point, considering that Luke apparently wrote after and knew the Gospel of Mark![20] A logical development, in other words, is not the same as a chronological development. If there was development on certain important points, it does not appear to have happened in one neat straight line. It would appear to be more of a zig-zag. It would be of the same *genus*, but not of the same *species*, as the process by which the church developed its answer, over a period of time, by fits and starts, to the question of which books should be allowed into the NT canon.[21]

Having said this, the NT theologian should be concerned about some versions of the "development" argument as it is often stated. A frequent version of this is that Paul developed in his thinking, and that this can be demonstrated from his letters.[22] The beginning student in a "liberal" academic institution is often subjected to this argument as if it were dogma. Those in conservative contexts will reject it out of hand as incompatible with the inspiration and unity of Scripture. What needs to be noted by both students is that this kind of development is extraordinarily difficult to prove one way or another.

Another danger, not unrelated to the first, is the temptation to arrange the NT developmentally according to the expectation of Christ's return. It is often said that in the earlier writings (especially those of Paul) Christ was expected to return at any minute; later on, however, when the hope began to wane with the delay of the parousia, writers such as Luke, the author of 2 Thessalonians,

---

19. See R. N. Longenecker, "On the Concept of Development in Pauline Thought," in *Perspectives on Evangelical Theology,* ed. K. S. Kantzer and S. N. Gundry (Grand Rapids: Baker, 1979), 195–207.

20. Markan priority is still the consensus of modern opinion. See the discussion of Scot McKnight, *Interpreting the Synoptic Gospels* (Grand Rapids: Baker, 1988), 33–44.

21. On the important question of canon and authority, see F. F. Bruce, *The Canon of Scripture* (Downers Grove, Ill.: Inter-Varsity, 1988); and D. G. Dunbar, "The Biblical Canon," in *Hermenutics, Authority, and Canon,* ed. D. A. Carson and J. D. Woodbridge (Grand Rapids: Zondervan, 1986), 299–360.

22. This is not always the way the problem is stated. Often apparent differences in the canonical letters of Paul are used to deny the authenticity of some of those letters. See, e.g., J. Charlot, *New Testament Disunity* (New York: E. P. Dutton, 1970), 54–55.

and the author of Ephesians relaxed that hope by pushing the parousia further into the future and replacing it with an emphasis on the present.[23] As we become more aware of the complexities of biblical language and imagery, and how dangerous it is to take NT statements concerning Christ's return with a flat-footed literalness,[24] we will also understand that many of the conclusions concerning the late dating (and hence authorship) of some of the writings must now be reevaluated as to their validity.

These are only some of the problems which confront one who aspires to the task of NT theology. In the end the interpreter can surmount them only if he or she is simultaneously a historian, a linguist, a literary critic, a psychologist, a sociologist, and even an artist. This may sound daunting, but the task is within the bounds of realistic performance if only the interpreter is especially careful to avoid two dangers.[25] First, there is the danger of *modernizing* the text, in which case one assumes that there is *no* culture gap between the first and twentieth centuries. For example, Paul is interpreted as though he were a twentieth-century Englishman or American. Second, there is the danger of *archaizing* the text—assuming that first-century people were totally different from us. Naturally, we must recognize that the human race has changed considerably since the days of Nero. On the other hand, technological advances aside, the same hopes, fears, and needs which drive and tear at the hearts of people today, drove and tore at the hearts of Jesus, Paul, and the other NT writers.

Method in Madness? Four Representative Approaches to New Testament Theology

If, after having confronted the challenges above, the student is not too discouraged to proceed, we may next look at four representative approaches to NT theology by four different writers.

---

23. See Dunn, *Unity and Diversity*, 345–46: "Is the implication not fairly clear that in Colossians we see Paul turning away from the urgent hope of an imminent parousia which previously drove him on, to a more tranquil and settled hope which now reckoned with a longer interval before the parousia, with more continuing human relationships (3.18–4.1), and so focused attention more on what Christ had already accomplished?"

24. G. B. Caird, *The Language and Imagery of the Bible* (Philadelphia: Westminster, 1980), 243–71.

25. See Caird, *New Testament Theology*, chap. 1.

1. Bultmann

Perhaps the most famous NT theology ever written is that of Rudolf Bultmann.[26] Bultmann, heavily influenced by the early thought of Martin Heidegger, was not satisfied that NT theology be an antiquarian exercise. He wanted deeply for it to speak to modern human experience. This is seen best in his program of "demythologization," which is made necessary because "the cosmology of the New Testament is essentially mythical in character. The world is viewed as a three-storied structure, with the earth in the center, the heaven above, and the underworld beneath."[27] Thus if the NT is to be a relevant book today it must be "demythologized" and interpreted "existentially," that is, made relevant to our experience. Consequently Bultmann drove his famous wedge between the historical Jesus and the Christ of faith, the latter of whom is not rooted in history but comes perennially in the present. With this in view it followed that Bultmann did not think that the message of the historical Jesus belonged within a NT theology: "The message of Jesus is a presupposition for the theology of the New Testament rather than a part of that theology itself."[28] Hence Part One of his work, while it includes a treatment of the message of Jesus (derived largely from form critical criteria), falls more into the category of prolegomena, with the main part divided between the theology of Paul and the theology of the Johannine Epistles.

Bultmann saw little continuity between Jesus and Paul in their theology. Paul in fact was the true founder of Christian theology, not Jesus. The center of Paul's theology was his anthropology rather than his theology or Christology. In Bultmann's scheme Paul was primarily an existentialist in his understanding of human life in this world. On the other hand, Bultmann depicted John as representing a final break with the historical Jesus. John's Jesus was a Gnostic revealer who imparted timeless truths but did not act in the mundane realm of history.

Bultmann has been heavily criticized both by conservative

---

26. R. Bultmann, *Theology of the New Testament*, trans. K. Grobel, 2 vols. (New York: Charles Scribner's Sons, 1951, 1955).
27. Idem, "New Testament and Mythology," in *Kerygma and Myth*, ed. H. W. Bartsch, trans. R. H. Fuller (New York: Harper and Row, 1961), 1.
28. Idem, *Theology of the New Testament*, I, 3.

and nonconservative scholars.[29] Perhaps his greatest defect was his extraordinarily uncritical acceptance of the idea that first-century people accepted with naive literalness their images of God and the universe. It is now being recognized that figures such as Jesus and Paul were as aware of the metaphorical nature of their language as are sophisticated "moderns" like Bultmann.[30] Also, it was Bultmann's misfortune that his denial of the possibility of the miraculous, based on the old Newtonian principle of natural law, was being made about the same time that Albert Einstein's revolutionary impact was beginning to be felt.

2. Jeremias

Those students who are dissatisfied with Bultmann will feel more at home with the work of Joachim Jeremias.[31] For Jeremias the historical, Aramaic-speaking Jesus is recoverable by modern research tools. His first volume (of an originally projected two-volume work), subtitled *The Proclamation of Jesus*, turns the form critical approach of Bultmann on its head by saying that it is the inauthenticity rather than the authenticity of the sayings of Jesus which must be demonstrated.[32] For Jeremias the historical Jesus dominated a NT theology to the degree that "Jesus is the Kyrios and the Kyrios stands above his messengers. The Kyrios above is the beginning and end, the center and measure of all Christian theology."[33] For him the Christology of the later NT writers was implicit in the understanding of Jesus regarding his own person and mission; that understanding, furthermore, was rooted in the Son of man title, which derived from Daniel 7:13 rather than extrabiblical sources. Thus those who tend to see Jesus as the true founder of Christian theology will greet Jeremias' investiga-

---

29. See G. Hasel, *New Testament Theology: Basic Issues in the Current Debate* (Grand Rapids: Eerdmans, 1978), 87–92.

30. Caird, *Language and Imagery*, 144–59, argued persuasively that the ancients were more aware of the metaphorical nature of their language than is sometimes appreciated.

31. J. Jeremias, *New Testament Theology I: The Proclamation of Jesus*, trans. J. Bowden (New York: Charles Scribner's Sons, 1971).

32. Ibid., 37.

33. From Jeremias's second German edition, I, 295, quoted in Hasel, *New Testament Theology*, 110.

tion warmly; others who drive a wedge between the historical Jesus and the Christ of faith will find it less congenial.

3. Caird

Another thematic approach to New Testament theology is that of G. B. Caird. In its general orientation to the question of the historical Jesus, Caird's *New Testament Theology* resembles that of Jeremias. But in terms of its comprehensive structure and its eventual tracing of the origins of NT theology to the involvement of Jesus in the political fortunes of the Jewish nation, it is different from any other treatment of the subject thus far.

Caird chose for his work a historical model: the apostolic conference held at Jerusalem between Paul, Barnabas, Peter, James, and John (Gal. 2:1–10). But his re-creation of "the apostolic conference table" is as much an exercise of the imagination as it is of historical scholarship. "Around the table sit the authors of the New Testament, and it is the presider's task to engage them in a colloquium about theological matters which they themselves have placed on the agenda . . . As the chairperson looks round the conference table and tries to fit a face and a personality to each of the members, some will inevitably stand out more readily than others."[34] It is the task of the NT theologian, Caird said, to "set the biblical writers discussing among themselves." "Having asked a question of John and having received a provisional reply, he will turn to the other gospels, Paul, Hebrews and Revelation and put the same question to them. He will then turn back to John, not to obliterate or minimize the distinctiveness of his thought, but to see whether, in the light of the other answers, he has missed something in his original estimate of John."[35] Thus in no way can it be said that Caird's recreation of the NT conference table is whimsical; it is in fact a serious enterprise of historical scholarship.

Caird, known for his previous lucid exposition of the NT Testament writers, stood firmly in the tradition of C. H. Dodd, Jeremias, and (to a lesser extent) T. W. Manson. Yet his extraordinary fastidiousness with words and the precision with which he ana-

---

34. Caird, *New Testament Theology,* Introduction.
35. Ibid.

lyzed NT texts, not to mention the fertility of his imagination, ultimately placed him outside all external influences. This is particularly seen in his unique decision to write a NT theology "backwards"—beginning with the theology of the NT writers and concluding with a treatment of the theology of Jesus. For Caird one of the great mistakes of modern research has been the tendency to be in too much of a hurry to progress from the particular to the universal. Hence the ultimate chapter is an attempt to anchor the origins of NT theology not in theological abstractions but firmly in the involvement of Jesus in the bitter Jewish political disputes of A.D. 30. And in doing so his work represents the polar opposite of Bultmann's approach: the theology of Jesus becomes the goal of a NT theology, not its "presupposition."

4. Guthrie

A fourth approach to doing a NT theology is that of Donald Guthrie. Guthrie, an evangelical from Great Britain, published his massive tome of over a thousand pages in 1981.[36] Seen in terms of its extraordinary industry, Guthrie's work can only be greeted as a major contribution. But seen in terms of its usefulness as an introduction to the subject, we encounter problems. Previously known for his lucid and useful *New Testament Introduction*, with its even-handed survey of the opinions of those who do not share his viewpoint, Guthrie appears less balanced in his discussion of NT theology. His approach is clearly stated: the scholar "is not at liberty to pick and choose [from the NT]. He must take all or nothing."[37]

Those who subscribe to Guthrie's particular understanding of NT unity will undoubtedly greet his work warmly. Others will feel that problems are glossed over at points, and that each evangelist, for instance, does not come out as having any distinctive theology of his own. "If, for instance," says Guthrie, "the theology of each evangelist is more important than the teaching of Jesus which each records, this would indicate a collection of different theologies rather than the notion of a unified NT theology."[38]

---

36. D. Guthrie, *New Testament Theology* (Downers Grove, Ill.: Inter-Varsity, 1981).
37. Ibid., 30.
38. Ibid., 71.

But will those who do not share Guthrie's approach to the question of unity wonder if this begs the question? Is not the very issue that a NT theology must address, not only in its introduction,[39] but throughout the course of the work, the problem of theologies *within* theology? Has Guthrie predetermined the outcome? Here one will need to make up his or her own mind. But one thing is certain: there is little in Guthrie's work of the "give and take" of theological discussion which one finds in some other writers. Guthrie's homogenizing inclination implies that if a NT writer is silent on a subject, he must be taken to have believed in it. Thus both Paul and John undoubtedly believed in the virgin birth, since "it was so deeply impressed on the consciousness of Christians that it became unnecessary to mention it repeatedly."[40] Only Matthew and Luke record this belief, and, historically speaking, that hardly speaks against the doctrine. However, if NT theology is construed to be an essentially historical and descriptive discipline, without dogmatic beliefs predetermining the evidence of each writer, then it is difficult to see how it could be claimed that the virgin birth was "deeply impressed" on the mind of Paul or John. The virgin birth was apparently not part of the apostolic kerygma as it appears in the speeches in Acts, and it is certainly possible, historically speaking, that Paul may not have been exposed to the traditions which eventually surfaced in Matthew and Luke.[41] This is simply one example from Guthrie's work which once again underscores the question of whether all of the NT writers understood everything from the beginning in the same way.

Guthrie's *New Testament Theology* represents the summit of a distinguished and illuminating evangelical scholarly career. What impact it will have in the long run will be judged differently by students and scholars alike according to their respective postulates.

This brief survey hardly exhausts the literature of the subject

---

39. See Guthrie's very useful introductory section (pp. 49–59) on different theologies within the NT.

40. Ibid., 374.

41. It is sometimes said that Paul must have known of the virgin birth since Luke, who was his companion, recorded the belief. But most scholars would date Luke's Gospel long after the death of Paul, and thus it is at least possible that he came across the tradition in the post-Pauline period.

at hand. Other major contributors who might have been included are L. Goppelt,[42] A. Richardson,[43] J. D. G. Dunn,[44] G. E. Ladd,[45] Hans Conzelmann,[46] W. G. Kümmel,[47] and Leon Morris.[48] Each has made his own distinctive contribution to the ongoing debate. For evangelicals Ladd and Morris may represent an interesting—and perhaps less tendentious—alternative to Guthrie. In any case, despite its daunting challenges, NT theology is likely to be a topic which will continue to attract the most ambitious, seasoned, and talented biblical scholars for years to come.

Proof in the Pudding: New Testament Theological Analysis in Action

An awareness of the tasks, problems, and organization of NT theology is essential to every student of the Bible. There is, however, no substitute for learning by example. We shall therefore turn to some instances of NT theological analysis in action as it concerns five NT writers: Mark, Luke, John, Paul, and the author of Hebrews. These are in no way intended to represent any kind of exhaustive survey; they are more like "depth soundings" at various points to illustrate the NT theologian at work.

1. Mark

It is well known that Mark's theology is concerned primarily to show that Jesus is the Christ, the strong Son of God (1:1; 3:11; 5:7; 15:39; see also 14:61). Consequently "Mark's christology is a

---

42. L. Goppelt, *Theology of the New Testament*, trans. J. E. Alsup, ed. J. Roloff, 2 vols. (Grand Rapids: Eerdmans, 1981–82).

43. A. Richardson, *An Introduction to the Theology of the New Testament* (New York: Harper & Row, 1958).

44. Dunn, *Unity and Diversity* (see n. 13 above).

45. G. E. Ladd, *A Theology of the New Testament* (Grand Rapids: Eerdmans, 1974).

46. H. Conzelmann, *An Outline of the Theology of the New Testament*, trans. J. Bowden (New York: Harper & Row, 1969).

47. W. G. Kümmel, *The Theology of the New Testament*, trans. J. E. Steely (Nashville: Abingdon, 1973).

48. L. Morris, *New Testament Theology* (Grand Rapids: Zondervan, 1986).

high christology, as high as any in the New Testament, not excluding that of John."[49] It is usually thought that the Gospel was written to the church at Rome soon after the great fire of A.D. 64, and that Mark sought to answer a question which stemmed from his readers' suffering: Why, if Jesus is the Son of God, do his followers have to suffer? Mark's answer is twofold: (1) Jesus was the Son of God not in spite of his sufferings, but *because* of them; and (2) the disciple will drink of the same cup as the master (Mark 10:39); hence, since Jesus suffered, the disciple should also expect to suffer.[50]

There are good reasons for accepting this reconstruction, and for saying that Mark's Gospel is really an extended passion narrative.[51] And, as such, Mark is frequently preparing his readers for the story of Jesus' suffering and death long before it actually occurs.

In Mark's account of Jesus' baptism (Mark 1:10–11), for example, we are told that upon coming up out of the water Jesus "saw the heavens opened and the Spirit descending upon him like a dove; and a voice came from heaven, 'You are my beloved Son, with whom I am well pleased.' " Now one of the first things noted by any beginning student of the NT is that the word used by Mark for "open" is the violent term *schizō*, literally "cracked" or "ripped." The Greek word used by Matthew and Luke, on the other hand, is the ordinary word for "open," *anoigō*. That this usage by Mark is theological rather than simply stylistic is indicated when we come to the passion narrative proper, where Mark uses the same word for the veil of the temple, which was *"ripped in two, from top to bottom"* (Mark 15:38 [italics added]). This ripping takes place immediately before the Roman centurion confesses his faith that Jesus is the "Son of God," and it can hardly be accidental that the ripping in both cases is connected with a confession of Jesus' divine sonship. The logical link of the two passages is that they both concern a revelation of what had previously been hidden from human eyes. And in the case of the centurion, the logic of the

---

49. V. Taylor, *The Gospel According to St. Mark*, 2d ed. (London: Macmillan, 1966), 121.

50. P. J. Achtemeier, *Mark*, Proclamation Commentaries (Philadelphia: Fortress, 1975), 41–50.

51. R. H. Lightfoot, *The Gospel Message of St. Mark* (Oxford: Clarendon Press, 1956), esp. 48–59.

sequence seems to suggest that even though it took place several miles away, the centurion's confession is the result of the ripping of the veil. Here the centurion speaks not as an individual but as a representative of the whole Roman world: what was hidden from the entire Jewish nation (cf. Mark 4:11–12) was revealed to a Gentile, and not only to a Gentile, but to a centurion, the symbol of Roman justice! Here the meaning of the rending of the veil appears to come very close to the statement in Ephesians 2:14 that the effect of Christ's death is to "break down the middle wall of partition" that separated Jew and Gentile.[52] The confession of the centurion signals the ripping apart of the barrier which kept Gentile eyes (and Jewish ones for that matter) from seeing into the true nature of God—and messiahship. True Christhood does not consist in the exercise of earthly power, but in suffering. Of course, the temptation of the redaction critic is to say at this point that the confession of the voice at the baptism and that of the centurion—not to mention the veil— are theology, and therefore not history. But this argument is not easy to follow. Mark could be interpreting history theologically.[53] It is, on the other hand, possible to take at least the rending of the veil as a theological comment of the writer on the centurion's statement (in the sense of Mark 7:19b or Eph. 2:14) without surrendering either a high view of Scripture or the historical reliability of the account.

Here the conservative critic will undoubtedly object: "But where does one draw the line? Are you not opening a Pandora's box?" To this I would simply answer that there is no magic touchstone, no guarantee, given us to determine the outcome of such questions in advance. It must result from the application of theological sense, literary sense, and common sense. What it should *not* result from is a previously formulated hermeneutical principle which regulates that each statement in the NT be taken historically and literally, without attention also being given to the writer's particular theology.

---

52. See Caird, *Language and Imagery of the Bible*, 185–86.

53. For another example of this possibility, cf. the treatment of the parable of Mark 12:1–12 by Matthew and Luke (Matt. 21:33–46; Luke 20:9–19) as discussed by J. A. T. Robinson, "The Parable of the Wicked Husbandmen," *New Testament Studies*, 21 (1974–75): 443–61, reprinted in *Twelve More New Testament Studies* (London: SCM, 1984), ch. 2.

2. Luke

What of Luke? Here opinions will vary. The British scholar J. M. Creed,[54] for instance, claimed that Luke has no theology of his own, only that which he has taken over from his sources. While there is something to be said for this view, it probably overstates the case.[55] Luke appears, for example, to have had a strongly defined interest in the Holy Spirit and the role of the Gentiles and Jews in historical eschatology.

Since most scholars still believe that one of Luke's sources was Mark, one aspect of his theology which may be compared with that of his sources is his Christology. As I have intimated above, NT scholars often draw a line between a so-called low or functional Christology, and a high or ontological one—the former stressing what Jesus *does*, the latter stressing who Jesus *is*. And Luke's Christology seems to be of the former kind. He preserves the Marcan tradition that Jesus is the Son of God, but unlike Mark, it is not for him a supernatural, numinous title, but something which comes to him via his descent from Adam (Luke 3:38). After the healing of the son of the widow of Nain (7:11–17), the crowd says, "A great prophet has arisen among us," and "God has visited his people" (7:16). There is no reason to believe that Luke thought these expressions to be inadequate. For him Jesus can be described as "a man approved of God" (Acts 2:22). Even the high christological title "Son of God" (Luke 1:35) seems to focus more on the mode of Jesus' generation than on any metaphysical status he might possess.[56]

Particularly interesting is his treatment of the centurion's statement which, as we have just seen, is also in Mark. In Luke's Gospel the confession of Jesus' divine sonship appears in the form "truly this man was innocent" (Luke 23:47). This appears to be in line with Luke's apologetic interest to show that Christianity presents no threat to the Roman Empire—a motif found repeatedly in Acts.[57] If Luke used Mark as a source, as the majority

---

54. J. M. Creed, *The Gospel According to St. Luke* (London: Macmillan, 1930), lxxi.
55. A useful discussion of the distinctiveness of Luke's theology is found in I. H. Marshall, *Luke the Historian and Theologian* (Grand Rapids: Zondervan, 1970), and in L. Morris, *New Testament Theology*, 144–221.
56. J. D. G. Dunn, *Christology in the Making* (Philadelphia: Westminster, 1980), 50–51.
57. See Guthrie, *New Testament Introduction*, 350–52.

of scholars still believe, then it is significant that Luke was willing to sacrifice the stronger, christological idea ("Son of God")
for the comparatively weaker apologetic one ("innocent"). In
other words, for Luke the phrase "truly this man was innocent"
is a perfectly adequate confession for the centurion to be making
at the foot of the cross. This is a point which, if accepted, appears to take J. M. Creed's theory one stage further; at times
Luke's theology is actually *less* than that of his sources!

3. John

The Fourth Gospel continues to be an enormous problem for
those who deal with the question of history and theology. When
we turn from the Synoptics to John we become immediately
aware that we have entered a different theological landscape.
This is evident when the author places the beginning of the
story not at the birth of Jesus or the preaching of the Baptist, but
with God "in the beginning" (John 1:1). We are also faced with a
whole new vocabulary. Instead of emphasizing the kingdom of
God, John focuses upon various word-themes: light, life, world,
truth, glory, darkness, love, hate, rebirth, and belief. Long dis-
courses replace the parables, and there are no warnings against
hellfire, no exorcisms, no lepers to be cleansed, and no secrecy
theme with regard to Jesus' messiahship. John also gives a different ordering of events in the life of Jesus: the cleansing of the
temple, for instance, is placed at the beginning of the story (John
2:13–22), not at the end (cf. Mark 11:15–17).[58]

And yet this is only one side of the picture. The Fourth Gospel remains one of the mysteries of the NT precisely because it
contains an amazingly large amount of information which appears accurate in relation to the topography of Palestine and the
particular details of Jesus' life. This is one reason why Brown[59]
suggested that John's Gospel went through at least five editions,

---

58. See R. E. Brown, *The Gospel According to John* (i–xii). The Anchor Bible (Garden City,
N. Y.: Doubleday, 1966), 118: "We suggest that the edition of the Gospel led to the transposition of the scene from the original sequence. . . ." For Brown the cleansing is placed where it
is in order to relate it to the prophecy of Mal. 3:1, the first part of which ("I send my
messenger to prepare the way before me") is fulfilled by John, and the second part ("The
Lord whom you seek will suddenly come to his Temple") by Jesus.

59. Ibid., xxxiv–xxxix.

with the theological elements added late in the first century. But here one must be cautious. What is increasingly disturbing is that the two bodies of literature with which the Fourth Gospel is continually compared are Philo of Alexandria and the Dead Sea Scrolls; and both of these belong to the first half of the first century. The parallels with Philo are at times especially striking; and it is worth considering that both Philo and Qumran were not apparently in vogue (at least there is no evidence to this effect) at the time when John's Gospel is supposed to have been written (ca. 90–95).

This in turn raises the enormous theological question of John's sources. Even admitting that John's Gospel was compiled last, a tradition attributed to Clement of Alexandria,[60] can we conclude that the *sources* of the Fourth Gospel are earlier than those of the Synoptics? C. H. Dodd[61] has demonstrated to this writer's satisfaction—and that of many others—that in John we have a tradition of the sayings of Jesus that is entirely independent of the Synoptics and that is markedly more political in its theological tone. Thus many of its sayings could possibly have more of an authentic basis than is often allowed.

One way to approach this problem, although it is by no means certain, is to say that in John we have two different phenomena working simultaneously: early sources of the life of Jesus plus an equally early attempt to "targumize" the sayings of Jesus. The Targums were long, extended Aramaic paraphrases of the Hebrew Scriptures which made the Scriptures relevant to the Aramaic-speaking people of Palestine. Before we object to this too quickly in the name of a high view of Scripture or out of a concern for the issue of historicity, we might do well to recall that, as already noted, all translation involves interpretation, and it is largely a question of the freedom of the translator. Here we need to consider as well the possibility of paraphrase. In terms of freedom, paraphrase is one step beyond translation, and this was the special territory of the targumist. Probably the closest contemporary analogies to the Targums are J. B. Philipps' *The New Testament in Modern English* and Kenneth Taylor's *The Living Bible*. In the case of the latter, many people read it as the

---

60. Cited in Eusebius, *Ecclesiastical History* vi.14.7.
61. *Historical Tradition in the Fourth Gospel* (Cambridge: Cambridge University Press, 1963).

Word of God, when in fact, *The Living Bible* is a vastly free and expansive rewriting of the English Bible with the translator's own theological biases often intruding into the text.[62] And there is no prima facie reason for saying that this could not have been the way in which John's Gospel was accepted in the first and second centuries, that is, as a free paraphrase of the life of Jesus.

4. Paul

The general outlines of Paul's theology are fairly clear.[63] Paul saw the human race as sinful, objectively wretched, and in need of salvation (Rom. 3:23; 5:12–21). The old covenant was a dispensation of death. It had failed as a means of bringing salvation (2 Cor. 3:7). Jesus, on the other hand, has "redeemed us from the curse of the law, by becoming a curse for us" (Gal. 3:13, NIV; cf. 2 Cor. 5:21). For Paul Jesus was "the Lord" (Rom. 10:9) who "emptied himself and took on the form of a slave" (Phil. 2:7) and who became the cosmic Christ (Col. 1:15–20). Christians are now "in Christ" (e.g., Rom. 8:1; 2 Cor. 5:17), just as once they were "in Adam" (1 Cor. 15:22). The church, furthermore, is Christ's body (e.g., Rom. 12:5; 1 Cor. 12:12–27), and his resurrection is the "firstfruits" of the resurrection of Christians (Rom. 8:23; 1 Cor. 15:20–23). Christians will one day meet Christ in the air upon his return (1 Thess. 4:17). As for the Jews, they are presently hardened against the gospel, but will one day be saved (11:25–32) along with the Gentiles (Rom. 11:11–24).

This all seems rather clear. However, when we try to fill in the outline, the complexity of Paul's theology begins to emerge. Again we may choose one example. Did Paul believe in the personal preexistence of Christ? Since the time of Lightfoot,[64] scholars have almost uniformly regarded Colossians 1:15–20 and Philippians 2:5–12 as indicating such a belief. Recently, however,

---

62. See, e.g., Heb. 5:7 in *The Living Bible*, where the word "premature" is inserted before "death," with a footnote explaining that Jesus was already dying and was afraid that he might not make it to the cross in time!

63. See, e.g., J. A. Fitzmyer, *Paul and His Theology: A Brief Sketch*, 2d ed. (Englewood Cliffs, N. J.: Prentice-Hall, 1989).

64. J. B. Lightfoot, *Paul's Epistle to the Colossians and Philemon* (London: Macmillan, 1884), and *Paul's Epistle to the Philippians* (London: Macmillan, 1927), q.v.

writers such as Dunn[65] and J. A. T. Robinson[66] have questioned that these passages support such a belief. They argue that in Colossians 1:15–20 Jesus embodies God's personified Wisdom (which is preexistent, but only as an attribute of God), but that he himself does not actually preexist. Similarly, in Philippians 2 Paul is said to be drawing a parallel between the human Christ and a figure such as Adam, with no indication of personal preexistence.

Which view is right? Lightfoot's or Dunn's? In the long run it may be difficult to decide with certainty. Some will feel that arguments which claim that Colossians 1:15–20 does not indicate personal preexistence are stronger than those for Philippians 2.[67] Others will undoubtedly claim that the evidence for preexistence in both texts is strong. In any case, the debate is likely to continue.

5. Hebrews

Hebrews is, by any criterion, one of the most mysterious writings in the NT.[68] Like one of its favorite characters, it comes to us "without father, without mother, without genealogy" (Heb. 7:3). We know virtually nothing about its date, author, or recipients. Consequently it has become a fruitful source of debate for anyone attempting to understand its logic and historical circumstances. Again, a christological example may help to illustrate the point.

Why does the author spend so much time on the subject of Christ and the angels in chapter 1? After an impressive opening (1:1–3), which touches upon almost every major Christian doctrine, the statement "having become as much superior to angels as the name he has obtained is more excellent than theirs" (1:4) seems at best anticlimactic. Why should he say such a thing? There are those who think the question is answered by claiming that the author is combating a defective view on the part of his

---

65. See Dunn, *Christology in the Making*.

66. *The Human Face of God* (London: SCM, 1973). See his chapter on "God's Man."

67. For arguments against Phil. 2:5–11 meaning what Dunn takes it to mean, see L. D. Hurst, "Re-enter the Pre-Existent Christ in Phillipians 2.5–11?" *New Testament Studies* 32 (1986): 449–57.

68. L. D. Hurst, *The Epistle to the Hebrews: Its Background of Thought* (Cambridge: Cambridge University Press, forthcoming), introduction.

readers, who think of Christ as an angel, or who tend to worship angels.

While such speculative reconstructions are popular, in the end they are totally unnecessary. If one approaches the question from within the author's own theology, it will be readily seen that one of the underlying purposes of Hebrews is to show that the new covenant is superior to the old. This is done by demonstrating the superiority of its great mediator to all those who mediated the old. Hence Moses (3:2–6), Aaron (7:11–14), and even the covenant itself (8:7–13) are shown to be weak when compared with Christ and the covenant he brings. Now, in such a scenario would it not be necessary to discuss the appeal of angels as well? They not only mediated the law at Sinai (2:2), but they were placed over humankind "for a little while"(Ps. 8:5 [LXX]; Heb. 2:7). For this author Christ has fulfilled the psalm representatively, and in Christ we can see humankind "crowned with glory and honor" (Heb. 2:9), a reversal of conditions under the old covenant. Thus it is often necessary to read specific NT passages in the context of an author's overall thinking, a practice that is infinitely preferable to constructing a hypothetical external situation which will explain an otherwise "hidden" meaning.[69]

In the context of one essay it is obviously impossible to treat every theological question raised by the NT writers. Hopefully, what has been presented above will be sufficient to sensitize the beginning student to the kinds of things which concern NT theologians. Ultimately the best way to begin learning the discipline is not to read what NT theologians are saying—too much of their work is contradictory—but by learning to read the NT itself.

Why Bother? Final Reflections on Unity and Diversity in New Testament Theology

By now we will begin to see "dialogue" as an attractive model for the discipline of NT theology. Such a term helps us to see that the theology of the NT was, and continues to be, a "give-and-take" exercise. Certainly when we approach the NT, from what-

---

69. See R. N. Longenecker, *Biblical Exegesis in the Apostolic Period* (Grand Rapids: Eerdmans, 1975), 181.

ever background we may come, it serves us well to reflect on the apparent fact that no one writer had the total truth. Each had a piece of the truth, and we need the composite picture gleaned from them all if we are to see Jesus as he really was.

There will be those, of course, who will claim that this smacks of subjectivity. Were not the writers of the NT wholly inspired by God, and thus did not each of them have the *same* truth? To this we may say two things. First, to have the same truth does not mean to have the *whole* truth. Even the idea of inspiration does not insure knowledge of the whole truth. The prophets, while inspired, diligently "searched and inquired about this salvation" (1 Pet. 1:10). And even Jesus, from the Christian point of view the most Spirit-inspired person who ever lived, did not appear to have known everything. As a child he grew in wisdom (Luke 2:52), he had to learn obedience (Heb. 5:8), and he did not know things both trivial (e.g., who touched him [Mark 5:30–34]) or important (such as when his parousia would occur [Mark 13:32]— a point of ignorance not shared with many modern writers on the subject of eschatology). He could be surprised (Matt. 8:10) and troubled in soul (John 12:27).

Second, it is an unfortunate fact that most Christians today who accept Christ's humanity have not really grappled with it as a historical fact. Those who adhere tenaciously to the Council of Chalcedon's decision in A.D. 451 that Jesus was both fully human and fully divine often do so without realizing that the council's statement was no solution at all, but the result of an impasse. In effect the council said that, after all of the fine philosophical distinctions have been made, we simply affirm both sides of Christ's person. And what is extraordinary is that when the church made a statement that was largely formulated from philosophical deliberations based upon Greek terms and ideas, it uttered something profoundly biblical.

Biblical paradox is that phenomenon by which one holds two apparently contradictory things in tension. A good example is Isaiah 45:6–7:

> I am the LORD, and there is no other.
> I form the light and create darkness,
> I create good and I create evil;
> I am the LORD, who do all these things.

The biblical writers never felt the need to harmonize these apparent contradictions in God's nature. To them he is love; but he is also wrath, "a consuming fire" (Heb. 12:29). Does that mean that God is sixty percent love and forty percent wrath? No. He is one hundred percent love and one hundred percent wrath—simultaneously.

Some of those who participated in Christian debate in the late second and early third centuries could not tolerate this. They could not accept a God of "paradox" who in any way changes or appears to contradict himself. They ordered things, subordinated them, ranked them according to importance. The biblical writers, on the other hand, on the whole tended to think in terms of what grammarians call "parataxis"[70]—laying things side by side—the way a child says, "And I went to the store, and I bought a piece of candy, and I came home." Philosophers will say "Having been to the store, I bought a piece of candy, after which I came home." They rank things. Fortunately, those who rendered their verdict at Chalcedon did not allow Hellenistic logic to become master, and retained the element of mystery in the person of God and Christ which might otherwise have been lost had the philosophers won the day.

Modern NT theologians, like the statesmen of Chalcedon, should be careful not to fall prey to the rationalistic impulse when dealing with God and his ways. As they plot the many areas of unity and diversity within NT thought, they must be careful to allow for the possibility that they might be getting things wrong, and that perhaps there is something ultimately elusive about the biblical God and his dealings with humankind. As usual, Paul put the point rather well:

> O the depth of the riches
> and wisdom and knowledge of God!
> How unsearchable are his judgments
> and how inscrutable his ways!
> For who has known the mind of the Lord,
> or who has been his counselor? (Rom. 11:33–34)

---

70. See Caird, *Language and Imagery of the Bible*, 117–21.

There was no systematic syllabus of Christian theology handed out in the early church which then simply needed to be explicated in subsequent lectures. When we look at examples of the primitive Christian gospel (e.g., 1 Cor. 15:3; the speeches in the Book of Acts), we find some startling omissions. There one finds no virgin birth, no trinitarian formulas, no statement of Jesus' eternal person. This might lead us to believe that in the early church there were some things that were understood from the beginning, while others developed and were a subject of considerable discussion. This is not to imply that things such as the virgin birth or the doctrine of the Trinity could not have been present early in germinal form. It is simply to say that there appears to have been a process, a fluidity of thought and freedom in which the early church debated a number of subjects, and in the NT we have a window to that debate. It must have been an explosion in terms of the mental energy which was being released.

In addition to this is the undeniable fact that the early church did not have the NT. It had the OT, a number of oral reports, and preaching, not all of which harmonized (see Luke 1:1–4). But the early Christians knew they had the Holy Spirit, and for them truth had not yet been fossilized and put into neat display cases for future generations to admire.

Of course, the NT writers were intensely interested in the historical and biographical details of the life of Jesus, something that radicals like Bultmann and their followers are not able to admit. But apart from the broad outlines of Jesus' life (such as his choosing of the Twelve, his conflict with the religious authorities, and his ensuing death and resurrection), the interpretation of that life and its meaning for the church seems to have come under considerable discussion.

The NT is remarkable for many things, not the least of which is its unity. Its main focus is that in Jesus God has intersected the eternal with the finite, and that by raising Jesus of Nazareth from the dead he has begun the end times. In the historical we can see the ultimate encapsulated. And it is remarkable how many NT writers say that the eschaton is near without saying that the end of the world is also thereby near. God's mighty work for the NT writers is centered not in the future but in what God has already done in the death and raising to life of his son. This is the meeting point, the nexus, of NT thought. And although the further away from the nexus one gets, the greater the variety of NT thinking becomes, Jesus' death and resurrection is always the center which fuses our attention. C. H. Dodd[71] has drawn our attention to a common principle of selection and interpretation of certain key OT passages in the light of the life and death of Jesus. Is this the true unity of the NT? We may never know for certain, but what we can know is that other issues are not as important as they may appear. As Caird put it, "The question we must ask is not whether these books all say the same thing, but whether they all bear witness to the same Jesus and through him to the many-splendored wisdom of the one God." Caird went on,

> If we are persuaded that the second Moses, the Son of Man, the friend of sinners, the incarnate Logos, the first-born of all creation, the Apostle and High Priest of our calling, the Chief Shepherd, and the lamb opening the scroll are the same person in whom the one God has achieved and is achieving his mighty work, we shall neither attempt to press all our witnesses into a single mould nor captiously complain that one seems at some points deficient in comparison with one another; we shall rejoice that God has seen fit to establish his Gospel at the mouth of so many independent witnesses.[72]

Some students may be tempted to throw up their hands at this point and ask why we should even attempt the task if so much of it is doomed to imprecision. To this I would venture three simple answers. First, he or she has no choice. Any thinking person is duty-bound to use his or her intellect to try to sort out the questions that the NT Scriptures present. We who are privileged to study such things in depth have a duty to explain to our fellows what in the NT may be timeless and what may be time-bound. Second, it is a privilege, to use Caird's image, to "chair an apostolic conference on faith and order." And third, it is *exciting*. What could be more boring than being seated at a dinner party with nine or ten guests, all of whom are agreed on every subject, at every single point? It is in fact the unanswered

---

71. C. H. Dodd, *According to the Scriptures* (Welwyn, Herts: James Nisbet, 1952).
72. Caird, *New Testament Theology*, Introduction.

questions posed by the diversity of the NT that turn out to be as fascinating as the uniformity that it so obviously displays.

Oliver Cromwell is reported to have said to the British Parliament, "I beseech you, my brethren, from the bowels of Jesus Christ, to consider the possibility that you might be mistaken." Somebody else has said that when everyone is thinking alike, the probability is that nobody is thinking. To those for whom a perfect harmony is the criterion of all truth, the NT will tend to be read that way, and the interpreter will have no serious areas of uncertainty. Those trained in the Hebrew "paratactic" approach to truth, on the other hand, will be more open to the possibility of areas of uncertainty. This does not mean that Christians will shut off their minds, put away their books, and surrender themselves to uncertainty whenever a tension surfaces. How often hard work reveals the tensions to be illusory! It does mean, on the other hand, that if all of the things in the NT cannot be reduced to a single key, Christians may take comfort in knowing that its melodies and countermelodies provide a deeper harmony for those attuned to it. And by listening to that wondrous music, with its occasionally dissonant tones, they may find enough courage and intellectual stamina to meet their God and their world triumphantly, amidst all of the ambiguities which have confronted ancients and moderns alike.

7

The Function of the Old Testament in the New

Craig A. Evans

One of the first things that beginning students observe is that when the OT is quoted in the NT, the citation often is not verbatim. Moreover, these citations often appear to have been interpreted in a sense other than what is found in the OT context. Sometimes writings are quoted or alluded to that are not found in the OT at all. These observations testify to a phenomenon that may be called "biblical pluralism."

Biblical pluralism manifests itself in four important areas:

Canon. When the NT was written there was not universal agreement as to the exact contents of the OT. Books that some viewed as authoritative (i.e., canonical), others did not. Although the vast majority of NT citations of the OT comes from the thirty-nine books of the Jewish Bible, there are many allusions to, and even a few citations of, the apocryphal writings.[1]

---

1. Even today there is no universally accepted canon of Scripture among Christians. Only Jews and Protestant Christians restrict the OT to thirty-nine books. Roman Catholics accept twelve of the apocryphal books (and additions), Greek and Russian Orthodox accept seventeen, though not the same seventeen, while Copts and many eastern Christians accept still more of the apocryphal books. Even in the NT canon there is diversity. For recent studies see R. T. Beckwith, *The Old Testament Canon of the New Testament Church and Its Background in Early Judaism* (Grand Rapids: Eerdmans, 1985); B. M. Metzger, *The Canon of the New Testament: Its Origin, Development, and Significance* (Oxford: Clarendon, 1987). For a theological discussion of canonical pluralism see J. A. Sanders, *Torah and Canon* (Philadelphia: Fortress, 1972); idem, "Adaptable for Life: The Nature and Function of Canon," in

The juxtaposition of the two Testaments in one Bible is itself the most dramatic evidence of canonical pluralism.

Versions. Related to canonical pluralism is textual pluralism. When the NT was being written, the OT existed in Greek and in Hebrew, and, as is becoming increasingly evident, in Aramaic as well. All three of these versions are represented by NT citations of the OT. Of these, the most influential is the Greek version, whose text (the LXX) underlies at least half of the citations. Thus, when a NT writer wished to quote the OT, he was not necessarily limited to one version. At times this textual pluralism aided biblical exegesis (such as is clearly evident in Matthew, John, Paul, and Hebrews).

Exegesis. NT exegesis of the OT is pluralistic. Sometimes new meanings are assigned to OT passages; and in some cases the same passage is interpreted and applied in two or more ways in the NT (a phenomenon that may be called "multivalency"; compare the function of Gen. 15:6 in Gal. 3:6 and James 2:23, or Ps. 2:7 in Acts 13:33 and Mark 1:11). When the NT writer finds a new meaning for an OT passage, this is usually called resignification. That such resignification frequently takes place in the NT will become apparent in the examples below.[2]

Theology. The NT, as well as the OT, is theologically pluralistic. That is, the testaments contain *theologies,* not just one *theology.* No one can read Paul, John, Hebrews, and James, and come away without a sense of the diversity of biblical theology.[3]

The study of the function of the OT in the NT opens the door to appreciation of biblical pluralism, for such study touches on all four aspects of this phenomenon. Indeed, a proper assessment of the function of the OT in the NT cannot be made apart from the recognition of this phenomenon. If the study of the OT in the NT is reduced to an effort to demonstrate that only one

---

Magnalia Dei: The Mighty Acts of God," ed. F. M. Cross, et al. (Garden City, N.Y.: Doubleday, 1976), 531–60; reprinted in J. A. Sanders, *From Sacred Story to Sacred Text* (Philadelphia: Fortress, 1987), 9–39; idem, *Canon and Community: A Guide to Canonical Criticism* (Philadelphia: Fortress, 1984).

2. W. C. Kaiser's claim (*Toward an Exegetical Theology* [Grand Rapids: Baker, 1981], 57) that resignification was "avoided when the New Testament writers were engaged in serious exegesis" strikes me as special pleading. All of the examples that will be considered in this essay reflect serious exegesis on the part of the NT writer, and in several cases resignification is clearly evident.

3. See J. D. G. Dunn, *Unity and Diversity in the New Testament: An Inquiry into the Character of Earliest Christianity* (Philadelphia: Westminster, 1977).

OT canon was known and accepted, that only one OT version was accepted, and that only one meaning of the text was sought, then the exegesis of the NT writers will likely be missed, perhaps even distorted. In the discussion that follows, the phenomena of biblical exegesis will be surveyed (part I), a method will be proposed for assessing and allying these phenomena to the task of NT exegesis (part II), and several examples will be studied (part III).

I. Phenomena

Jewish Exegesis[4]

Jewish exegesis is rooted in the adaptation, expansion, and interpretation of Israel's sacred tradition. The discipline known as tradition criticism is really the study of how sacred tradition was formed, interpreted, and passed on before a stabilized, canonical text of Scripture emerged. But even when a stabilized text emerged, early exegesis usually did not formally comment on the older text, but rewrote the tradition itself. This early form of exegesis has been called the "rewritten Bible." In its earliest stage, the focus is on the story, not on the text. The biblical text places only minimal limits on the rewriting of the story. What is considered irrelevant is omitted, while traditions not found in the text are freely added. This is clearly seen in Chronicles, Jubilees and the Genesis Apocryphon. These writings have retold the biblical story, and in doing so often diverge widely from the biblical text. Such rewriting is seen in the NT when Matthew and Luke retell the story of Jesus. Although both have made use of Mark, neither felt constrained to follow the Marcan text closely. This type of biblical exegesis, however, falls outside of the concerns of the present essay. This essay is concerned with exegesis that presupposes a stabilized, canoni-

---

4. See G. Vermes, "Bible and Midrash: Early Old Testament Exegesis," in *The Cambridge History of the Bible*, vol. 1, *From the Beginnings to Jerome*, ed. P. R. Ackroyd and C. F. Evans (Cambridge: Cambridge University Press, 1970), 199–231; idem, *Scripture and Tradition in Judaism* (Leiden: Brill, 1973); D. Patte, *Early Jewish Hermeneutic in Palestine* (Missoula, Mont.: Scholars, 1975); D. J. Moo, *The Old Testament in the Gospel Passion Narratives* (Sheffield: Almond, 1983), 5–78.

cal text. Exegesis of this nature may be described in the following five categories.

1. *Targum*.[5] When the canon of Scripture was viewed as more
or less closed, the focus became increasingly textual. The Bible
was still rewritten, but the text, as the primary and perhaps
controlling point of reference, was sometimes paraphrased. This
form of exegesis, a descendant and relative of the rewritten Bible, appears as "targum," the Aramaic paraphrase of Scripture.
Through paraphrase, text and interpretation are combined.
(Even the LXX is a paraphrase, and so in a sense is a targum.)
Many of the paraphrastic NT quotations of the OT exemplify
this form of Jewish exegesis, and at many points reflect specific
targumic traditions (compare Mark 4:12 with Tg. Isa. 6:10, or
Luke 6:36 with Tg. Ps.-J. Lev. 22:28).[6]

2. *Midrash*.[7] Midrash (lit. "interpretation"; from Heb. *dāraš*,
"to search"; see John 5:39) should not be viewed as exegesis that
is somehow different from, or at odds with, peshat ("plain" or
"literal"). Peshat refers to the obvious, contextual meaning of a
passage, an idea that midrash itself encompasses. Midrash
means searching the text for the obvious and more. In reference
to the study of Scripture, a student of Hillel once said: "Turn it
and turn it again for everything is in it; and contemplate it and
grow grey and old over it and stir not from it for than it thou
canst have no better rule" (Mish. *'Abot* 5:22). The key statement
here is, "for everything is in it." This reflects the conviction of

---

5. See J. Bowker, *The Targums and Rabbinic Literature* (Cambridge: Cambridge University
Press, 1969). Various editions and translations of portions of the targum are available. Cur-
rently the Aramaic Bible, a nineteen-volume series directed by M. McNamara, is being published by Michael Glazier, Inc. This set will offer an English translation of all the targums. To
date four volumes (Former Prophets, Isaiah, Jeremiah, and Ezekiel) have appeared.

6. See M. McNamara, *The New Testament and the Palestinian Targum to the Pentateuch*
(Rome: Pontifical Biblical Institute, 1966); idem, *Targum and Testament* (Grand Rapids: Eerd-
mans, 1972); R. le Déaut, "Targumic Literature and New Testament Interpretation," *Biblical
Theology Bulletin* 4 (1974): 243–89; J. T. Forestell, *Targumic Traditions and the New Testament*
(Chico, Calif.: Scholars, 1979).

7. See S. Zeitlin, "Midrash: A Historical Study," *Jewish Quarterly Review* 44 (1953): 21–36;
A. G. Wright, *The Literary Genre Midrash* (Staten Island, N.Y.: Alba, 1967); R. le Déaut,
"Apropos a Definition of Midrash," *Interpretation* 25 (1971): 262–82; M. P. Miller, "Midrash,"
Interpreter's Dictionary of the Bible: Supplementary Volume, ed. K. Crim (Nashville: Abingdon,
1976): 593–97; R. Block, "Midrash," in *Approaches to Ancient Judaism*, ed. W. S. Green (Mis-
soula, Mont.: Scholars, 1978), 29–50; G. G. Porton, "Defining Midrash," in *Study of Ancient
Judaism*, ed. J. Neusner (New York: Ktav, 1981), 55–94; R. T. France and D. Wenham, eds.,
Studies in Midrash and Historiography (Sheffield: JSOT, 1983); J. Neusner, *What is Midrash?*
(Philadelphia: Fortress, 1987).

the midrashist. Scripture is to be searched and contemplated until the answer is found.

Hillel followed seven rules (or *middoth*) for studying Scripture ('Abot R. Nat. 37; t. Sanh. 7:11). The most significant for NT study include *qal wahomer* ("light and heavy"), where what is true in a less important case will certainly be true in a more important case (see Matt. 7:11; Rom. 5:10); *gezera shawah* ("rule of equivalence"), where passages clarify one another if they share common vocabulary (see Rom. 4:7–8; 11:7–10); *kelal upherat* ("general and specific"), where a general rule may be deduced from a specific passage, and vice versa (see Rom. 13:8–10; Gal. 5:14). Jewish exegesis is halakic (i.e., concerned with legal matters, from *halak*, "[how to] walk") and haggadic (i.e., homiletical, from *haggadah*, "homily" or "popular discourse"). The former was chiefly the product of the academies, while the latter was chiefly the product of the synagogue. Midrash often takes the form of a running commentary. One of the best examples in the NT is seen in John 6:25–59 (commenting on Exod. 16:4; Ps. 78:24; cf. John 6:31).[8]

3. *Pesher.*[9] Scripture at Qumran was viewed as containing mysteries in need of explanation. The "pesher" was the explanation of the mystery: ". . . the pesher of the [scripture] concerns the teacher of righteousness to whom God made known all the mysteries of the words of his servants the prophets" (1QpHab 7:4–5). It was assumed that the text spoke of and to the Qumran community, and that it spoke of eschatological events about to unfold. As in NT exegesis (see Mark 12:10–11 [citing Ps. 118:22–23]; 14:27 [citing Zech. 13:7]; Acts 2:17–21 [citing Joel 2:28–32]), pesher exegesis understands specific biblical passages as fulfilled in specific historical events and experiences.[10]

---

8. For a survey of examples see M. Gertner, "Midrashim in the New Testament," *Journal of Semitic Studies* 7 (1962): 267–92.

9. See W. H. Brownlee, "Biblical Interpretation among the Sectaries of the Dead Sea Sect," *Biblical Archaeologist* 14 (1951): 54–76; F. F. Bruce, *Biblical Exegesis in the Qumran Texts* (Grand Rapids: Eerdmans, 1959); C. Roth, "The Subject Matter of Qumran Exegesis," *Vetus Testamentum* 10 (1960): 51–68; J. A. Fitzmyer, "The Use of Explicit Old Testament Quotations in Qumran Literature and in the New Testament," *New Testament Studies* 7 (1961): 297–333; M. P. Horgan, *Pesharim: Qumran Interpretation of Biblical Books* (Washington: Catholic Biblical Association, 1979); G. J. Brooke, *Exegesis at Qumran: 4QFlorilegium in its Jewish Context* (Sheffield, JSOT, 1985).

10. For a major comparison of pesher with NT exegesis, see K. Stendahl, *The School of St. Matthew and Its Use of the Old Testament* (Philadelphia: Fortress, 1968).

4. *Allegory.*[11] Allegorical interpretation involves extracting a symbolic meaning from the text. It assumes that a deeper, more sophisticated interpretation is to be found beneath the obvious meaning of the passage. The allegorist does not, however, necessarily assume that the text is unhistorical, or without a literal meaning. His exegesis is simply not concerned with this aspect of the biblical text. The best known first-century allegorist was Philo of Alexandria, whose many books afford a wealth of examples of the allegorical interpretation of Scripture, primarily of the Pentateuch.[12] Allegorical interpretation is found in Qumran and in the rabbis. There is even some allegory in the NT. The most obvious example is Galatians 4:21–31, where Sarah and Hagar symbolize two covenants. Another example is found in 1 Corinthians 10:1–4, where the crossing of the Red Sea symbolizes Christian baptism (though this aspect may be typological as well), and the rock symbolizes Christ.

5. *Typology.*[13] Typology is not so much a method of exegesis as it is a presupposition underlying the Jewish and Christian understanding of Scripture, particularly its historical portions. Typology is based upon the belief that the biblical story (of the past) has some bearing on the present, or, to turn it around, that the present is foreshadowed in the biblical story. Unlike allegory, typology is closely tied to history. Even midrashic exegesis reflects this understanding of Scripture. J. L. Kugel has recently described midrash as reflecting an "obsession with past events and the necessity of having them bear on the present."[14] He later says that Jewish exegesis wished to make the present "partake of (indeed, be continuous with) that comforting world of biblical history in which events made sense."[15] This is typological thinking, and to a certain extent it underlies pesher and allegorical exegesis as well.

Popular Jewish eschatological expectation presupposed a typological understanding of Scripture. For example, in the messianic age, it was believed, the great wonders of the past would be

---

11. See J. Z. Lauterbach, "The Ancient Jewish Allegorists," *Jewish Quarterly Review* 1 (1911): 291–333.

12. See S. G. Sowers, *The Hermeneutics of Philo and Hebrews* (Richmond: John Knox, 1965).

13. L. Goppelt, *Typos: The Typological Interpretation of the Old Testament in the New* (Grand Rapids: Eerdmans, 1982); Patte, *Early Jewish Hermeneutic*, 159–67.

14. J. L. Kugel, *Early Biblical Interpretation* (Philadelphia: Westminster, 1986), 38.

15. Kugel, *Early Biblical Interpretation*, 46.

reenacted. But typology is not without biblical precedent; it is rooted in the OT itself. The great event of the exodus serves as a type for the postexilic return to the land of Israel (Isa. 43:16–17). David is a type of the righteous king who would some day rule over restored Israel (Isa. 11:1–3, 10; Jer. 23:5–6; Zech. 3:8). Jubilees 5 likens the time of evil preceding the flood to the time that will precede the messianic age. The latter typology is particularly interesting, since Jesus himself makes a similar comparison (Matt. 24:37–39 par. Luke 17:26–27). Elsewhere Jesus compares the judgment that fell on Sodom with the coming eschatological judgment (Luke 17:28–30), the experience of Lot's wife with the one who loses his life (Luke 17:32–33), and Elijah with John the Baptist (Mark 9:13). Best known is the comparison of Jonah's experience with that of Christ's burial and resurrection (Matt. 12:40; Luke 11:30). Of all the writings in the NT, Hebrews makes the most extensive use of typology.

The OT in the NT[16]

The OT is quoted or alluded to in every NT writing except Philemon and 2 and 3 John. It appears in the NT in every conceiv-

---

16. In addition to the books listed in the selected bibliography, see R. Rendall, "Quotation in Scripture as an Index of Wider Reference," *Evangelical Quarterly* 36 (1964): 214–21; G. W. Grogan, "The New Testament Interpretation of the Old Testament: A Comparative Study," *Tyndale Bulletin* 18 (1967): 54–76; D. E. Aune, "Early Christian Biblical Interpretation," *Evangelical Quarterly* 41 (1969): 79–96; C. K. Barrett, "The Interpretation of the Old Testament in the New," in *Cambridge History of the Bible*, 1: 377–411; M. Black, "The Christological Use of the Old Testament in the New Testament," *New Testament Studies* 18 (1971): 1–14; D. M. Smith, "The Use of the Old Testament in the New," in *The Use of the Old Testament in the New and Other Essays*, ed. J. Efird (Durham: Duke University, 1972), 3–65; D. Hagner, "The Old Testament in the New Testament," in *Interpreting the Word of God*, ed. S. J. Schultz and M. A. Inch (Chicago: Moody, 1976), 78–104; B. Lindars, "The Place of the Old Testament in the Formation of New Testament Theology," *New Testament Studies* 23 (1976): 59–66; J. D. G. Dunn, *Unity and Diversity*, 81–101, 395–97; E. E. Ellis, "How the New Testament Uses the Old," in *New Testament Interpretation: Essays on Principles and Methods*, ed. I. H. Marshall (Grand Rapids: Eerdmans, 1977), 199–219; E. E. Ellis, *Prophecy and Hermeneutic in Early Christianity* (Grand Rapids: Eerdmans, 1978), 147–253; M. Wilcox, "On Investigating the Use of the Old Testament in the New Testament," in *Text and Interpretation*, ed. E. Best and R. McL. Wilson (Cambridge: Cambridge University Press, 1979), 231–43; A. T. Hanson, *The New Testament Interpretation of Scripture* (London: SPCK, 1980); S. E. Balentine, "The Interpretation of the Old Testament in the New Testament," *Southwestern Journal of Theology* 23 (1981): 41–57; W. C. Kaiser, *The Uses of the Old Testament in the New* (Chicago: Moody, 1985); B. Lindars, "Old Testament Quotations in the New Testament," *Harper's Bible Dictionary*, ed. P. J. Achtemeier (San Francisco: Harper & Row, 1985), 723–27; M. Black, "The Theological Appropriation of the Old Testament by the New Testament," *Scottish Journal of Theology* 39 (1986): 1–17; D. A. Carson and H. G. M. Williamson, eds., *It Is Written. Scripture Citing Scripture* (Cambridge: Cambridge University Press, 1988), 191–336.

able manner. It is quoted with introductory formulas (e.g., "it is written") and without. It is paraphrased and alluded to. Sometimes the allusions comprise no more than a word or two. Other times the NT reflects OT themes, structures, and theology. The NT writers appeal to the OT for apologetic, moral, doctrinal, and liturgical reasons. Only the gospel itself makes a greater contribution to NT thought. (For further discussion see the examples in part III below.)

II. Method

In order to perceive how the NT writer has understood the OT passage which he has quoted, or to which he has alluded, one must reconstruct as closely as possible the first-century exegetical-theological discussion surrounding the OT passage in question. How was the OT passage understood by early Christians and Jews? To answer this question every occurrence of the passage should be examined. This involves study of the ancient versions themselves (the MT, LXX, targums) and, through the use of concordances and cross-references, citations of the passage elsewhere in the NT, OT, Apocrypha, pseudepigrapha, Qumran, Josephus, Philo, and early rabbinic sources. Some of these sources will prove to be utterly irrelevant; others may significantly clarify the NT writer's exegesis. For example, the citation and interpretation of Psalm 82:6–7 in John 10:34–36 cannot be adequately explained by an appeal to the OT context alone. But when rabbinic interpretation of this Psalm is considered (Sipre Deut. § 320 [on 32:20]; Num. Rab. 16.24 [on 14:11]), its relevance to the Johannine context becomes clear. The examples in part III below will provide further illustration.

To assess properly the function of the OT in the NT the following questions must be raised:

1. What OT text(s) is(are) being cited? Two or more passages may be conflated, and each may make an important contribution.
2. Which text-type is being followed (Hebrew, Greek, Aramaic)? What are the meanings of these versions? How

does the version that the NT has followed contribute to the meaning of the citation?

3. Is the OT citation part of a wider tradition or theology in the OT? If it is, the citation may be alluding to a context much wider than the specific passage from which it has been taken.

4. How did various Jewish and Christian groups and interpreters understand the passage in question? This question is vital, for often the greatest help comes from comparing the function of the OT in these sources.

5. In what ways does the NT citation agree or disagree with the interpretations found in the versions and other ancient exegeses? Has the Jesus/Christian tradition distinctively shaped the OT citation and its interpretation, or does the NT exegesis reflect interpretation current in pre-Christian Judaism?

6. How does the function of the citation compare to the function of other citations in the NT writing under consideration?

7. Finally, what contribution does the citation make to the argument of the NT passage in which it is found?

If these questions are carefully considered, one's exegesis will be in large measure complete. The following examples will illustrate what is to be gained from this approach.

III. Examples

Jesus[17]

Assessing the function of the OT in Jesus' teaching is complicated by the question of authenticity, for it is commonly held that many of the OT quotations and allusions found in the sayings of Jesus derive from the early church and not from Jesus

---

17. For general studies see R. T. France, *Jesus and the Old Testament* (London: Tyndale, 1971); J. W. Wenham, *Christ and the Bible* (London: Tyndale, 1972); B. D. Chilton, *A Galilean Rabbi and His Bible* (Wilmington, Del.: Glazier, 1984).

himself.[18] This negative assessment has been promoted in part by the historical skepticism of many form and redaction critics, and especially by the predominant use of the dissimilarity criterion. Since the dissimilarity criterion calls into question tradition that overlaps with known tendencies of the early church and of first-century Judaism,[19] the presence of the OT naturally falls under suspicion. This is so, because such tradition may derive, according to this criterion, from typical Jewish usage of the OT (e.g., the discussion of Deut. 6:4–5; see Mark 12:28–34), on the one hand, or from Christian apologetic (e.g., Ps. 118:22–23; see Mark 12:10–11), on the other. In my judgment, however, this critical criterion is defective and in need of revision.[20] One would expect that the early church would tend to preserve tradition that it found relevant (and if Jesus had said nothing relevant, the founding of the church would then be inexplicable), while parallels with Judaism are exactly what we should expect, given the Jewishness of Jesus and the first-century Palestinian setting of his ministry.[21] Recent scholarship has supported the claim of authenticity for the following two examples of Jesus' teaching in which the OT figures significantly.

1. Alluding to Isaiah 6:9–10, Jesus explained why the secret of the kingdom of God was given to his disciples and why for nondisciples ("outsiders") everything was parabolic: ". . . so that they may indeed see but not perceive, and may indeed hear but not understand; lest they should turn again, and be forgiven" (Mark 4:11–12).[22] Comparison of verse 12, with the three

---

18. One's view of Jesus' messianic consciousness, of course, often determines the question of the authenticity of tradition in which messianically interpreted OT material appears. If one holds that Jesus did not view himself as Messiah, then tradition in which OT messianic material appears is usually regarded as inauthentic.

19. R. Bultmann, *The History of the Synoptic Tradition*, trans. J. Marsh (New York: Harper & Row, 1963), 205; J. M. Robinson, *A New Quest of the Historical Jesus* (London: SCM, 1959), 116–19; R. H. Fuller, *Foundations of New Testament Christology* (New York: Scribner's, 1965), 18; N. Perrin, *What is Redaction Criticism?* (Philadelphia: Fortress, 1969), 71.

20. See M. D. Hooker, "On Using the Wrong Tool," *Theology* 75 (1972): 570–81; D. L. Mealand, "The Dissimilarity Test," *Scottish Journal of Theology* 31 (1978): 41–50; R. H. Stein, "The 'Criteria' for Authenticity," in *Studies of History and Tradition in the Four Gospels*, ed. R. T. France and D. Wenham (Sheffield: JSOT, 1980), 225–63, esp. 240–45; C. A. Evans, "Authenticity Criteria in Life of Jesus Research," *Christian Scholars Review*, forthcoming.

21. This is recognized and cogently argued in Hooker, "Wrong Tool," 574; Chilton, *A Galilean Rabbi*, 86–88; and E. P. Sanders, *Jesus and Judaism* (Philadelphia: Fortress, 1985), 16–17.

22. Although Mark 4:11–12 is now found in the context of the parable of the sower (vv. 1–9), it is probable that this logion originally had a wider application (compare its usage in John 12:40; Acts 28:26–27). J. Jeremias (*The Parables of Jesus*, trans. S. H. Hooke [New York:

OT versions discussed above readily shows that the word "forgiven" reflects the targum, and not the Hebrew or the LXX.[23] Further examination of the targum reveals that the prophetic word was to be spoken to those "people who indeed hear but do not understand, and indeed see but do not know" (Isa. 6:9). The insertion of the relative "who" has changed the meaning of the passage significantly. The word of obduracy is now directed only to those "who . . . do not understand," not to the whole people, as the Hebrew text clearly implies. So it is in Jesus' usage; the word of obduracy only applies to the outsiders. Those who have refused to follow him will suffer the fate of obduracy described in Isaiah 6:10: "Make the heart of this people fat . . . lest they . . . repent and be forgiven." It is clear then that the targum of Isaiah is important for the interpretation of Mark 4:11–12.[24]

2. In his parable of the wicked vineyard tenants (Mark 12:1–9), the contents and context of which reflect bitter animosity between Jesus and the religious authorities of his day, Jesus alluded to Isaiah's song of the vineyard (Isa. 5:1–7).[25] The vocabulary in verse 1 that alludes to Isaiah 5 ("vineyard," "planted," "hedge," "wine press," etc.) is not derived exclusively from either the LXX or the Hebrew.[26] Moreover, using these Isaianic materials in a parable directed against the temple establishment reflects an understanding that cannot wholly derive from either the LXX or the Hebrew. Why should Jesus' opponents have understood his parable as directed against them (Mark 12:12), since Isaiah 5:1–7 is directed against all of Judah? The targum, however, provides the

---

Scribner's, 1971], 15–17) has, and I think plausibly, suggested that the logion originally applied to the entirety of Jesus' ministry, and not merely to his parables. He has also suggested that "in parables" in 4:1 in all likelihood originally meant "in riddles."

23. See Chilton, *A Galilean Rabbi*, 90–98.

24. The case for the authenticity of this logion is easily made, even against the strict demands of the dissimilarity criterion. Jesus' harsh word against the "outsiders" may have embarrassed the later evangelists Matthew and Luke who in various ways mitigate the severity of the passage. This argues against seeing the early church as the creator of the saying. Furthermore, the saying does not represent Jewish understanding of the text (see Mek. Bahodeš 1 [on Exod. 19:2]; b. Roš. Haš. 17b; Meg. 17b; y. Ber. 2:3; Seder Elijah Rabbah 16 [82]). Consequently, the saying is dissimilar to tendencies in both Judaism and early Christianity.

25. The allusion is quite clear, if the Isaianic words of v. 1 are retained as authentic. Even if they are not, the reference to "vineyard" (v. 1), and the question, "What will the owner of the vineyard do?" (v. 9), certainly allude to Isaiah's song of the vineyard.

26. See. C. A. Evans, "On the Vineyard Parables of Isaiah 5 and Mark 12," *Biblische Zeitschrift* 28 (1984): 82–86, esp. 85 n. 18. E. Schweizer's claim (*The Good News According to Mark* [Atlanta: John Knox, 1972], 239) that the allusion to Isaiah 5 is septuagintal, thus proving that the Marcan parable is a creation of the early Greek-speaking church, is incorrect.

missing link. According to its paraphrase, God built an "altar" and a "sanctuary" (instead of a "watchtower" and "wine vat") for his people.[27] But because of his people's sin, God will destroy their "sanctuaries." This threat of the destruction of the temple and altar makes the Isaianic passage particularly relevant for the temple authorities of Jesus' day. In view of the targum's interpretation, therefore, Jesus' use of Isaiah 5 in his parable is particularly appropriate, and the hostile reaction of his religious opponents is perfectly understandable.[28]

Matthew[29]

Matthew's citations of the OT, customarily introduced with a fulfillment formula (1:22; 2:15, 17, 23; 4:14; 8:17; 12:17; 13:14, 35; 21:4; 27:9), are among the most controversial in the NT. The two considered below offer an assortment of difficulties and so, for the purpose of this essay, make excellent test cases.

1. In 2:13–15 the evangelist tells the story of the holy family's flight to Egypt, the place where they were to remain "until the death of Herod" (v. 15a). Jesus' departure from Egypt, Matthew tells us, fulfills the prophecy: "Out of Egypt have I called my son" (v. 15b). The quotation comes from Hosea 11:1b, but from the Hebrew, not the LXX (". . . I called his children"). Matthew's Greek translation is quite literal, but his application is problematic. Hosea, as the context makes quite clear, is looking back to the exodus, not to a future deliverance. Indeed, the Hosean context is judgmental, not salvific. Moreover, God's "son" is Israel (see Hos. 11:1a), not Israel's Messiah. If Hosea 11:1 is not messianic, why has the evangelist applied the passage to Jesus?[30] The reference in Hosea 11:1a to Israel as a "child"

---

27. The same exegesis appears in Tos. Me'il 1:16; Tos. Sukk. 3:15, where the tower and wine vat are explicitly identified as "temple" and "altar," respectively. In 1 Enoch 89:56–73 the first and second temples are also referred to as towers.

28. For further discussion, see Chilton, *A Galilean Rabbi*, 111–16.

29. For general studies see R. O. Coleman, "Matthew's Use of the Old Testament," *Southwestern Journal of Theology* 5 (1962): 29–39; J. J. O'Rourke, "Fulfillment Texts in Matthew," *Catholic Biblical Quarterly* 24 (1962): 394–403; N. Hillyer, "Matthew's Use of the Old Testament," *Evangelical Quarterly* 36 (1964): 12–26; R. H. Gundry, *The Use of the Old Testament in St. Matthew's Gospel* (Leiden: Brill, 1967); Stendahl, *The School of Matthew*; R. S. McConnell, *Law and Prophecy in Matthew's Gospel: The Authority and Use of the Old Testament in the Gospel of St. Matthew* (Basel: Reinhardt, 1969).

30. The claim of S. V. McCasland ("Matthew Twists the Scriptures," *Journal of Biblical*

(Heb. נַעַר) or "infant" (LXX νήπιος) may explain in part why the evangelist perceived the relevance of this passage for the infancy narrative. But by itself the text is neither messianic nor predictive. However, when read in the light of the similar passage from LXX Numbers 24:7–8a ("There shall come a man out of his seed, and he shall rule over many nations . . . God led him out of Egypt"), its messianic and predictive potential becomes clear. Matthew is not appealing to Hosea 11:1b only, but to LXX Numbers 24:8a as well.[31] Appealing to one text, interpreted in the light of another, is a form of exegesis that is not foreign to Jewish exegetical practices of the time. A messianic application of the text is also facilitated by the assumption that references to David may sometimes be taken as references to all of Israel. This is seen clearly in Midr. Pss. 24:3: "Our Masters taught: In the Book of Psalms, all the Psalms which David composed apply either to himself or to all of Israel." The midrash goes on to say that in some instances the Davidic Psalm may have application for the "age to Come" (the messianic age).[32] If David and Israel were thus identified, and if David was also understood as a type for the Messiah (see Matt. 1:1, 17), it is not hard to see how Matthew saw messianic potential in Hosea 11:1. The saying of Rabbi Johanan, though uttered in the post-NT era, probably reflects what many assumed in the first century: "Every prophet prophesied only for the days of the Messiah" (T. B. Ber. 34b). Moreover, rabbinic exegesis of Hosea 11:1 itself may shed further light on

---

Literature 80 [1961]: 143–48, esp. 144–45) that the evangelist "misunderstood" the passage is not helpful, for no explanation is offered. We should assume that Matthew followed the exegetical conventions of his day, and therefore Matthean exegesis should be assessed accordingly. McCasland's essay throughout betrays a limited understanding of first-century exegesis and application of Scripture.

31. So B. Lindars, *New Testament Apologetic* (Philadelphia: Westminster, 1961), 216–17. Kaiser (*The Use of the Old Testament*, 50) objected to this interpretation, since the Hebrew of Num. 24:8a reads: "Water shall flow from his buckets." Since Matthew quotes from the LXX (see Matt. 13:14–15), and so obviously is familiar with the Greek version, such an objection is irrelevant. It should also be noted that Num. 24:7 is paraphrased messianically in Tgs. Onq., Ps.-J., and Neof. Moreover, since in all likelihood Matthew's portrayal of the visit of the magi ("We have seen his star" [Matt. 2:2]) also reflects Num. 24:17 ("A star shall come forth out of Jacob, and a scepter shall rise out of Israel"), the probability that Num. 24 (Balaam's prophecy) is part of the evangelist's exegesis of Hosea 11, coming only a few verses after the account of the magi, is greatly increased. Num. 24:17, it should be pointed out, was also applied messianically in Jewish interpretation (1QM 11:6; 4QTestim 12–13; T. Judah 24:7; Tgs. Onq., Ps.–J., and Neof.). Indeed, it is reported that Rabbi Akiba applied this verse specifically to Simon Bar Kokhba, the messianic claimant who led the second Jewish revolt against Rome (y. Ta'an. 4:5).

32. Quotation is from W. G. Braude, *The Midrash on Psalms*, 2 vols. (New Haven: Yale University, 1959), 1:338; see also Midr. Pss. 4:1; 18:1; b. Pesaḥ. 117a.

why Matthew would apply this OT passage to the infant Jesus. In several passages (Sipre Deut. § 305 [on 31:7]; Exod. Rab. 43:9 [on 32:7]; Num. Rab. 12:4 [on 7:1]; Deut. Rab. 5:7 [on 16:18]; Pesiq. R. 26:1–2) the rabbis understood Hosea's reference to "son" as a reference to Israel's innocence and youth, even infancy. Matthew has not exegeted Hosea 11:1 in a strict linguistic, contextual, and historical sense. His is an exegesis of "resignification," that is, finding a new element or dimension in the older tradition. This aspect of his exegesis conforms completely with what is observed in the Jewish exegesis of his day. Matthew has (re)interpreted Scripture in the light of what God has accomplished (or "fulfilled") in his Messiah.[33]

2. Matthew 27:3–8 states that the purchase of the potter's field with the betrayer's thirty pieces of silver fulfilled something spoken by Jeremiah (vv. 9–10). The citation, however, is based loosely on Zechariah 11:12–13, although it does parallel Jeremiah in places (18:1–3; 19:11; 32:6–15),[34] and possibly borrows from LXX Exodus 9:12 ("as the Lord directed") as well. We face here the same problem as above. The passages in Zechariah and Jeremiah are not predictions of the purchase of a potter's field with blood money, whether we take the parts of the quotation separately or in combination. Zechariah describes the prophet's actions of casting thirty pieces of silver into the temple treasury (or to the potter—the MT is uncertain), while Jeremiah makes mention of the potter, a place of burial, and the subsequent purchase of the

---

33. Kaiser (*The Uses of the Old Testament*, 50–53) has made a valiant effort to demonstrate that Matthew has not "added his own interpretation to the text" (p. 53). But his exegesis is not convincing. It is true that "son" in Hosea 11:1 is collective, but an appeal to the concept of corporate solidarity, in which Israel and her Messiah are identified, introduces an element that is quite foreign to the Hosean context (but not foreign to Matthew's way of thinking). Offering a similar exegesis, D. A. Carson ("Matthew," in *The Expositor's Bible Commentary*, ed. F. Gaebelein, 12 vols. [Grand Rapids: Zondervan, 1984], 8:92) argued that "son" is part of the OT "messianic matrix" and that Hosea "grasped the messianic nuances of the 'son' language already applied to Israel and David's promised heir." But nowhere in Hosea does "son" have a messianic, or even Davidic, nuance. There is simply nothing in Hosea 11:1 that is messianic (see the criticism offered by D. J. Moo, "The Problem of *Sensus Plenior*," in *Hermeneutics, Authority, and Canon*, ed. D. A. Carson and J. D. Woodbridge [Grand Rapids: Zondervan, 1986], 200). Hence it would appear that Matthew has indeed added his own interpretation to the text. For further discussion see G. M. Soarés Prabhu, *The Formula Quotations in the Infancy Narrative of Matthew* (Rome: Biblical Institute, 1976), 216–28; and R. H. Gundry, *Matthew: A Commentary on His Literary and Theological Art* (Grand Rapids: Eerdmans, 1982), 33–34.

34. Gundry (*Matthew: A Commentary*, 558; *Use of the Old Testament*, 122–27) thought that the evangelist was dependent on Jeremiah 19 rather than on Jeremiah 18:1–3; 32:6–15.

potter's field. As in the example above, Matthew has made use of two or more Scriptures, and in doing so has resignified them. Apparently he has understood the actions of the prophets Zechariah and Jeremiah in a typological or pesher sense; that is, by casting thirty pieces of silver into the temple treasury, and by purchasing the potter's field, Judas and the temple priests have reenacted the scriptural story.[35] In this sense, prophecy has been fulfilled. The evangelist's practice of finding new meaning in old tradition (whether OT or Christian tradition) may very well be reflected in a verse found only in his Gospel: "Every scribe trained for [or by] the kingdom of heaven is like a householder who brings out of his treasure what is new and what is old" (Matt. 13:52).

Mark[36]

Unlike Matthew and John, Mark rarely quotes the OT outside of what is likely the tradition that he received. Other than the conflated quotation of LXX Exodus 23:20, Malachi 3:1, and LXX Isaiah 40:3 at the opening of his account (Mark 1:2–3), and a few allusions in the passion (15:24, 29, 36), OT quotations are limited to statements of Jesus (4:12; 7:6–7, 10; 8:18; etc.). Even in the case of the citation in 1:2–3 and the allusions in the passion, it is likely that these are traditional elements as well. But this is not to say that the OT is unimportant to the evangelist. In many places OT passages and themes underlie the Marcan narrative.[37] One

---

35. One thing seems clear here. The Gospel tradition cannot be based on an inference from OT materials, as McCasland ("Matthew Twists the Scriptures," 145) thought. The awkward appeal to Zechariah and Jeremiah suggests just the opposite: the evangelist works from Gospel tradition to the OT. Carson ("Matthew," 563–64) made the same point.

36. For general studies see H. Anderson, "The Old Testament in Mark's Gospel," in *The Use of the Old Testament in the New and Other Essays*, 280–309; H. C. Kee, "The Function of Scriptural Quotations and Allusions in Mark 11—16," in *Jesus und Paulus*, ed. E. E. Ellis and E. Grässer (Göttingen: Vandenhoeck & Ruprecht, 1975), 165–88; W. S. Vorster, "The Function and Use of the Old Testament in Mark," *Neotestamentica* 14 (1981): 62–72.

37. For studies that claim to have found extensive OT typology underlying Mark, see A. Farrer, *A Study in St. Mark* (New York: Oxford University, 1952); U. Mauser, *Christ in the Wilderness: The Wilderness Theme in the Second Gospel and its Basis in the Biblical Tradition* (London: SCM, 1963). These studies, however, have not won general acceptance. For a different assessment of the function of the OT in Mark, see A. Suhl, *Die Funktion der alttestamentlichen Zitate und Anspielungen im Markusevangelium* (Gütersloh: Mohn, 1965); and E. Best, *The Temptation and the Passion: The Marcan Soteriology* (Cambridge: Cambridge University Press, 1965), 134–59. However the purpose of Mark's use of the OT is to be understood, one cannot deny that there are numerous allusions to OT passages and themes. See H. C. Kee, *Community of the New Age: Studies in Mark's Gospel* (Philadelphia: Westminster, 1977), 45–49.

scholar has suggested, for example, that the miracle stories of Mark 4:35–8:26 reflect God's mighty acts of deliverance eulogized in Psalm 107.[38] If this is so, then an important key for understanding the selection and ordering of synoptic materials may be at hand.[39]

A specific example of the allusive presence of the OT is found in the transfiguration story (9:2–8), which at numerous points parallels Sinai tradition. (1) The phrase "after six days" (v. 2) alludes to Exodus 24:16, where after six days God speaks. If such an allusion is not intended, the chronological reference at this point in the Marcan narrative is without meaning. (2) Just as Moses is accompanied by three companions (Exod. 24:9), so Jesus is accompanied by Peter, James, and John (Mark 9:2). (3) In both accounts, epiphany takes place on a mountain (v. 2; Exod. 24:12). (4) Moses figures in both accounts (Mark 9:4; Exod. 24:1–18). It is interesting to note that on one occasion Joshua (LXX "Jesus") accompanied Moses on the mountain (Exod. 24:13). (5) Jesus' personal transfiguration (Mark 9:3) probably parallels the transfiguration of Moses' face (Exod. 34:29–30). Matthew and Luke have apparently seen this parallel, for they draw a closer correspondence by noting the alteration of Jesus' face (Matt. 17:2; Luke 9:29). (6) In both accounts the divine presence is attended by a cloud (Mark 9:7; Exod. 24:15–16). Some believed that the cloud which had appeared to Moses would reappear in the last days (see 2 Macc. 2:8). (7) In both accounts the heavenly voice speaks (Mark 9:7; Exod. 24:16). (8) Fear is common to both stories (Mark 9:6; Exod. 34:30; cf. Tg. Ps.-J. Exod. 24:17). (9) Mark's "Hear him" (9:7), unparalleled in Exodus 24, probably

---

38. R. P. Meye, "Psalm 107 as 'Horizon' for interpreting the Miracle Stories of Mark 4:35–8:26," in *Unity and Diversity in New Testament Theology*, ed. R. A. Guelich (Grand Rapids: Eerdmans, 1978), 1–13, Meye (p. 7) suggested four categories for comparison: (1) deliverance from hunger and thirst in the wilderness (Ps. 107:4–9; Mark 6:30–44; 8:1–10, 14–21); (2) deliverance from imprisonment (Ps. 107:10–16; Mark 5:1–20; 6:13; 7:24–30); (3) deliverance from sickness (Ps. 107:17–22; Mark 5:21–6:5, 13, 53–56; 7:31–37; 8:22–26); and (4) deliverance from peril at sea (Ps. 107:23–32; Mark 4:35–41; 6:45–52). Other considerations also suggest that Mark 4:35–8:26 is a unified and edited section; see P. J. Achtemeier, "Toward the Isolation of Pre-Markan Miracle Catenae," *Journal of Biblical Literature* 89 (1970): 265–91; idem, "The Origin and Function of the Pre-Markan Miracle Catenae," *Journal of Biblical Literature* 91 (1972): 198–221.

39. One scholar recently has described the contents and arrangement of Mark's Gospel as a "gigantic midrash" on the Hexateuch and Lamentations; see J. D. M. Derrett, *The Making of Mark: The Scriptural Bases of the Earliest Gospel*, 2 vols. (Shipston-on-Stour: Drinkwater, 1985), 1:38. I view this thesis with much skepticism.

echoes Deuteronomy 18:15. Again Luke has likely noticed the parallel, for he makes the word order correspond to that of the LXX (see Luke 9:35). These parallels, especially that of the injunction to hear, may suggest that the voice that spoke with authority from Sinai now speaks through Jesus the Son.[40]

Luke-Acts[41]

The OT functions in the writings of Luke in ways that are clearly distinct from the other three Gospels. He does not punctuate the tradition with proof texts as do Matthew and John; rather, he punctuates his narrative with speeches that are often made up almost entirely of OT words and phrases (esp. the speeches in the birth narratives). Another distinctive feature is Luke's dependence upon the LXX. Indeed, the evangelist deliberately imitates the style of the Greek OT.[42] But this imitation does not simply involve style, it involves substance. One of the clearest examples of this imitation is seen in Jesus' birth narrative: (1) The angelic announcement of Luke 1:32–33 clearly alludes to the Davidic covenant (2 Sam. 7:9–16);[43] (2) The progress reports in Luke 2:40 and 2:52 echo the similar reports of the young Samuel (1 Sam. 2:26; 3:19; and that of John's in Luke 1:80). Indeed, at other points in the narrative there are echoes of the Samuel story (compare 1 Sam. 1:22 with Luke 2:22; 1 Sam. 2:20 with Luke 2:34); (3) The Magnificat itself (Luke 1:46–55;

---

40. The OT background of the transfiguration narrative does not reflect Sinai themes exclusively. Reference to "tabernacles," though probably reflecting Mosaic tradition (Lev. 23:42–43), does not reflect Sinai tradition; nor, of course, does the appearance of Elijah. For further details see W. L. Liefeld, "Theological Motifs in the Transfiguration Narrative," in *New Dimensions in New Testament Study*, ed. R. N. Longenecker and M. C. Tenney (Grand Rapids: Zondervan, 1974), 162–79.

41. For general studies, see T. Holtz, *Untersuchungen über die alttestamentlichen Zitate bei Lukas* (Berlin: Akademie, 1968); G. D. Kilpatrick, "Some Quotations in Acts," in *Les Actes des Apôtres*, ed. J. Kremer (Gembloux: Duculot, 1979), 81–87; E. Richard, "The Old Testament in Acts," *Catholic Biblical Quarterly* 42 (1980): 330–41; J. Jervell, *The Unknown Paul* (Minneapolis: Augsburg, 1984), 122–37; H. Ringgren, "Luke's Use of the Old Testament," *Harvard Theological Review* 79 (1986): 227–35; D. L. Bock, *Proclamation From Prophecy and Pattern: Lucan Old Testament Christology* (Sheffield: Sheffield Academic, 1987).

42. This has been commonly observed. See. W. G. Kummel, *Introduction to the New Testament*, trans. H. C. Kee (Nashville: Abingdon, 1966), 95, 98; J. A. Fitzmyer, *The Gospel according to Luke I–IX* (Garden City, N.Y.: Doubleday, 1981), 114–16; T. L. Brodie, "Greco-Roman Imitation of Texts as a Partial Guide to Luke's Use of Sources," in *Luke-Acts: New Perspectives from the Society of Biblical Literature Seminar*, ed. C. H. Talbert (New York: Crossroad, 1984), 17–46.

43. See Fitzmyer, *Luke I–IX*, 338.

compare also Anna's song in 2:36–38) is modeled to a certain extent after Hannah's song of thanksgiving (1 Sam. 2:1–10). These observations lead to yet another aspect of the function of the LXX in Luke. The evidence suggests that Luke arranged large portions of his narrative according to the contents and patterns of biblical material. One scholar has suggested that the Elijah/Elisha narratives (1 Kings 17–2 Kings 8) serve as a foil for much of Luke (chaps. 7–10, 18, 22–24) and Acts (chaps. 1–2, 5–9).[44] Others have argued that Luke's central section (10:1–18:14) has been arranged so as to correspond to Deuteronomy 1–26.[45] This work is still in its early stages, so it is not possible to offer a definitive assessment at this time; however, it does appear to be promising, and may set the pace for future Lucan research. Also, this approach is certainly in keeping with the evangelist's own understanding of Jesus' relationship to the OT (see Luke 24:25–26, 45–47; Acts 3:18; 17:2–3; 18:28; 26:22–23). The two OT citations that will be discussed appear to have paradigmatic value for Luke. Both occur at important points of inception in his Gospel, and both are illuminated more fully when we appeal to exegetical traditions of antiquity.

Two chapters of birth narratives notwithstanding, Luke viewed the ministry of John as the beginning of the Gospel story (see Acts 10:37: "beginning from Galilee after the baptism which John preached"; cf. 2:22), so it is likely that redactional activity at this point carries with it implications for his Gospel as a whole. Lucan redaction of Mark's opening citation (Mark 1:2–3; Luke 3:4–6) justifies this claim. Luke omits Malachi 3:1 par. Exod. 23:20 (which appears later in 7:27), but extends Isaiah 40:3 to verses 4–5,[46] so as to conclude: "and all flesh will see

---

44. T. L. Brodie, *Luke the Literary Interpreter: Luke-Acts as a Systematic Rewriting and Updating of the Elijah-Elisha Narrative in 1 and 2 Kings* (Rome: Pontifical University of St. Thomas, 1987); see also C. A. Evans, "Luke's Use of the Elijah/Elisha Narrative and the Ethic of Election," *Journal of Biblical Literature* 106 (1987): 75–83.

45. C. F. Evans, "The Central Section of St. Luke's Gospel," in *Studies in the Gospels*, ed. D. E. Nineham, (Oxford: Blackwell, 1955), 37–53; J. Drury, *Tradition & Design in Luke's Gospel: A Study in Early Christian Historiography* (London: Darton, Longman & Todd, 1976); J. A. Sanders, "The Ethic of Election in Luke's Great Banquet Parable," in *Essays in Old Testament Ethics*, ed. J. L. Crenshaw and J. T. Willis (New York: Ktav, 1974), 247–71; R. W. Wall, " 'The Finger of God': Deuteronomy 9.10 and Luke 11.20," *New Testament Studies* 33 (1987): 144–50.

46. Although the quotation is basically dependent on the LXX, it does reveal a few Semitic features. For this reason some have assigned the whole quotation to early tradition; see Bock, *Proclamation*, 94.

the salvation of God." This part of the quotation, found only in the LXX, obviously contributes to Luke's emphasis on the Gentile mission and the universal proclamation of the gospel (see also Acts 13:23–26; 28:28). Moreover, as is clear from usage at Qumran and elsewhere (1QS 8:12–14; 9:19–20; Bar. 5:7; As. Moses 10:1–5), Isaiah 40:3–5 is understood eschatologically (an understanding clearly presupposed by the NT), and not as a reference to Israel's postexilic restoration (the original import). It is apparent also that Luke weaves key words phrases from his citation (and Mal. 3:1) into the fabric of other parts of his Gospel.[47] Not only do some of these allusions apply to the Baptist, as one would expect (see 1:17, 76–79), but some of them apply to Jesus as well. This is seen in 2:30–31 ("my eyes have seen your salvation which you have prepared in the presence of [lit. "in the face of"] all peoples") and in 9:52 ("he sent messengers ahead of him [lit."before his face"]"). The important point is that Luke has applied this Isaianic text to Jesus, and not only to John (as in the other Gospels). The allusion in the Nunc Dimittis (Lk. 2:29–32) suggests that the theme of Isaiah 40 applies to the whole of Jesus' anticipated ministry, as much as it does to John's, while the allusion in 9:52 provides a specific example of this theme being actualized. Jesus is now on his way to Jerusalem, and he has sent messengers on ahead to prepare his way. What is important here is to realize that Luke has applied the promise of Isaiah 40:3–5 to Jesus as well as to John. For this reason, as well as for his universal concerns, Luke extended the citation to verse 5. Whereas the preparation of the way is John's task, the "salvation of all flesh" is accomplished only in Jesus, the Baptist's successor.

Luke's account of Jesus' Nazareth sermon (4:16–30) represents a reworking and expansion of Mark 6:1–6a (see Matt. 13:53–58). By placing this pericope at the beginning of Jesus' public ministry, rather than near its midpoint, as it is in Mark and Matthew, Luke no doubt wished to show at the outset what Jesus' ministry would entail. The theme of the pericope, therefore, probably reveals to a great extent Luke's emphasis. Lying

---

47. For a fuller discussion see K. R. Snodgrass, "Streams of Tradition Emerging from Isaiah 40:1–5 and Their Adaptation in the New Testament," *Journal for the Study of the New Testament* 8 (1980): 24–45, esp. 36–40.

at the heart of this pericope is the citation of Isaiah 61:1–2 and its interpretation. Comparison with the OT versions readily shows that the LXX has been followed, but not without important changes. One significant change is the insertion of a phrase from Isaiah 58:6. By alluding to this passage, the citation refers to the Messiah, not to the prophet (as clearly seen in the targumic paraphrase of Isa. 61:1).[48] Another significant change is the omission of the phrase, "and the day of vengeance." Since other parts of the Isaianic passage are omitted, this omission may at first seem inconsequential. But in view of the point that Jesus makes and the response of his audience, the omission is probably deliberate. Jesus goes on to interpret this popular passage as promising blessing for Israel's traditional enemies. Stories from the Elijah-Elisha narratives are cited to illustrate and to justify his interpretation. The crowd reacts with indignation, and the reason that they do is because they interpret Isaiah 61:1–2 differently. In all probability this Isaianic passage was understood to promise blessings for Israelites and judgment for Israel's enemies. What may be a particularly relevant example of this interpretation is found in 11QMelchizedek. In lines 9–10 we are told that the "acceptable year" refers to the last day when God's "king of righteousness" will execute judgment. In lines 15–16 the phrase, "the day of vengeance," whose usage elsewhere suggests that it was a technical expression at Qumran (see 1QS 9:23; 10:19; 1QM 7:5), is linked to Isaiah 52:7, which is revocalized so that the prophet proclaims not only peace (*šālôm*), but also retribution (*šillûm*)! The balance of this pesher makes it clear that blessings are for those of the Qumran covenant, and damnation for those outside of the covenant. The element of vengeance, according to Qumran, is one of the most important elements in Isaiah 61:1–2. Thus, when Jesus proclaimed that the Isaianic promise was fulfilled, the synagogue audience was pleased, for such fulfillment to them meant blessings for Israel and judgment for Israel's enemies. But when Jesus suggested that blessings, not judgment, were to be extended to these enemies (the reference to healing of the Syrian soldier may very well have drawn comparisons to the hated Roman soldiers), he

---

48. The targum of Isaiah 61:1 reads: "The prophet said, 'The spirit of prophecy . . . is upon me.' " So also the rabbis. See Bock, *Proclamation*, 108–11.

squarely contradicted what in all likelihood was the popular understanding of the passage. This is why "the day of vengeance" is omitted (though tragically it appears in Luke 21:22 predicting destruction not of Israel's enemies, but of Jerusalem). The Lucan Jesus was not interested in condemning Israel's enemies, but in redeeming them (as Luke demonstrates in Jesus' ministry to outcasts). Hence the people became indignant and tried to do away with him. Jesus was not rejected because of unbelief (as in the Matthean and Marcan accounts), but because he was viewed as a traitor.[49]

John[50]

At first glance John's use of the OT appears to be about the same as Matthew's. Like Matthew, John formally quotes the OT several times, many times in "fulfillment" of something. But in other important ways the OT functions in John quite differently. Even in the case of the quotation formulas, John's purpose runs along very different lines. Unlike Matthew, John's formulas appear to make up a pattern, a pattern that accentuates the theological development of the Gospel narrative. In the first half of his Gospel, the evangelist introduces Scripture in a variety of ways, though usually using the word "written" (1:23; 2:17; 6:31, 45; 7:38, 42; 8:17; 10:34; 12:14). In the second half he invariably introduces Scripture "in order that it be fulfilled"(12:38, 39–40; 13:18; 15:25; 19:24, 28, 36, 37).[51] What is the meaning of this pattern? The answer may be deduced from the summary in 12:37 and the citation that follows in verse 38: "Though he had done so many signs

---

49. For many more technical features in this exegesis, see J. A. Sanders, "From Isaiah 61 to Luke 4," in *Christianity, Judaism and Other Greco-Roman Cults*, ed. J. Neusner (Leiden: Brill, 1975), 75–106.

50. For general studies see C. K. Barrett, "The Old Testament in the Fourth Gospel," *Journal of Theological Studies* 48 (1947): 155–69; C. Goodwin, "How Did John Treat His Sources?" *Journal of Biblical Literature* 73 (1954): 61–75; R. Morgan, "Fulfillment in the Fourth Gospel," *Interpretation* 11 (1957): 155–65; F.-M. Braun, *Jean le Théologien: Les grandes traditions d' Israël et l' accord des Écritures selon le Quatrième Évangile* (Paris: Gabalda, 1964); E. D. Freed, *Old Testament Quotations in the Gospel of John* (Leiden: Brill, 1965); G. Reim, *Studien zum alttestamentlichen Hintergrund des Johannesevangelium* (Cambridge: Cambridge University Press, 1974).

51. The verb that is used is πληροῦν, except in 19:28, where the synonym τελειοῦν is used (possibly to complement τετέλεσται ["it is finished"] in vv. 28, 30). The citations in 12:39 and 19:37 are not exceptions, for they are connected to the citations that precede them (as πάλιν ["again"] makes clear).

before them, yet they did not believe in him, in order that the word of Isaiah . . . be fulfilled. . . ." The "signs" to which reference is made are those of the first half of the Gospel. The scriptural citations in the first half of the Gospel demonstrate that Jesus conducted his ministry in keeping with scriptural expectation ("as it is written"). For example, Jesus' zeal for the temple (John 2:14–22) is related to Psalm 69:9, the feeding of the five thousand (John 6:31) is related to Psalm 78:24, his appeal to the testimony of two witnesses (John 8:7) is related to Deuteronomy 17:6 (or 19:15), his claim to be God's Son (John 10:34) is related to Psalm 82:6, and his riding the donkey (John 12:15) is related to Zechariah 9:9. In some of these instances John could have introduced the OT citation as a fulfillment (cf. the citation of Zech. 9:9 in Matt. 21:4–5), but he did not. Not until Jesus is rejected, despite his signs, are the Scriptures said to be "fulfilled." In Jesus' rejection and crucifixion the Scriptures find their ultimate fulfillment. Far from proving that Jesus did not fulfill the Scriptures, and so could not be Israel's Messiah, Jewish unbelief and obduracy specifically fulfilled Isaiah 53:1 ("Lord, who believed . . . ?") and Isaiah 6:10 ("He blinded their eyes . . ."). With each action taken against Jesus, including the treachery of Judas, Scripture is fulfilled. Apparently John wished to show that in Jesus' passion, his "hour of glorification" (John 17:1), the Scriptures were truly fulfilled.[52]

Allusions to the OT also have an important function in the fourth Gospel. The opening words, "in the beginning," are meant to echo those of Genesis 1:1. According to John 1:1–2 the world is created through an intermediary, the Word (ὁ λόγος). This concept probably reflects Jewish exegesis of Genesis as seen in Targum Neofiti Genesis 1:1: "From the beginning with wisdom the Word [מימרא] of the Lord perfected the heavens and the earth"[53] (see also Prov. 8:22–31; Wisd. 8:3–4). Throughout the creation account it is the "Word of the Lord" that acts.[54]

---

52. For further details of this exegesis see C. A. Evans, "On the Quotation Formulas of the Fourth Gospel," *Biblische Zeitschrift* 26 (1982): 79–83.

53. There is some textual uncertainty here. The opening verse may actually read: "From the beginning with wisdom the Son of the Lord perfected. . . ."

54. In the past it has been frequently claimed that the targumic מימרא has nothing to do with John's prologue, since it is a circumlocution for the divine name and not a reference to an intermediary being. Recent studies, however, have offered compelling evidence and reasons for reassessing this claim; see Le Déaut, "Targumic Literature and New Testament Interpretation," 266–69; McNamara, *Targum and Testament*, 101–6. In my judgment, John has

Not only did the Word of the Lord create the light (Gen. 1:3), according to Targum Neofiti's expanded paraphrase of Exodus 12:24, "the Word of the Lord was the light and it shone" (see also the Frg. Tg.). Just as God sent light into the world at the time of creation, so at the time of redemption he sent his Son, the light of the world (John 8:12; 9:5), to enlighten humankind (John 1:4–5, 9).[55] Significant allusions are found elsewhere in the prologue. In verses 14–18 the Sinai story is contrasted with Jesus. Whereas the law was given through Moses, grace and truth were made available through Jesus the Messiah (v. 17). The words of verse 17, "grace and truth," are first mentioned in verse 14: "And the Word became flesh and dwelt among us, full of grace and truth." The phrase, "full of grace and truth," is probably an allusion to the words of Exodus 34:6 (רב חסד ואמת), uttered when God passed before Moses. Moses, however, was permitted no more than a fleeting glimpse of God's retreating backside (Exod. 33:20–23), for no one can see God and live (33:20; cf. also John 12:41 with Tg. Isa. 6:1). The only Son, in contrast, has not only seen God (so it is implied), but he eternally resides in the bosom (i.e., the "front side") of the Father (John 1:18; cf. Sir. 43:31). Hence Jesus is in a position to disclose God's will in a way that not even the great lawgiver himself can equal.[56]

---

taken over the *memra* concept in conjunction with ideas of the personification of God's wisdom. (Note that the targum says, "In the beginning with wisdom the Word. . . .") See esp. Sirach 24, where Wisdom says that she has come "forth from the mouth of the Most High" (v. 3), has existed from "the beginning" (v. 9), and has pitched her "tent" in Israel (v. 8) and rested in Jerusalem (v. 11). These wisdom parallels certainly form part of the background to the Johannine prologue. But the evangelist has chosen the masculine targumic appellation "Word," rather than the feminine "Wisdom."

55. For more details of this exegesis see M. McNamara, "*Logos* of the Fourth Gospel and *Memra* of the Palestinian Targum (Ex. 12:42)," *Expository Times* 79 (1968): 115–17; idem, *Targum and Testament*, 101–4.

56. For more on this exegesis see Hanson, *New Testament Interpretation of Scripture*, 97–109. For more on Moses in John see R. H. Smith, "Exodus Typology in the Fourth Gospel," *Journal of Biblical Literature* 81 (1962): 329–42; T. F. Glasson, *Moses in the Fourth Gospel* (London: SCM, 1963); P. Borgen, *Bread from Heaven: An Exegetical Study of the Concept of Manna in the Gospel of John and the Writings of Philo* (Leiden: Brill, 1965); W. A. Meeks, *The Prophet-King: Moses Traditions and the Johannine Christology* (Leiden: Brill, 1967). On John's allusive use of Isaiah see F. W. Young, "A Study of the Relation of Isaiah to the Fourth Gospel," *Zeitschrift für die neutestamentliche Wissenschaft* 46 (1955): 215–33; C. A. Evans, "Obduracy and the Lord's Servant: Some Observations on the Use of the Old Testament in the Fourth Gospel," in *Early Jewish and Christian Exegesis*, ed. C. A. Evans and W. F. Stinespring (Atlanta: Scholars, 1987), 221–36, esp. 226–36.

Paul[57]

Paul quoted the Scriptures some one hundred times and alluded to them many more times. Sometimes his quotations are
in verbal agreement with both the LXX and the Hebrew, sometimes with one against the other, and sometimes against both.[58]
In most of the latter cases the variations are insignificant (e.g.,
"God" instead of "the Lord"). In other cases the differences are
much more significant, usually having to do with the interpretation that Paul has given the OT passage. For example, in Romans 9:25–26 Paul cited Hosea 2:23; 1:10, and applied it to the
Gentiles. The OT passage, however, speaks of an estranged Israel once again restored to her God. Paul's point, of course, is
that if an estranged people (such as apostate Israel) can become
God's people, then so can another estranged people (such as the
Gentiles).

In 1 Corinthians 15:55 Paul cited Hosea 13:14, following neither the LXX nor the Hebrew (which read differently), and applied the passage in a novel way. In Hosea the question, "O
death, where . . . ?" anticipates certain death, not victory over
it. In the first line of Hosea 13:14 the question, "Shall I ransom
them from the power of sheol?," clearly expects a negative answer. Disobedient Israel will not be delivered from sheol. So
when the Lord asks, "O death, where are your plagues?" he is
unleashing death on his people, because "compassion is hid
from [his] eyes." Paul, however, has reversed the sense of the
passage, and in so doing has resignified it. Let us consider two
more examples in greater detail.

1. In Romans 11:26 Paul expressed his conviction that all Israel will someday be saved: "The Deliverer will come from Zion;
he will banish ungodliness from Jacob" (cf. Isa. 59:20). Paul's
quotation and interpretation involve two significant variations
from the OT. (1) In the second half of the quotation, he followed
the LXX against the Hebrew. In the Greek text, God turns away

57. For general studies see E. E. Ellis, *Paul's Use of the Old Testament* (Grand Rapids:
Eerdmans, 1957; reprint Baker, 1981); N. Flanagan, "Messianic Fulfillment in St. Paul,"
Catholic Biblical Quarterly 19 (1957): 474–84; A. T. Hanson, *Studies in Paul's Technique and
Theology* (London: SPCK, 1974), 136–278.
58. See Ellis, *Paul's Use of the Old Testament*, 150–52.

ungodliness,[59] while in the Hebrew, God redeems "those who turn from transgression." In the Hebrew text redemption is contingent on repentance (turning), and so is apparently selective. In the Greek, however, redemption is not contingent on repentance; all of "Jacob" is redeemed. The reading of the LXX obviously suits Paul's argument better, for he anticipates the salvation of "all Israel." (2) Paul said that the Deliverer will come "from [ἐκ] Zion." In this he differed from all OT versions. The Hebrew and Aramaic read "to [ל] Zion," and the LXX reads "for the sake of [ἕνεκεν] Zion." The modification in the LXX emphasizes the beneficial aspect of the Deliverer's advent, and so rules out the judgmental aspect that the second half of the verse in the Hebrew may imply. Paul, however, could not follow the LXX. To say that the Deliverer's advent is "for the sake of Zion" would undercut his argument that the Deliverer has come for the benefit of the Gentile, as well as for the Jew. Therefore, a different preposition was necessary. By saying that the Deliverer would come "from Zion," Paul did not limit eschatological benefits to Jews alone, and yet the implication of the passage is still retained that the Deliverer bears a special, and consequently a beneficial, relationship to Israel.

2. Our second example involves the allusion to Deuteronomy 30:12–14 (and 9:4a) in Romans 10:6–8. Paul's exegesis often strikes interpreters as odd. Whereas Moses spoke of God's "commandment" not being too far off (either up in heaven or beyond the sea), so that failure to obey it cannot be excused, Paul spoke of Christ. As unusual as Paul's exegesis appears, it is not entirely novel. The author of Baruch has alluded to this passage from Deuteronomy, and has applied it to Wisdom: "Who has gone up into heaven, and taken her, and brought her down from the clouds? Who has gone over the sea, and found her . . . ?" (Bar. 3:29–30). As already noted, comparison between Christ and wisdom was sometimes made. But Baruch's parallel usage leaves some components of Paul's exegesis unclear. McNamara rightly called attention to the paraphrase of Deuteronomy 30:12–13 in the Fragmentary Targum. He translated (with italics showing

---

59. The targum is in essential agreement with the LXX: "to turn the rebellious ones of the house of Jacob to the law." According to this rendering there is absolutely no doubt that all will be redeemed, even the rebellious.

departures from the Hebrew): "The Law is not in heaven that one may say: *'Would that we had one like the prophet Moses who would ascend to heaven and fetch it for us* and make us hear the commandments that we might do them.' Neither is the Law beyond the Great Sea that one may say: *'Would that we had one like the prophet Jonah who would descend into the depths of the Great Sea and bring it up for us* and make us hear the commandments that we might do them.' "[60] The point of the Hebrew is that the law has been given once and for all. There is no need for a prophet to ascend to heaven or to traverse the sea to obtain it. The Aramaic paraphrase illustrates this point with two biblical characters whose experiences roughly match the language of the passage. Moses, it was believed, had ascended to heaven when he received the law from God. For example, in Targum Pseudo-Jonathan on Deuteronomy 34:5 we are told that Moses "brought it [the law] from heaven"; and in Pesiqta Rabbati 4:2: "Moses went up to heaven" (see also Ps.–Philo, *Bib. Ant.* 15:6; 2 Esdras 3:17–18). These traditions are based on Exodus 19:3, 20, where God summons Moses to meet him on the mountain. The reference to the sea, of course, provides the link to Jonah. In fact, the targum's "descend into the depths" draws the OT passage into closer alignment with Jonah's experience, for the prophet did not go *across* the sea, but *down into* it (see the reference to "abyss" in Jonah 2:3; cf. v. 6). In the NT, of course, both Moses and Jonah are compared to Christ, specifically at points that are relevant to the traditions just reviewed. Like Moses, Jesus brought a new law from heaven (Mark 9:2–8; John 1:17; 3:13–14); like Jonah, Jesus descended into the abyss (Matt. 12:39–40; 16:4; Luke 11:29–30). Paul presupposed these Jewish and Christian traditions (cf. Eph. 4:8–10), and combined them in his own way. His point in Romans 10:4–13 is that Christ has accomplished salvation. All that is now required is faith. No one needs to ascend to heaven to bring Christ down, for he has already descended. No one needs to descend into the abyss to raise him up, for he has already been resurrected. Redemption has been accomplished. All that remains is the confession of faith (Rom. 10:8–10, citing

---

60. McNamara, *The New Testament and the Palestinian Targum*, 74–75.

and interpreting Deut. 30:14). By faith in what God has accomplished through Christ, God's righteousness may be obtained.[61]

In Paul's allusive use of Scripture we find examples of his boldest exegesis (see also 2 Cor. 3:7–18; Gal. 4:21–31). In these instances Paul did not formally quote Scripture, because to do so would not clarify his exegesis, and might even militate against it. Indeed, in the case of 2 Corinthians 3:16, a formal citation of Exodus 34:34 would confuse the apostle's point. Paul only alluded to those parts of the OT passage that were germane to his argument. But we should not assume that allusion to biblical words and phrases, instead of quotation, indicates a less serious level of exegesis. The exegesis of Romans 10 could hardly be more serious.

Hebrews[62]

One commentator has described Hebrews as "a homiletical midrash" on Psalm 110.[63] Although this is clearly an overstatement, it does rightly alert us to the pervasive influence of the OT in this writing. While several studies have looked to Philo[64] or Qumran[65] as the background against which Hebrews might be understood, the exegesis of its author is neither allegory nor pesher. Its author has developed his own style of typological exegesis, in which he compared Christ and the church against OT figures and institutions. Unlike midrash, pesher, or even

---

61. For more details of this exegesis, see McNamara, *The New Testament and the Palestinian Targum*, 70–78.

62. For general studies see R. Rendall, "The Method of the Writer to the Hebrews in Using OT Quotations," *Evangelical Quarterly* 27 (1955): 214–20; C. K. Barrett, "The Eschatology of the Epistle to the Hebrews," in *The Background of the New Testament and its Eschatology*, ed. W. D. Davies and D. Daube (Cambridge: Cambridge University Press, 1956), 363–93; G. B. Caird, "The Exegetical Method of the Epistle to the Hebrews," *Canadian Journal of Theology* 5 (1959): 44–51; F. C. Synge, *Hebrews and the Scriptures* (London: SPCK, 1959); M. Barth, "The Old Testament in Hebrews," in *Current Issues in New Testament Interpretation*, ed. W. Klassen and G. F. Snyder (New York: Harper & Row, 1962), 65–78; K. J. Thomas, "The Old Testament Citations in Hebrews," *New Testament Studies* 11 (1965): 303–25; F. Schröger, *Der Verfasser des Hebräerbriefes als Schriftausleger* (Regensburg: Pustet, 1968).

63. G. W. Buchanan, *To the Hebrews* (Garden City, N.Y.: Doubleday, 1972), xix, xxvii.

64. Sowers, *The Hermeneutics of Philo and Hebrews;* R. Williamson, *Philo and the Epistle to the Hebrews* (Leiden: Brill, 1970).

65. Y. Yadin, "The Dead Sea Scrolls and the Epistle to the Hebrews," in *Aspects of the Dead Sea Scrolls*, ed. C. Rabin and Y. Yadin (Jerusalem: Hebrew University, 1958), 36–55; G. Howard, "Hebrews and the Old Testament Quotations," *Novum Testamentum* 10 (1968): 208–16.

allegory, typology is primarily interested in biblical *events* and not the biblical *text*. Hebrews' author cited or alluded to the OT approximately sixty times, usually following the LXX, and often citing the Psalter.[66] His most important typological comparisons include Moses-Christ (3:2–6), Melchizedek-Christ (7:1–28), and old covenant-new covenant (8:1–9:28). This author's quotation formulas vary considerably. Scripture is the utterance of the Holy Spirit (3:7), or of Moses (12:21). Usually the author introduced Scripture as "he says" or "he said" (1:5, 6, 7, 13; 2:12; 3:15; 4:3, 4, 7; 5:5; 6:14; 7:21; 8:5, 8; 9:20; 10:5, 8, 15, 30; 11:18; 13:5), as though God himself spoke it. From this we may infer that the author of Hebrews believed Scripture to be the Word of God. The familiar formulas, "as it is written," "as the Scripture says," or "in order that it be fulfilled," do not appear. Many times the citation is woven into the text without an introduction. The following examples reveal the importance of the LXX for this author's biblical exegesis.

1. In 1:6 the author of Hebrews cites a line from Deuteronomy's Song of Moses (Deut. 32:1–43) and applies it to Jesus the "first-born": "Let all angels of God worship him." This reading, however, does not match exactly what is found in LXX Deuteronomy 32:43: "Let all sons of God worship him . . . and let all angels of God strengthen him." It is possible that the author replaced "sons" with "angels," perhaps under the influence of LXX Psalm 96:7 ("worship him, all ye his angels"). But the most probable explanation is that the author of Hebrews has followed the text of the Song of Moses, as it appears in the collection of Odes (in Codex A) appended to the Psalms. Odes 2:43 agrees exactly with his citation (Odes 2 = Deut. 32:1–43). Since the Odes are linked to the Psalter, and since the author of Hebrews shows a marked preference for the Psalms, it is likely that this is the text that has been followed. Unfortunately, the MT offers no guidance, for it has no equivalent (nor do the targums). However, a Hebrew equivalent does appear in 4QDeut^a: "Let all gods [אלהים] worship him."[67] The LXX sometimes translates אלהים

---

66. See S. Kistemaker, *The Psalm Citations in the Epistle to the Hebrews* (Amsterdam: van Soest, 1961).

67. 4QDeut^a is a fragment consisting of Deut. 32:37–43. At other points it agrees with the LXX. For text and discussion of implications for reconstructing the original Hebrew, see P. W. Skehan, "A Fragment of the 'Song of Moses' (Deut 32) from Qumran," *Bulletin of the*

as "angels" (Ps. 8:5; 96[97]:7), and sometimes בני האלהים as "angels of God" (Job 1:6; 2:1) or simply as "angels" (Job 38:7).[68] It is likely, therefore, that LXX Deuteronomy 32:43 par. Odes 2:43 does ultimately derive from the Hebrew. There remains, however, a significant contextual problem. In Deuteronomy 32:43 who is speaking, and of whom is he speaking? Throughout verses 20–42 God is speaking in the first person, but not in verse 43. This verse, in both the MT and LXX, appears to be Moses' concluding injunction to praise. According to the MT, the nations are enjoined to praise *his* (God's) *people* (עַמּוֹ). But according to the LXX, the heavens are to rejoice *with him* (ἅμα αὐτῷ = עַמּוֹ), and the angels are to worship *him*. In all likelihood, the LXX translator intended "him" to refer to God. But the author of Hebrews apparently understood verse 43 as spoken by God, not by Moses. Taken this way, God has enjoined the heavens to rejoice with him (Messiah), and the angels to worship him (Messiah). This sense will not work in the MT. But because the LXX reads "him," instead of "people," the exegesis in Hebrews is made possible. Messiah, of course, is sometimes called God's "first-born." According to Rabbi Nathan (Exod. Rab. 19:7 [on 13:2]), God told Moses: "I will make King Messiah a first-born], as it says: 'I will make him first-born' " (see Ps. 89:27; see also Ps. 2:7 and 2 Sam. 7:14, which are cited in Heb. 1:5). Moreover, in at least one midrash, Deuteronomy 32:43 is interpreted as pertaining to the "age to come" (Sipre Deut. § 333 [on 32:43]). An eschatological interpretation of this verse would only further facilitate the exegesis of Hebrews. Elsewhere in the NT, Jesus is called first-born (Rom. 8:29; Col. 1:15, 18). The former text, which described Christ as "first-born among many brethren," is particularly relevant, for Hebrews also speak of Christ's "brethren" (Heb. 2:11–12, 17). Finally, citing a passage about angelic worship of Christ in connection with his being brought "into the world" may reflect nativity tradition (see Luke 2:13–14). The citation of Deuteronomy 32:43 apparently does not reflect the typological exegesis that is otherwise characteristic of Hebrews. Instead this OT passage has been christologically resignified.

American Schools of Oriental Research 136 (1954): 12–15. For more details see Buchanan, *Hebrews*, 15–18.

68. The rabbis, however, understand אלהים in Ps. 97:7 as heathen gods, not angels (Midr. Pss. 97:2 [on 97:7]; see also 31:4 [on 31:1]).

2. Hebrews 2:12–13 cites Psalm 22:22 and Isaiah 8:17b–18a: " 'I will proclaim your name to my brethren, in the midst of the congregation I will praise you.' And again, 'I will put my trust in him.' And again, 'Here am I, and the children God has given me.' " The citations follow the LXX closely, and the LXX follows the MT closely as well. The first citation is taken from Psalm 22, a lament psalm that was applied to Jesus in his passion (Mark 15:24, 29, 34, etc.), though verse 22 is cited only here in Hebrews. As the Evangelists before him, the author of Hebrews has understood the psalm christologically, and, as the psalm itself requires, has understood the reference to "brethren" in a metaphorical sense. Hebrews uses this citation to support the point that Christ is not ashamed to call Christians "brethren" (Heb. 2:11; see Luke 8:21, where Jesus calls his disciples "brethren"). It is appropriate to the context in Hebrews that Psalm 22:22 begins the triumphant section of the psalm, in which the psalmist praises God. The "congregation" (ἐκκλησία) is doubtlessly understood as referring to the Christian church. The connecting formula, "and again," implies that the citation that follows contributes to the same idea. This citation is taken from Isaiah 8:17b. Although some have argued that it derives from 2 Samuel 22:3, the fact that Isaiah 8:18a immediately follows it makes it clear that Isaiah is in view. In this passage, the prophet Isaiah expressed his confidence in God (as opposed to the foolhardy policies of Ahaz). The words of the prophet have been appropriated as the words of Christ. He will put his trust in God. Isaiah 8:18a, given as the third citation, actually follows Isaiah 8:17b in the LXX without a break. In Hebrews it is separated with the second use of the formula, "and again." This break in continuity may point to a development in the logic of the argument. The idea seems to be that because Christ has put his trust in God, he and his children are the result. Since the citation of Isaiah 8:18a is broken off, we should not assume that the remainder of the verse is in mind (i.e., "I and my children . . . are signs and portents in Israel . . ."). What is actually cited in Hebrews could be translated, "Behold, I and the children, which God has given me, exist." In the OT context, of course, the prophet Isaiah referred to himself and to his literal children, Shear-Jashub (Isa. 7:3), Maher-Shalal-Hash-Baz (8:3), and possibly Immanuel (7:14). The author of Hebrews probably understood these children as the righteous remnant, which in his

time made up the church. His exegesis has again resignified passages from the OT.

Conclusion

As the above examples make evident, NT writers frequently found new meanings in OT passages. This happened, not because of careless exegesis or ignorance, but because of the conviction that Scripture speaks to every significant situation. This is especially so, if the situation is believed to have eschatological significance. The Scriptures are accordingly searched for clarification. The NT writers were rarely concerned with the question of what happened or what the text originally meant. The NT writers, as also their contemporary Jewish exegetes, were chiefly interested in what the Scriptures meant and how they applied. The life, death, and resurrection of Jesus became for early Christians the hermeneutical key for their interpretation and application of the Jewish Scriptures. Since the Scriptures could be relied on for clarification of eschatological events, and since Jesus was the eschatological agent, there could be no doubt that the Scriptures were fulfilled in him.

There is therefore no need either (1) to criticize the NT writers for not always providing the kind of exegesis that we moderns value so much and think is valid, or (2) to foist unnatural interpretations upon the Scriptures in order to demonstrate that the NT writer has given the OT passage no other sense than what we moderns believe to have been the original. While liberal scholars are sometimes guilty of the first, conservative scholars are sometimes guilty of the second. In both cases modern principles of exegesis are set up as the standards by which the exegesis of the NT writers is to be measured. In the final analysis, the legitimacy of the NT writers' employment of the OT is tied to the legitimacy of their faith in Jesus.

Selected Bibliography

Background

Cohen, S. J. D. *From the Maccabees to the Mishnah.* Philadelphia: Westminster, 1987.

Gruen, E. S. *The Hellenistic World and the Coming of Rome.* 2 vols. Berkeley: University of California Press, 1984.

Hengel, M. *Judaism and Hellenism.* 2 vols. Philadelphia: Fortress, 1974.

Leaney, A. R. C. *The Jewish and Christian World 200 BC–AD 200.* Cambridge: Cambridge University Press, 1984.

Safrai, S. and M. Stern, eds. *The Jewish People in the First Century.* 2 vols. Philadelphia: Fortress, 1974, 1976.

Schürer, E. *The History of the Jewish People in the Age of Jesus Christ (175 BC–AD 135).* Revised and edited by G. Vermes and F. Millar. 3 vols. Edinburgh: T. & T. Clark, 1973–87.

Textual Criticism

Aland, K. and B. *The Text of the New Testament: An Introduction to the Critical Editions and to the Theory and Practice of Modern Textual Criticism.* Translated by E. F. Rhodes. Grand Rapids: Eerdmans, 1987.

Fee, G. D. "The Textual Criticism of the New Testament." In *Expositor's Bible Commentary.* Vol. 1. Edited by F. E. Gaebelein, 419–33. Grand Rapids: Zondervan, 1979.

Finegan, J. *Encountering New Testament Manuscripts: A Working Introduction to Textual Criticism.* Grand Rapids: Eerdmans, 1974.

Metzger, B. M. *Manuscripts of the Greek Bible: An Introduction to Palaeography.* New York: Oxford, 1981.

————. *The Text of the New Testament: Its Transmission, Corruption, and Restoration*. 2d ed. New York: Oxford, 1968.

————. *A Textual Commentary on the Greek New Testament: A Companion Volume to the United Bible Societies' Greek New Testament*. 3d ed. New York: United Bible Societies, 1971.

Greek Grammar

Blass, F., Debrunner, A. *A Greek Grammar of the New Testament and Other Early Christian Literature*. Translated and revised by R. W. Funk. Chicago: University of Chicago, 1961.

Moule, C. F. D. *An Idiom Book of New Testament Greek*. 2d ed. Cambridge: Cambridge, 1963.

Robertson, A. T. *A Grammar of the Greek New Testament in the Light of Historical Research*. Nashville: Broadman, 1934.

Turner, N. *Syntax*. vol. 3. In J. H. Moulton, *A Grammar of New Testament Greek*. 4 vols. Edinburgh: T. & T. Clark, 1963.

Zerwick, M. *Biblical Greek: Illustrated by Examples*. Rome: Biblical Institute, 1963.

Word Study

Barr, J. *The Semantics of Biblical Language*. Oxford: Oxford, 1961.

Brown, C. *The New International Dictionary of New Testament Theology*. 4 vols. Grand Rapids: Zondervan, 1975–85.

Caird, G. B. *The Language and Imagery of the Bible*. Philadelphia: Westminster, 1980.

Kittel, G., and Friedrich, G. *Theological Dictionary of the New Testament*. 10 vols. Translated by G. W. Bromiley. Grand Rapids: Eerdmans, 1933–1976.

Louw, J. P. *Semantics of New Testament Greek*. Philadelphia: Fortress, 1982.

Silva, M. *Biblical Words and their Meaning: An Introduction to Lexical Semantics*. Grand Rapids: Zondervan, 1983.

New Testament Sociology

Gager, J. *Kingdom and Community*. Englewood Cliffs, N.J.: Prentice Hall, 1975.

Malherbe, A. *Social Aspects of Early Christianity*. 2d ed. Philadelphia: Fortress, 1983.

Malina, B. J. *The New Testament World: Insights from Cultural Anthropology*. Atlanta: John Knox, 1981.

Meeks, W. *The First Urban Christians*. New Haven, Conn.: Yale University Press, 1983.

Theissen, G. *The Social Setting of Pauline Christianity*. Philadelphia: Fortress, 1982.

New Testament Theology

Bultmann, R. *Theology of the New Testament*. 2 vols. New York: Charles Scribner's, 1951, 1955.

Caird, G. B. *New Testament Theology*. Completed and revised by L. D. Hurst. New York: Oxford, forthcoming.

Dunn, J. D. G. *Unity and Diversity in the New Testament*. Philadelphia: Westminster, 1977.

Guthrie, D. *New Testament Theology*. Downers Grove, Ill.: Inter-Varsity, 1981.

Ladd, G. E. *A Theology of the New Testament*. Grand Rapids: Eerdmans, 1974.

Old Testament in the New Testament

Dodd, C. H. *According to the Scriptures*. New York: Scribner's, 1952.

Ellis, E. E. *Paul's Use of the Old Testament*. Grand Rapids: Baker, 1981.

Lindars, B. *New Testament Apologetic*. Philadelphia: Westminster, 1961.

Longenecker, R. N. *Biblical Exegesis in the Apostolic Period*. Grand Rapids: Eerdmans, 1975.

Shires, H. M. *Finding the Old Testament in the New*. Philadelphia: Westminster, 1974.